THE DEVIL YOU KNOW

ENCOUNTERS IN FORENSIC PSYCHIATRY

DR. GWEN ADSHEAD
AND EILEEN HORNE

SCRIBNER

New York   London   Toronto   Sydney   New Delhi

To Laura,
whose Spirit brought us together

Scribner
An Imprint of Simon & Schuster, Inc.
1230 Avenue of the Americas
New York, NY 10020

First Scribner trade paperback edition August 2022

SCRIBNER and design are registered trademarks of The Gale Group, Inc.,
used under license by Simon & Schuster, Inc., the publisher of this work.

For information about special discounts for bulk purchases,
please contact Simon & Schuster Special Sales at 1-866-506-1949
or business@simonandschuster.com.

The Simon & Schuster Speakers Bureau can bring authors to your live event.
For more information or to book an event, contact the Simon & Schuster Speakers
Bureau at 1-866-248-3049 or visit our website at www.simonspeakers.com.

Manufactured in the United States of America

1   3   5   7   9   10   8   6   4   2

Library of Congress Cataloging-in-Publication Data is available.

ISBN 978-1-9821-3479-2
ISBN 978-1-9821-3480-8 (pbk)
ISBN 978-1-9821-3481-5 (ebook)

The reason for evil in the world is that people are not able to tell their stories.

CARL JUNG, *Freud Letters*, Vol. 2

CONTENTS

INTRODUCTION

In that distant time when people on airplanes used to talk to each other, I'd sometimes get asked what I did for a living. "I'm a psychiatrist and psychotherapist who works with violent offenders," I would reply. Mild curiosity would shift to amazement. "You mean you actually talk to those people?" This could lead to an impromptu lecture about what a waste it was to bother with such monsters; or I'd get more of a bemused "But they can't be helped, aren't they born that way?" The occasional British fellow passenger might lean in and offer, sotto voce, "Frankly, I think Parliament ought to bring back hanging." Nowadays, on the rare occasions when anyone starts up a chat while we're fastening our seatbelts, I'm inclined to tell them I'm a florist. But I think that everyone who is both fascinated and repelled by human cruelty deserves a better and more honest response about the treatment of violence and those who perpetrate it, and that is my aim with this book.

The title comes from the Latin proverb which suggests that the devils we know are less risky than the ones we don't. If my fellow passengers were a therapy group, I might test out their symbolic thinking skills by asking them to consider this saying, and what it suggests to them. I'd have high hopes of a hypothetical "airplane seatmate" therapy group, likely a chatty, sociable bunch. We could open up a discussion by talking about the familiar devils of religion or fantasy. "What about the devil we don't know?" I might prompt. "Who is that for you?" "Obviously, it's something alien," someone might offer, "like one of those terrible people you work with." In

1

time, I hope the group would come to discover that it could also signify a cruel and belittling self that lives in all of us. Accepting that won't come easy for some; to paraphrase the beautiful words of Lear's daughter, "We ever but slenderly know ourselves."

In the following stories I will show what it is that my colleagues and I do with "those people," and how and why listening and compassion can make a difference. I don't judge those who might disagree, just as I don't judge my patients, and I completely understand why people have strong opinions about my work. Everyone is fascinated by what we call "evil," that human capacity for violence and cruelty—more than enough proof of this is found in the mirrors that are our news and entertainment media.[1] Even as global data show violence of all kinds trending steadily ever-downward in the modern era, our appetite to know more about it has increased. I include myself in this; I chose this career, after all.

Back when I was in medical school in the 1980s, psychiatry was still a specialism that was often overlooked or discounted, despite wide acknowledgment since classical times that a healthy mind was essential to a healthy body. (And, as a colleague of mine likes to say, "Psychiatrists are doctors who look after the only part of the body that votes.") As a student, I briefly considered pursuing orthopedic surgery, probably because I wanted to fix things and was attracted by its pragmatic effectiveness. But I was also drawn to psychiatry and its relationship with human identity and communication; I thought it would be profoundly stimulating, both intellectually and emotionally. I saw that the complexity and power of the human mind were immense and that changing minds had significance both personally and politically.

Over the centuries, humans have often turned to the current technologies for metaphors about the mind, and I guess the most common one we hear these days is that of the mind as a computer: a machine where identity is "hardwired." Data about thoughts or emotions are "processed" and "filed"; we "switch modes" when carrying out different functions. Such a model of the mind lends itself to some kinds of research but has little to say about the complexity of human experience, especially in the relational space in which we all live our lives. Physicists like Carlo Rovelli tell us that the universe is relational, therefore so the mind must be, and if that is the case, then we need better metaphors, ones that reflect the organic, ever-evolving nature of psychological experience.

I prefer to think of the mind as a coral reef: ancient, layered, and mysterious, not without shadows and risk but containing a nourishing diversity; it might appear chaotic, but it is a complex and structured ecosystem, endlessly fascinating and essential to human life. Under environmental stress, many reefs will bleach out and wither, but science has also shown they can be responsive to intervention and made more resilient. As a student, I soon learned that the study of psychiatry would require a "deep dive" below the surface, into a darkness where things of great beauty as well as danger might appear. It would take time to acclimatize myself and learn to breathe easy.

Since then, a long professional voyage has continually inspired in me the awe and wonder that I associate with the ocean and its hidden depths—I love that e. e. cummings idea that it is "always ourselves that we find in the sea."[2] It has been immensely rewarding work, and often unpredictable; it has shown me how good and evil, ideas of right and wrong, as well as identities like victim and perpetrator, are not set in stone and can coexist. When I started out, I thought the work I was doing was about making people feel better, but time has taught me that it was about helping them to better know their minds, which is quite another matter. The process is not painless for my patients, and there has been turbulence for me too along the way. I have found that it is inevitable that I will experience some distressing feelings, though they tend toward deep sadness and frustration more than horror or disgust. It is my job to recognize those responses and hold them with a kind of compassionate detachment, what Buddhists might describe as "hovering in the Bardo."

As my psychiatric training went on, I found out about forensic work, which looks at the mind's darker modes that sometimes give rise to risk. The word "forensic" derives from the Latin *forum*, a place to hear legal disputes. Beyond providing assessments, making diagnoses and coordinating the care of patients like any other medical specialist, forensic psychiatrists address how a society responds to and treats those people who break the criminal law. The work raises fascinating ethical and legal questions about responsibility, agency, and blame for actions done when people are mentally unwell. Many forensic psychiatrists work in secure hospitals as members of a team of professionals providing coordinated care; they are like "dive buddies" who discuss a plan and share responsibility for each other's safety. I am by nature a collaborator, as demonstrated by my work as a group therapist (and, indeed, by the writing of this book), so forensic work seemed an ideal choice for me.

Once I qualified in forensic psychiatry, I soon realized that I wanted to train as a psychotherapist as well. In the early years of the profession, most psychiatrists were also therapists, but by the late twentieth century these were seen as separate disciplines and it was considered unusual for a psychiatrist to also offer psychological therapy. Like other medical specialists, they would generally act as case managers, with an overview on assessment and treatment. But, for me, the art of psychiatry was in the dialogue and the story of people's lives: I wanted to work in depth with them and provide time and space for reflection. In the course of my further training to become a therapist I got involved in particular areas of research such as maternal violence, trauma and group work, as well as medical ethics and the treatment of doctors. These and much more are woven into the tapestry of the lives that follow. An important thread throughout has been my study of childhood attachments in relationships and their association with later violence. This had a major influence on my thinking about human behavior, as I will show.

Every violent crime is a tragedy, for the victims and their families as well as for the perpetrators. I am not here to argue that any violent action should be excused, or that our prisons and secure hospitals should be emptied. I firmly believe in justice and consequences within a humane legal framework, and given some of the terrible things I have seen and heard, I have no doubt that a subgroup of violent offenders belong in secure settings. I also comprehend why some people feel a need to condemn the perpetrators of violence: revenge is a basic human impulse, a kind of wild justice that keeps us stuck in our fear and anger, mirroring the very cruelty we claim to abhor. This can be painful; there is wisdom in that popular notion that hating someone else is like taking poison and waiting for them to die. And, as Gandhi and others have observed, it is a measure of a just society that we treat the worst of us with compassion.

Over the years, I've come to think of my patients as survivors of a disaster, where they are the disaster and my colleagues and I are the first responders. I meet them at a turning point in their lives and help them to come to terms with a new identity, which may feel indelible; as one of my patients memorably put it, "You can be an ex–bus driver but not an ex-murderer." The work we do requires people to take responsibility for their life story, which can be a difficult and lengthy process. This is done in the context of shifting political agendas which shape mental health resources and outcomes. I well remember how, not long after I started out in my forensic career in the early 1990s, our then prime minister in the UK, John Major, famously said, "Society needs to condemn a little more and understand a little less." Mandatory minimum sentences and the wave of mass incarceration that followed, coupled with drastic cuts to mental health care services, have had far-reaching and dire social consequences both in the UK and around the world. Much has been written and said about this elsewhere by people far more expert than me; I will just say that we imprison far too many people, essentially to feed the public appetite for punishment, when only a small percentage of them are too cruel or risky to rehabilitate in the community.

I have spent my working life, more than thirty years to date, employed within the UK's National Health Service (the NHS). For much of that time, I've been based at Broadmoor Hospital in Berkshire, about fifty miles west of London. Broadmoor was built in 1863 as part of a Victorian system of asylums (from the Greek, meaning "refuge"), which were venues where "criminal lunatics" could be cared for, sometimes indefinitely. With its mock-Gothic appearance and a history of housing some of the UK's most notorious violent criminals, Broadmoor has long held a particularly lurid position in the British imagination. On a training visit there back in my student days, with all the certitude and ignorance of youth I too thought it was an antiquated and even a barbaric place. When I actually came to work there, I quickly found otherwise. Our secure hospitals fulfill such an important and humane function, and I'm glad to say that most other developed countries have similar psychiatric facilities that either admit people from prison or offer an appropriate alternative for those who need it.

Today, places like Broadmoor are no longer seen as oubliettes for people who cannot be helped and will never be released; on the contrary, the emphasis is on rehabilitation and recovery, with an average stay of five years. At Broadmoor there are around two hundred patient beds now, less than half the number there were when I first joined. Many more people are now sent to medium- and low-security hospitals, where I've also worked over the years. Most of the patients in any of these institutions have either been committed by a judge after trial, or transferred from prison for treatment because their mental health deteriorated, or (rarely) transferred from community psychiatric outpatient care because of the risk they pose to others.

As some of the following chapters describe, I've also spent time working with people inside prisons as an NHS employee. Our mental health services in the UK are mandated to work in prison with inmates with psychiatric problems, and have been since the 1990s. "Inreach teams" do their best to support and treat the unprecedented and ever-growing number of prisoners, and I have seen at first hand how demand for mental health care in prisons far exceeds capacity, and how incarceration exacerbates mental illness. This is a recognized crisis that needs urgent attention. An estimated 70 percent of people in UK prisons today are said to have at least two mental health issues, ranging from depression to substance abuse and addiction or psychosis. The law-and-order policies introduced in recent years have contributed to sharp increases in the overall prison population, doubling in the UK since I started training as a doctor, while in the US it has more than tripled. Although crime rates in general have fallen in that period, the steep rise in imprisonment rates over time (which is higher in England and Wales than anywhere in Western Europe) means that the relative number of people with mental health issues who are incarcerated has also risen.[3]

These numbers are a reflection of serious problems of social and racial inequity in our world, coupled with increasingly punitive approaches to offenders, rather than any causal link between mental illness and crime. The vast majority of people with mental illness will never break any laws at all, not so much as getting a parking ticket, and sadly they are far more likely to be victims of crime. The small cohort of people with an existing mental illness who do end up in prison after committing acts of violence do not do well there; conditions are difficult enough for someone of sound mind and body. The lack of resources means that only 10–20 percent of prisoners will get the help and treatment they need, if they are judged to be grossly mentally ill. Even then, they may wait a long time for it; triage for the mind is not as straightforward as it is for broken limbs or gunshot wounds.

My therapist colleagues and I have to live with the moral ambiguity and complexity of knowing how flawed and compromised the system is. We are part of a democracy, where the people vote for governments and our laws reflect the will of the majority; that means offenders are being treated this way on our behalf. Every time I work with one person in difficulties, there are many more just like them that I will never reach. Knowing this doesn't mean I can throw my hands up in protest and walk away; all doctors go toward suffering and make what difference they can. There are also many people who refuse our help even when it is offered; psychological therapy cannot be forced on anyone.

Little has been written about the field of forensic psychiatry for the public; usually, mental illness and the treatment of violence are mythologized and misrepresented, often in fictional form or in true crime depictions which tend to ignore our common humanity. Recently I started to feel a sense of urgency about coming forward at what seems to be a moment of reckoning in the world on so many fronts. The intense debates raging around us daily via rapid communication technologies, about a number of pressing social issues, all seem to me to be shot through with fear. And what is more fearsome than a "monster" who commits a violent crime?

Like a silvered shark darting through shadows around the reef, the violent offender is perceived only as a predator. This person who was once a child like any of us, with shared ideas of joy and sorrow, is drowned in polarity and the public noise of condemnation.

I have lectured for years about concepts of violence and evil, and have enjoyed writing for academic and professional audiences throughout my career. More recently I've done some talks in the public sphere, and I felt ready to invite a wider audience to come with me into the kind of therapy sessions where I have learned so much about the mind. But the work I do can be halting and disjointed; some people find it hard to talk about their feelings or thoughts, while others cannot grasp what is real. To translate my experience, I joined forces with my good friend Eileen Horne, a dramatist and storyteller, professions that—like my own—have long been occupied with making sense of the senseless and using imagination to generate compassion. Together we charted the arc of my professional life, with a range of stories that would also allow some reflection on tectonic changes in the NHS and developments in psychological therapies and the justice system over three decades. My experience has been in the UK, but reference is made when relevant to research, data, and professional practices in other countries, particularly the US.

There is a gender balance in the book, even though women represent under 5 percent of the offender population.[4] This is because I've been much involved in research into female violence and have worked with many violent women, and it was vital to ensure their voices were heard. About 25 percent of the chapters feature people of color, roughly proportionate to the prison and secure hospital populations, a telling fact when our most recent census indicates that people of color make up 13 percent of the UK's general population. It would be dishonest to overlook how toxic relationships of culture, ethnicity, and race exist within our criminal justice system and foster bias and prejudice (including my own) in the forensic services.

Finally, although most of my work has been with homicide perpetrators in secure hospitals, I include discussion here of other violent offenses such as arson, stalking, and sexual offenses, committed by people I've treated in prison or while on probation. Two chapters are about people who haven't even been charged with a crime, where I had to consider their potential risk. In each instance, I talk about how I met the patient and in what capacity, how our interactions developed (including my missteps), as well as reporting other revelations, challenges, and occasional threats. Some common issues that arise in therapy will be familiar to many readers, like the struggle to put trauma in the past tense, the need to let go of old ways of being or identities that are no longer useful, and the search for healthy ways to manage and communicate anger or despair. Sometimes there is progress, sometimes problems are intractable, just like in real life. Along the way, I take on popular notions of familiar diagnoses like narcissism and psychopathy and explore myths around "telegenic" offenses like serial killing and Munchausen's syndrome by proxy.

Each chapter covers different ground, but an important theme here and in all forensic work is the common risk factors for violence. A colleague of mine helpfully describes the enacting of violence as a bicycle lock. A combination of stressors aligns: the first two "numbers" are likely to be sociopolitical, reflecting attitudes to masculinity, vulnerability, or poverty; bluntly, most violence in the world is committed by young, poor males. The next two may be specific to the perpetrator, such as substance abuse or varying kinds of childhood adversity. The final "number," the one that causes the lock to spring open and release an act of harmful cruelty, is the most intriguing. It tends to be idiosyncratic, something in the action of the victim which has meaning only to the perpetrator: this might be a simple gesture, a familiar phrase, even a smile. At the center of my work with offenders is always a search for that meaning, and how it may fit with the whole history of their lives, their self-narrative. Finding it can be like tracking an elusive quarry, a darting, tiny fish in a twisting maze of coral. It requires time and an opening of the mind, a willingness to look and a little light.

One of my most influential teachers and mentors was Dr. Murray Cox, another medical psychotherapist at Broadmoor. He always spoke about the importance of listening out for the unconscious poetry that may be heard even from those who seem dangerously alien. A favorite example he would give came from a patient who once said, "I'm blind because I see too much, so I study by a dark lamp."[5] This remarkable metaphor sums up my purpose in writing this book. We can all be blinded sometimes, whether by fear, intolerance, or denial. The person sitting next to me on the airplane who regards my patients as monsters may also "see too much" when they watch the news and read the daily headlines on Facebook or in their Twitter feed. I am inviting readers to venture well below that surface level, in deep dives down to where dark stories hold much enlightenment. Together we will encounter individual people, not data points or mythical creatures, and I will show how their lives have informed mine and what they might teach us.

This won't be easy. It takes a radical kind of empathy to sit with a man who has decapitated another person, or a woman who stabbed a friend dozens of times, or someone who abused their own child, for example. As they go through the therapeutic process, you may well ask, "What right do they have to emotions like love or sorrow or regret?" (I think of Shylock crying, "If you prick us, do we not bleed?") To comprehend them will require imagination, going where they walk to see what they see; it was the great oceanographer Jacques Cousteau who said, "The best way to observe a fish is to become a fish." Some things I will ask you to look at will be hard to unsee, but I know from my own experience that gaining insight into experiences that are alien to us is transformative, and I will be by your side, working to turn suffering into meaning. Chapter by chapter, as the light grows stronger, I hope the reader will be able to visualize new possibilities for acceptance and change.

Dr. Gwen Adshead

AUTHORS' NOTE

These stories are set in the context of mental health care as it is delivered by the UK's National Health Service. As many readers will be aware, the NHS was founded after the Second World War on the principle that health care should be provided by the state and funded from the public purse, because all citizens benefit from a healthy population. But the costs of the NHS have risen as people live longer, and the techniques and medicines doctors use have become ever more expensive, so successive governments have tried to move the NHS toward a more market-based model in order to cope. Health care in the UK is becoming a commodity that people buy and sell, closer to the US model of care; more and more of those who can afford it choose to buttress their diminishing NHS access with private health insurance policies. Continued restructuring has focused on driving down costs, mainly by cutting services, so that today's NHS delivers much less value than it used to, especially in relation to the provision of mental health care, as many of our stories indicate. References to NHS "trusts" in the stories that follow signify the individual business units (similar to the US model of HMOs) that were set up in every region of the UK following a massive restructuring in 2001.

We touch on a wide range of issues relating to offending, mental health, forensic psychiatry, and the treatment of mental disorders, each a vast research topic in its own right. This is not a textbook or a comprehensive review, nor is it meant to be a claim to expertise in all the subjects that arise. Given the complexity of the extensive literature and debates about the human mind, it seemed best to us to offer for each chapter just a few notes with suggested reading, as well as some references for data sources or direct quotes. These appear at the end of the book and are intended as signs on a path for those who want to know more.

When the word "offender" appears in the text, it is not pejorative or used to dehumanize; this is a term of law denoting people who have been convicted of a criminal offense. The word "normal" also arises often, usually in quotes because it is a loaded adjective which defies easy definition in a world of billions. The authors make no assumptions about what is "normal" in any categorical sense for any group of people or institution; one of the first things that psychiatrists discover in training is that "normal" is rather like tofu in a spicy soup, gaining flavor from its context. Apparent normalcy may well be a veil that hides risk, as more than one of these patients I describe will demonstrate.

Another key word we have held in mind throughout the writing is "privilege," in two senses. First, it is a true privilege to bear witness to people taking risks in order to share what Shakespeare called "our naked frailties," and we are respectful of that. Second, privilege is a vital medico-legal concept, meaning that patient information and conversations with them should be kept for private knowledge. The duty to protect privacy in forensic work extends beyond the offenders with whom we work to their victims and both sets of families, and these stories have been constructed with honor and respect for all. Rather than describe individual medical cases, we have drawn from many encounters and case studies over the years to create composites. We believe the eleven mosaic portraits presented here provide clinical and psychological insight and accuracy, though not the particulars of any individual or case.

Dr. Gwen Adshead and Eileen Horne
December 2020

THE DEVIL
YOU KNOW

TONY

"Who wants to see a serial killer?" We were in the weekly psycho-therapy department meeting at the hospital, where referrals are discussed and allocated. Most people had taken on a new case, and we were on to the last few. There was some brief laughter in response to the chair of the meeting's ironic query, but nobody volunteered. "Really? No takers?" I was itching to raise my hand, but as the most junior person in the room, I worried that I might be seen as professionally naive or as having a prurient interest. I could sense the invisible collective shrug of my colleagues around the table. The public, stoked by popular entertainment and the media, are endlessly fascinated by those rare people who commit multiple homicides. But within my profession they generate much less interest. Rehabilitation into the community is never going to be an option for them. As one of my colleagues remarked to me, "What have they got to talk about except death?"

I had a lot to learn. It was the mid-1990s, and I had recently started at Broadmoor Hospital, an NHS facility set amid rolling hills and woodland in a picturesque area of southeast England, not far from Eton College and Windsor Castle. After qualifying as a forensic psychiatrist a few years earlier, I had welcomed an oppor-tunity to come and work part-time as a locum (or "temp" doctor, filling in as necessary) at Broadmoor while I was completing my additional training as a psychotherapist. To build up my skills, I needed to spend as many hours as I could giving one-on-one ther-apy to patients while I was under supervision. It seemed to me that a man going nowhere would have a lot of time—and if he wanted to talk about death, well, that was on my curriculum.

It may be surprising that we were having this discussion at all. Attitudes to, and the resourcing of, mental health care for offenders, whether they are in the hospital or in prison, vary considerably around the world. My European and Antipodean colleagues work in systems similar to the UK's, where some individual therapy is offered, but many other countries have none. I've found my American colleagues in particular always remark on the differences. Having visited a number of different countries to observe firsthand how things work, I've been struck by the fact that it is those that have known military occupation within the last century, like Norway and Holland, that have among the most humane, progressive attitudes to the mental health treatment of violent offenders. Some studies suggest that experience makes it easier for them to understand these fellow human beings as rule-breakers who are ill rather than "bad people."

"I'll take the referral," I said. "What's his name?" I looked to my supervisor as I spoke, hoping he'd support me. He smiled his agreement. "Knock yourself out, Gwen," one of the senior doctors chipped in. "I saw one of these guys in prison for years. All he did was drone on and on about his art classes and how good he was at painting still lifes . . ." That comment actually struck me as intriguing, but before I could ask about it, the chair was handing me the referral letter, saying, "He's all yours. Tony X . . . killed three men, decapitation, I think. Oh—and by the way, he asked for therapy." The older colleague gave me a knowing look: "Mind how you go."

It was only later that my supervisor, a man of huge experience, told me he had only ever seen one serial killer himself, and that was for a psychiatric assessment, not long-term therapy. I was glad I would be able to access any knowledge and support he could offer as I went forward. To this day I greatly value that sense of being held by my colleagues and miss it when I'm working outside of institutional environments. I confessed to him that as a trainee, I thought I was lucky to get such an opportunity. Now I was beginning to feel a bit daunted. I went away to prepare as best I could, but soon realized that while there were a lot of lurid reports out there about serial killers, there was little available on how to talk to one, and nothing about how to offer him therapy.

By definition, serial killers kill repeatedly, but there is no official agreement about the number of victims required for membership of this macabre club. Historically, there had been quite a debate about this, with some consensus reached around three or more, although public attention has always inevitably been given to the smaller subset of preternatural individuals who kill dozens of people in separate events. It was a little disconcerting to read about the medical professionals within their number, who had easy access and the means to carry out their crimes, often going unchecked and unsuspected for years. A cooling-off period or gap between killings is also an accepted criterion, and their victims are not thought to be randomly chosen. Spree killers, who may take the lives of a great many people in one day, tend not to be included in this category, and for some reason I've never fully understood, neither do the politicians and leaders responsible for the deaths of thousands or even millions of their fellow men.[1]

From the vast volume of fiction, film, and TV devoted to the subject it would be easy to get the impression that killing multiple people is a common crime that's happening all the time, everywhere. The data provide a different picture. There is evidence that serial killing can and does happen around the world, with reported instances on every continent, but even allowing for underreporting, poor or deliberately opaque data, and the ones that got away, we know that this kind of multiple-event homicide is vanishingly rare. I can't give you definitive figures for this crime any more than I can for most other forms of violence; nothing is certain but uncertainty in this field, for a variety of reasons, from underreporting to different standards of classification and methods of data collection over time and different geographies. A search engine query about global figures for serial killing offers more than six million articles and answers. The majority of these will agree that serial killers are overwhelmingly male and an endangered species, falling into decline in recent years; this is in line with global crime statistics of all kinds, which demonstrate a slow decrease in all violence over the last quarter century.

One recent study that focused on the last hundred years, led by Professor Mike Aamodt at Radford University in Virginia in 2016, created a database which showed there were 29 serial killers caught and identified in the US in 2015, versus a peak of 145 per year during the 1980s.[2] Some FBI figures I've seen quoted put those numbers at a much higher level (over 4,000 in 1982, for example[3]), which only emphasizes the difficulty of data collection and a lack of universal criteria for comparison; but every source I've found supports the idea of a diminishing number. Some credit for this must go to improved detection and surveillance methods, and specialist units set up by different law enforcement groups to study and deter the perpetrators. Another major contributor is probably the widespread use of mobile phones and social media, which makes it much harder for people (whether victims or predators) to disappear without trace.

Law enforcement sources don't publish country-by-country comparative lists of serial killers, but drawing from the same Radford study, the US is at the head of the pack by a considerable margin, claiming nearly 70 percent of all known serial killers in the world, and this is borne out by other sources I've looked at, from Wikipedia to various journalistic pieces. By contrast, England, which comes in second place, is at 3.5 percent, South Africa and Canada are next at about 2.5 percent, and China, with its vastly larger population, has just over 1 percent of the total. I don't know why the US dominates in this way, but theories abound, from ideas about the lack of gun regulation there to their decentralized law enforcement to the dangers of American ultra-individualism. It may well be that the Americans are just better at detecting and telling us about them, thanks to a free press and a relatively open government. But the number of serial killers caught in the US per year is still tiny relative to the country's total population of more than three hundred million, and it is also dwarfed by their "regular" homicide numbers. In one large American urban center, such as Chicago or New York, four hundred murders in just a single year are considered unremarkable. By contrast, that figure represents two-thirds of the annual homicide rate across the whole of England and Wales.

At the time I met Tony, I knew that there had been a few serial killers admitted as patients to Broadmoor, people with tabloid-generated pseudonyms like Ripper or Strangler. Although the majority of homicide perpetrators admitted to the hospital had killed only a single victim when mentally ill, these few repeat killers contributed to Broadmoor's public status as a kind of grim receptacle of unspeakable evil. I knew that reputation, and it was enhanced by the hospital's appearance as a red-brick Victorian fortress, although when I first went to work there, in 1996, the process of modernization had begun. I remember being struck at first by the seemingly endless doors and airlocks and gates, which required a complex assortment of keys that had to be drawn each morning at security and attached to my person at all times by a big, heavy leather belt. Initially it was cumbersome, but I got used to it. I actually developed a sentimental attachment to the extra-large belt I was given when I was pregnant with my first child, and I have it still.

Once inside the gates, my early impression was of a university campus, with different buildings scattered about and walkways between them. There were carefully tended gardens and flowering trees. Best of all there was the terrace, which had a magnificent view over four counties. I've always thought it was a massive act of kindness to give those men and women a place to walk, with a perspective that invited broader thinking and hope. There were high red-brick walls that circled the perimeter of the grounds; I've always seen them as a valuable divider between my personal and professional life, enabling me to leave my work behind each night, to be held securely until my return.

On the day of my first session with Tony, I arrived early to check in with the ward staff and make sure that the room I'd booked to work in hadn't been snagged by someone else; as in every hospital I'd ever worked in, there were not enough therapy rooms at Broadmoor and there was always competition for space. I also wanted to set it up to my liking, with the chairs placed well apart, the patient's by the window and mine nearest the door. "Never let the patient block your exit" was a bit of lore I picked up as a trainee, and I stick to it even now. There's also something important about allowing a respectful space for reflection between the participants; that notion of social etiquette we refer to as "not getting into someone else's space" is just as important in therapy, if not more so. I fussed about with the angle of the chairs, as if exactly the right placement might help me make a connection with this stranger.

I felt nervous and knew I was flying by the seat of my pants. For one thing, I didn't have a lot of information about him, beyond what I'd been able to glean from the referral letter. There was still a records department at the hospital in those days, and a clinician had the authority to walk in and request to pull files on their patient, but then, as now, there wasn't a complete record. We could assemble a collage of their family background, education, medical history, police files, trial proceedings, or prison documentation, but always with gaps. Ultimately, we knew we could only really get to know a person by speaking with them and hoping they would open up to us.

Today, such background documentation is held on computers, not piled into dusty box files, but that doesn't mean there's a button to press or a code to type in that will unlock a trove of valuable material. If anything, it is harder to get useful details now, in this era of increased information governance and new legal privacy protections, than when I started out. We jump through hoops and have to rely on a range of people in different functions who may or may not be disposed to assist us. Sometimes I feel a little like one of those hapless private eyes in fiction who must manage to charm a friendly cop or otherwise shuffle around begging for reliable information in order to uncover clues. Maybe this is one reason why I enjoy reading detective novels so much in my leisure time: it is pure pleasure to sit back and let someone else do the problem-solving.

I was not even clear about what I was hoping to achieve with Tony that first day, or what the work would entail. How would we ever know if he was "better"? And what would that mean for a man who had three life sentences and was unlikely to be released until he was an old man, if ever? I was also having some qualms about "practicing" on another human being's mind as part of my education. If what I was offering was pointless for him but helpful for me, wasn't I mirroring some of his own cruelty and exploitative behavior? I reminded myself that he must have had some need or purpose in requesting therapy, and I would have to find out what that was, even if it might not be straightforward. Deceit is a hallmark of psychopathy, which is a severe disorder of the personality that I knew was associated with serial killers. I realized it was possible Tony wanted therapy merely to help fill the chasm of time that he faced in custody. "If that is the case," I thought selfishly, "I won't learn much." Maybe I'd been foolish to take this work on— but it was too late to back out now. Out of the corner of my eye, I could see through the reinforced glass in the door that a man was approaching, escorted by a nurse, and it was time to begin.

"Mr. X? Good morning, I'm Dr. Adshead, thank you for coming to—" He interrupted me, his voice gravelly and a little brusque. "Tony." It sounded like he might be anxious too. He allowed me to usher him in and direct him to the chair by the window, composing himself in a comfortable position without meeting my eyes. Gaze aversion is useful for all of us as a way to regulate intimacy, and I wouldn't expect someone to make full eye contact at first. On the other hand, I knew Tony had worked as a waiter before his conviction, a role that required him to engage and to look strangers in the eye. I wondered in passing if he had made good tips. Was he charming to his customers? To his victims? I was conscious he might try to charm me.

I began by running through some important guidelines for therapy in secure settings. Chief among these was the principle that while he could expect some degree of doctor-patient confidentiality, if he told me anything that suggested a risk to himself or others, I would need to share it with the team looking after him. Our work together would be part of the care that his team was providing, and I explained that I'd be liaising with those team members on a regular basis, including the nursing staff, the team psychologist and the consultant psychiatrist overseeing his care. All of this was part of an effort to keep him safe and ensure continuity. Our meeting would last for fifty minutes, I told him, and we would need to adhere to that each time we got together.

I tend to keep to this boundary even though forensic hospitals are very different from Sigmund Freud's comfortable consulting rooms. He initiated the fifty-minute session, or "therapeutic hour," perhaps so that he could meet patients on the hour without them crossing over in the waiting room, or maybe he just wanted a break. Unlike Freud or most psychotherapists working in private practice, I don't see people back to back in the course of my work, so I don't need that buffer. Every day is different, but it would be unusual for me to see more than two or three patients in a day, partly because each session has to be written up in detail afterward, and also because I have to make time to liaise with the other colleagues who work with the patients I see. I had learned by this time that the first five or ten minutes after a session are invaluable for jotting down memorable phrases or ideas that emerged in the session, while they are fresh in the mind. I don't take notes while people are talking, not least because it can make the interaction seem more like an interrogation than a conversation; it's also not a good idea if the patient is paranoid, for obvious reasons. Most forensic therapists train themselves to memorize their sessions. When I was working with Tony, I was still honing this skill, and I was anxious to work hard at recalling some of the exact words people used in order to retain key images, metaphors, and their language of self. I found it helped me to divide the session into three chunks, to try to keep things from getting jumbled in my memory. That wasn't always straightforward, and it would remind me of Larkin's observation (paraphrasing Aristotle) that the novel, like a tragedy, has "a beginning, a muddle and an end."

Tony nodded along as I talked him through the preliminaries, seeming neither concerned nor particularly interested. I thought he had the look of an actor—not a leading man, more the nondescript fellow hovering behind the powerful boss's shoulder. His hairline was receding, but his bare forearms and hands were furred with black curls, with more sprouting from the neck of his T-shirt. He was short and stocky, verging on overweight; it is difficult for our patients to avoid putting on extra pounds, as exercise is somewhat limited, the food is starchy, and certain medications cause weight gain. He wasn't showing any hostility or resistance, but after I'd finished my explanations he stayed silent. He just sat there with me for a long, long time, probably several minutes, and I wasn't sure what to do.

Today, I'm not sure I'd let such a silence run for so long, especially in a first session with a patient who could be anxious or paranoid and might experience it as threatening. But at that stage in my training, I'd learned that a psychotherapist shouldn't speak first, instead letting the patient start the session as they chose. I waited, and after a bit, I found I didn't mind the silence. Nor apparently did Tony, who sat idly picking a hangnail on his thumb, not looking at me. And yet I had a sense he was taking the time to size me up, considering whether he could trust me. Eventually, I thought of a way out. "What kind of silence is this for you?" I asked. He jerked his head up, startled. Then he broke into a friendly, open smile. I could see how attractive he might be, how he would easily convince you to order the daily special or another glass of wine. "Nobody's ever asked me a question like that before."

I told him therapy could sometimes involve odd questions, trying to hold eye contact with him as I said it. His eyes were so dark they appeared almost black, as if the pupil were a broken yolk that had spread into the iris. He let his gaze drift off to one side, over my shoulder, toward the glass panel in the door just behind me, which looked out on the corridor. There were sounds of life out there, underscored by the hum of the ward TV, which was always on—usually tuned to MTV in those days. I heard people talking, a low and indistinct murmur some way off. Closer to hand, someone's voice rose in complaint to a staff member outside, and we both listened until they moved off. Then he answered me: "I was thinking that it was kind of peaceful in here." I thought I detected the careful diction that I associate with those for whom English is their second language. "This ward is so noisy," he said. "Is it?" I asked. I had the sense he wasn't just talking about that moment, that he had a larger point to make.

"There's a man in the room next to mine who keeps shouting in the night and—" He stopped himself, as if he needed to monitor what he said, perhaps wanting to make a good impression and not appear to be a whiner. "I mean, I don't want to complain, it's better here than in prison, but I don't sleep well . . . so it's nice to sit quietly for a bit. And Jamie, that's my primary nurse, he said this was a good thing for me to do, and he's a good guy. I trust him." I thought, but didn't say to Tony, "But there's no reason for you to trust *me* at this point," and made a mental note to talk to Jamie as soon as possible. Tony's comment reflected how important the role of the primary nurse can be; they offer individual support sessions to their patients and usually have the best understanding of their state of mind. My work has to be integrated with the work of the nurses, who spend so much more time with the patient than I do, and I have come to rely on their observations and greatly respect their insights.

Over time, as this case and others will illustrate, I've seen just how essential it is for the nurses and the therapist to work in tandem so nothing is missed—much like teachers and parents must liaise to help children develop and grow. This is not to say our patients are childish (although some seem stuck in their memories of childhood), but the demands of a secure environment inevitably limit patients' autonomy and liberty, which can leave them feeling like children and dependent on professionals to help them get what they want.

At no time in this initial interview did I form the impression that Tony was in the secure hospital by design, as some happy alternative to prison. The media seem eager to perpetuate the idea that criminals try to cadge their way into secure psychiatric hospitals as a cushy alternative to prison, but the reality is very different. Life in these hospitals is psychologically demanding. In prison it is possible to withdraw and to some extent fade into the anonymity and monotony of routines, but in secure units choice and privacy are severely limited, and professionals like me come around all the time, asking difficult questions about mood and feelings. In fact, most offenders don't want to be sent to psychiatric services (there's an unpleasant phrase for this: being "nutted off") because it's stigmatizing, and unlike most prison sentences, it can be indefinite.

I asked Tony if he could tell me more about his problems with sleeping. He'd been depressed, and insomnia is a curse of anxiety and mood disorders, but I was intrigued that he'd mentioned it to me so quickly. "I have nightmares." This was an opening. Most of us don't tend to introduce the idea of a dream or nightmare to another person without wanting to unburden ourselves. There are some entrenched stereotypes of therapists interpreting dreams to explain people's minds to them, but the best therapists follow where the patients lead and assume that the patient is the expert on their own mind. But back then, I was like a student driver in psychotherapy, keen to do everything by the book, and for a brief moment I thought, rather wildly, that maybe I ought to delve into Tony's dream like a "proper" analyst. Was that what he wanted? But when I asked if he could tell me more about his nightmares, Tony shook his head emphatically. Silence resumed. I sat back in my chair, trying to look relaxed and to convey with my body language that I was fine with his reticence. It is never easy for two people who don't know each other to talk about dreadful things.

My mind wandered to memories of other first sessions, to my colleagues and mentors discussing how to talk and listen to people who've killed. Soon I was miles away, only to be pulled back into the room when he spoke again. His voice had challenge in it. "So how does this work? We just sit here? Aren't you going to ask me more questions?" It appeared that he wasn't comfortable anymore with the peace in the room and was using inquiry to disrupt it. I responded that it could take a while for us to get to know each other and become comfortable, and in the meantime it was possible that silences might come and go, and could feel different at different times. I reminded him that he'd said he liked it before and asked if that had changed. "Now I feel a bit tense for some reason," he answered. I mentally punched the air at this seemingly innocuous reply, because it revealed that Tony had the capacity to notice his mental experience and could describe how it altered over time. He had also answered a direct question without defensiveness. Every time I see anyone as a therapist, I want to know, Are they curious? Are they willing? Are they interested in their own mind? These were good signs.

I knew that it was sometimes easier for people to respond to questions at the start of therapy, so I asked another one. I wanted to know if he saw any connection between his tension and the nightmares he had spoken about. He folded his arms across his broad chest, and I had the thought that he wanted to block me — he was also covering his heart, as if protecting it from some perceived threat. "I don't want to talk about the nightmares. It will be upsetting for me, and I don't see how it will help." Well, that was clear enough. I didn't try to reassure him. It's a strange paradox in psychology that reassurance can convey to a patient that the therapist doesn't really want to hear about whatever is worrying them; this might be just as applicable in other environments — at work, in school, or in the home — whenever people are in close dialogue about emotive subjects. I knew I needed to show that I was there to listen to whatever he had to say, when he was ready, even if it was difficult. Changing the subject, I reminded him I was there at his request, asking him bluntly, "Can you tell me, why did you want to see a therapist?" Again, I was still finding my way in this work, and with the benefit of many more years of experience, I doubt I would ask a "why" question so early, because it can feel too intrusive. But once again, he answered me readily: "Because I think . . . I know I have to try and understand what I did, and I guess that this kind of talking might help. I told you — that's what Jamie said."

I used this mention of his nurse to go on and explore what he thought about the team looking after him more generally, then asked for his account of how it was that he had been transferred to the hospital. He told me he had been ten years into his life sentence in a high-security prison when he'd been attacked on a landing by some other prisoners, who called him a nonce — pejorative prison slang for sex offender. Tony stammered a little as he described to me how three men had jumped him, holding him down and stabbing him with a homemade weapon, which he later found out was a sharpened toothbrush. He had needed emergency surgery and was fortunate to survive. When he recovered physically, he became depressed, particularly as he had considered one of the three attackers to be a friend. He made a serious suicide attempt, and this led to him being diagnosed with severe depression, and ultimately his transfer from prison to the hospital for treatment.

As our first session closed, I asked him if that tense feeling had gone. He said it had, and he would be willing to meet me again, adding, "It wasn't as bad as I thought it would be." Music to the forensic psychotherapist's ears. Later, I sought out Jamie to introduce myself and ask him more about those sleep issues. A quietly spoken, graceful man with a warm smile, he told me he had come to mental health nursing after being a landscape gardener, and it seemed to me his observations had the precision of detail of a horticulturalist describing his flowers. He took time to think about my question about Tony's nightmares, adding some insight about their impact on others. "It's a problem for us, because the man in the next room complains about Tony shouting out in his sleep, waking him all the time. But there's not much we can do. There aren't any spare rooms to move him to." I was puzzled by his comments. As I made my laborious way back to the admin building, airlock by airlock, gate by gate, I was struck by a sudden thought: Were the man who shouted and the man who complained about the shouting the same person? Were they both Tony?

I came away from that first encounter not knowing what to make of Tony. The received idea about serial killers is that they are all psychopaths—but I wasn't sure if that really applied to him. It didn't feel like it, but perhaps I might not know. The concept of psychopathy is a complex one and first emerged in psychiatric discourse in the 1930s, really taking hold after the Great Depression and the Second World War. There was a rising social concern about isolated men, many of them emotional casualties of economic ruin and war who seemed disconnected from social norms, with callous states of mind that caused them to treat others as "things," instead of as fellow humans. By the 1970s, this kind of antisocial behavior would be defined in *DSM-3*, the third edition of the *Diagnostic and Statistical Manual of Mental Disorders*, which is published periodically by the American Psychiatric Association. This behavior is similarly described in the *ICD*, the *International Classification of Diseases* handbook published by the World Health Organization. Both the *DSM* and the *ICD* include a version of what is called antisocial personality disorder (ASPD), and most people argue that psychopathy is a severe form of this.

In 1941, an American psychiatrist, Hervey Cleckley, published a landmark study called *The Mask of Sanity*,[4] which brought the idea of the "psychopath" into popular usage. It is ironic to think that Cleckley was working on his book at the same time as the Nazi government in Germany was developing its Final Solution—the mass slaughter of Jewish citizens—at the Wannsee Conference in January 1942, soon after *The Mask of Sanity* was published. I've always wondered what Cleckley would have made of that gathering, had he known anything about it. Would he have described them all as psychopaths?

Cleckley studied a group of people who appeared "normal" and might even have had a certain charm, but who showed no concern about other people's feelings. Many of the subjects had been referred by their parents or partners, who complained about their repeated lies, manipulative nature, and emotional shallowness and insincerity, as well as their apparent disregard for social mores or rules. Crucially, these men and women did not seem to experience remorse or care about the distress they caused their families; they would promise to change their ways, but they never did. It is important to note that few of Cleckley's psychopaths were seriously violent or cruel; some may have served brief sentences for fighting or theft, but not for severe violence. It is also striking that the three women he chose to include as examples of female psychopaths appeared to qualify because they did not obey the social rules for women at the time; a main indicator of their psychopathy was a lot of extramarital sex.

In the 1970s, Professor Robert Hare, a Canadian criminal psychologist, used the behavioral characteristics of Cleckley's subjects to devise a measure of psychopathy, the Hare Psychopathy Checklist.[5] He applied this to a large sample of prisoners convicted of violent crimes and found that a minority of them, about a third, scored highly on his scale, with key recurrent features, such as lack of emotion and deceitfulness. Their criminal behavior was extreme in its violence and variety, and they would reoffend more often than those with lower scores. Hare's work excited tremendous interest and generated studies around the world. The academic field of psychopathy is huge, and ideas are still evolving; the jury is still out on the causes of psychopathy and what we can do about it.

The best guess is that psychopathy arises from a complex interplay between genetics and environment, but there's still more to be discovered about this, I'm sure. I've been less interested in the causes than in ideas for the treatment of psychopaths, which first began to appear in the 1960s and 1970s. Evidence began to accrue that people with psychopathy could, if they had at least some capacity for self-reflection, respond well to structured prison programs that combined group and individual therapy.[6] Working with individuals still has to be approached with caution, however, because of the risk of the therapist being conned and exploited.

By the time I met Tony, almost twenty years after Hare's checklist was first devised, there was a new twist: some researchers were beginning to question whether psychopathy existed at all, and if it did, whether criminal rule-breaking was a necessary feature of a typical psychopath. The suggestion arose that there could be countless successful psychopaths in our society: those charming, intelligent, and ruthless people who are running our banks and other industries or invading smaller countries.[7] The complexity here is that this effectively makes psychopathy the same as being tough and exploitative, so it should be a common diagnosis in contemporary cultures like ours. But, at least according to the available data, that does not seem to be the case. It is also unclear to me what applying this label to people achieves if they haven't broken the law, beyond implying that they are especially mean and nasty, which we knew already.

How might any of this thinking apply to Tony and people like him? By definition, the psychopaths we see in prison and secure hospitals are social failures, not successes, and obviously lack the intelligence to avoid detection. I suspect that the most able criminal psychopaths would never use violence themselves (although they might get someone to do it for them) because doing so jeopardizes their welfare. Over the course of my life, the psychopaths I've encountered have been neither exceptionally bright nor socially able nor at all charming. They are usually so unempathic that they cannot see the effect they have on others, which is why they end up sabotaging themselves. They are unlikely to ask for therapy because they don't want to demean themselves by requesting our help—and they think they know everything anyway. On that basis alone, Tony wouldn't have met the criteria for psychopathy, no matter how many people he had killed.

I expected to work with him over the long haul, gradually building a therapeutic alliance, or what pioneering British psychiatrist and psychotherapist John Bowlby called a "secure base."[8] It might take a year before we had the kind of trust that enabled Tony to open up. I decided to return to the issue he had raised at the beginning: even though he'd said that he would rather not talk about his nightmares, I wanted to find out more about the link between them and the problem of the man who shouted. I was fascinated by the idea that Tony might have located himself in the "shouting man," using a psychological mechanism called projection, by which we transfer our uncomfortable feelings or wishes to another person, like an image cast onto a screen. I recognized that I would have to go carefully because projection is a defense that involves distorted "reality testing." This term, which I will return to, describes the ability to distinguish between what is real and what is not, and whether someone can judge and respond to situations appropriately. We all have this faculty, but it is diminished or impaired in those who experience psychosis.

The "shouting man" projection might mean Tony was more unwell than he appeared, and I sensed that his resistance to talking about his nightmares was an indication of the emotional quality and power of the defense. If that wall came down too quickly or abruptly, he might get in touch with horrible feelings that he could not process, and he could become suicidal again. My supervisor and I also talked about whether the nightmares could stand for something else in Tony's mind, and whether it was possible that "the man next door" represented some idea or person he needed to keep behind a barrier. We discussed how I needed to support Tony and let him go at his own pace, so that he might be able to tell me about the things he most feared. We eventually made some progress when, several months into our work together, Tony told me he was ready to speak about the content of his nightmares.

They were always the same, he began. He was strangling a handsome young man who was attempting to scream, and he had to shut him up. He was increasing the pressure on the throat, seeing the panic and terror in his victim's eyes, and feeling a soaring sense of power, "a high." Suddenly, the young man's face became his late father's face, distorted by rage. Tony's voice shook as he described how it then transformed into a kind of male Medusa head, with snakes framing a terrible angry mouth. In the dream, he always tried to stop the head from speaking, but it would shout at him. The words were indistinct, he said, but he knew they were "something sneering and nasty," and he felt both terrified and frustrated that he couldn't comprehend their meaning. He felt he had to find out, and that was the point at which he would wake up, in a sweat, his heart racing, and hear the man next door crying out.

This nightmare took us directly into talking more about his offenses and his family. I knew some bare facts, but I wanted to hear them directly from him. He began by saying he grew up in a Catholic household with his English father and a fragile, beautiful Spanish mother who was helpless in the face of her husband's violence toward her and the children. Tony told me he remembered hiding under his mother's clothes in the wardrobe to escape from his father's fists, and how he loved the sweet smells and soft fabrics, as a kind of antidote to his father's abusive masculinity. Sometimes he would try things on or play with her makeup when he was alone, which is a normal part of development, as young people explore what it means to be masculine and feminine. It did make me think about whether Tony had identified more with his mother than his father, but that didn't seem to fit when he described to me how, as he approached adolescence, he began to despise his mother, rejecting her affection and hating her weakness.

At secondary school, he struggled with self-esteem and thought himself ugly; this was something I would hear again from people who had experienced childhood abuse and neglect, including Marcus, another patient in this book. There have been studies showing how such children will react to their images in a mirror with agitation and hostility. They also tend to have difficulty in developing a "social brain," meaning they are unable to interact well with others and may have persistent problems with mood swings and temper control. It was unsurprising to hear that young Tony did not make many friends in his class. It is often said that quiet, tough children like this—the loners with troubled home lives—are resilient; indeed, that is an adjective which is regularly applied to all children, as if they were hardy plants. It is more accurate to say that a child who has lacked basic nurturing, living in an emotional drought, goes into a state of dormancy, or hibernation. They may detach from the reality of their world to protect themselves, and like a plant under stress from acid rain, or one that is planted in poor soil, their minds cease to grow and flower.

Tony told me that his response to difficulties at school was to start working out, building up his muscle mass. Soon he began to lash out and bully other boys, finding that it aroused him sexually. This association is something I hear regularly from sexual offenders, and it is supported by a wide body of research over many decades. Advances in neuroscience tell us that the areas of your brain that "light up" when you are fearful, aroused, or excited are all situated close together and use the same neuronal networks. As Tony talked about the sexual arousal he experienced when he bullied others, I had a sense that it might be a defense mechanism for him: he could feel phallic and strong by making other children feel afraid. He could get rid of his own horrible feelings of fear related to his father by projecting them onto another person. I've heard many patients describe something similar, telling me how their violence helped them feel safer and somehow satisfied. While this may be hard for most of us to relate to, we have probably all known at some time a feeling of *Schadenfreude*, or satisfaction at someone else's misfortune, the word literally being a combination of the German words for harm and joy. This too is a coping mechanism, a flicker of relief prompted by someone else's suffering. In Tony's case, this flicker would become a roaring flame.

Young Tony had sufficient empathy and social awareness to be concerned about these feelings. He was also still ambivalent about his sexual attraction to other men. He told me he knew it would be anathema to his strict Catholic parents, who thought homosexuals belonged in hell. His father called gay males "fairies" and was scathing about any sign of femininity in men. Still, Tony would fantasize about what it would be like to be with another man and to control him—someone who was both beautiful and weak. I thought of his mother and father's power relationship and the scared little boy who witnessed their interactions through the slats in the wardrobe. When he got into fights at school, Tony told me his father always responded by praising him, saying, "Now you're a real boy." It may seem like a long way from the Marquis de Sade to Pinocchio, but the little puppet boy leapt into my mind when he said this. I couldn't help but think of the love Pinocchio found that made him real and the link with his "father" Geppetto, who gave him life.

When Tony finished school, he wanted to train as a chef. His father disdained this ambition ("women do the cooking"), and so Tony left his provincial hometown, moving to London in the late 1980s. By day, he found work as a waiter in a trendy restaurant, where he thrived. When I was eventually able to locate his trial records, I saw testimony from his coworkers, who described him as popular and diligent, and who were stunned by his eventual arrest for serial murder. By night, he played the hard man in the local gay bars, butch and challenging. He was able to articulate to me that it suited him to oscillate between two identities: the pleasant waiter and the tough sexual predator. As he talked, I visualized his account of how he would end his shift at the restaurant, duck into an alley, and ditch his crisp white shirt and apron for the other Tony's singlet and leather jacket. This reminded me of other serial killers I had read about, who would carefully compartmentalize their cruelty from their everyday lives, an internal split screen that acts as another kind of defense mechanism, which is sometimes known as "doubling." The term was coined by Professor Robert Lifton in his 1986 study of Nazi doctors in the death camps, in which he describes how they would have an "Auschwitz self," one that was free of all moral standards, and a "human self" outside the camp, where they were principled, professional family men.[9]

This split was highlighted by the FBI in a 2008 symposium on serial murder.[10] Their research confirmed that contrary to portrayals in countless TV series and novels, these offenders are rarely loners and social misfits. Most of the subjects the FBI experts studied were employed, and they had social lives and families. They were usually described as "nice neighbors" and "friendly colleagues," which reminded me of expert testimony I had once heard about a serial killer that emphasized that "he had always paid his taxes." The good self acts as a double for the cruel alternate self, which is usually hidden, as in the ancient idea of the good person and their evil doppelgänger. *The Strange Case of Dr. Jekyll and Mr. Hyde* is a classic literary example of this.

In therapy, people tend to bring their better selves to the table, at least initially. I thought it might take time for Tony to reveal what Jung would have called his "shadow self" to me, but it emerged in the sessions quicker than I anticipated. I was at pains to be careful with him, but as happens when one is trying too hard, it was easy to make a rookie error. We were talking about his nightmares again one day, and in that context I asked if we could go back to what he had told me about his father's "abusive behavior"—a phrase he had used. I saw Tony's face darken; his heavy brows came together and he turned a fiery gaze on me. I felt anxious but also confused. I was sure he had described his father's cruelty in this way, so I had assumed this term was acceptable to him. What I had not understood was that for me to use his words gave them a reality he could not bear; he was too identified with his father, and his words in my mouth had unsettled him. His hands gripped the edge of the table between us, knuckles whitening. I almost flinched, worrying that he was going to upend the table or leap over it. My hand moved, ready to press the alarm on my belt. But instead he got to his feet, threw his chair aside, strode to the door, and left, slamming it behind him.

His abrupt departure made the staff worried and angry in equal measure. "What happened?" I sensed they really meant "What did you do to him?" Patients can sometimes react negatively as part of the process of working with a psychotherapist, and although the nurses know that, they also have to clear up the psychological mess left behind when the therapist goes home. An "upset" caused by therapy might make the patient riskier and more aggressive with staff or other patients, or it could even lead to self-harming.

I had to spend quite a bit of time explaining what had transpired and reassuring the staff that nobody was in danger; Tony was just annoyed with me, and annoyance and homicidal risk are not the same.

I wanted to make progress with him, to show that I was a good therapist, or at least had the makings of one if I could just shut up and listen. When I did speak, I would need to become more delicate, more careful with my words. I'd had this pointed out to me before in training, and I had been told it was something which took years of practice and a lot of trial and error. I told my supervisor that I felt a keen sense of disappointment in myself for my failure to "mentalize" or read Tony properly. He pointed out that this was another valuable lesson. We tend to focus on our patients' inability to mentalize others, because often they will have misread signals from their victims or got into conflict while in custody because they couldn't mentalize fellow offenders or staff, but it was worth experiencing how easy a trap this was for anyone to fall into—even a trained therapist. It is a faculty that can be developed and improved, he explained, in therapists as well as in the people we treat.

Tony and I were able to explore this together once his anger abated and he decided he was ready to return for another session, a few weeks later. We agreed that "upset" was necessary for minds to change and grow, and we talked about the dual meaning of the word: making someone unhappy versus knocking something over, thus revealing something new and perhaps uncomfortable underneath. I realized that I needed to let go of wanting to control such upsets. I was able to share with Tony something of what my supervisor had helped me to understand: that we needed to allow our minds to be different and in conflict—it might even be fruitful. I was relieved that my mistake and Tony's anger had not destroyed our work together, and we resumed our weekly meetings with a new understanding.

Tony continued to narrate his history, and after a few more months we approached the period when the killing began. His first offense had occurred after several years of what sounded like a wild life in the London gay scene. Just as the HIV epidemic was exploding, he started experimenting with all sorts of drugs and multiple sexual partners, living life with a "fiddling while Rome burns" nihilism. He got into the habit of "cruising" on his night off, every Thursday, looking to meet men in bars. He told me he liked younger ones who were "pretty" and "needy." He would entice them by acting gruff at first, and then let them think they had softened him. I had seen his disarming smile and thought his rough charm might be appealing to someone who was looking for masculine love and protection. I thought Tony might have been drawn to younger men who reminded him of his own vulnerability and need for care; perhaps when he killed them, he was killing off that part of himself. I was not surprised when he told me that he had been feeling depressed and suicidal around the time of his first offense.

Tony described to me how he would leave a bar with a man to have sex in an alley or park nearby. He said he never gave them his real name, so when he punched them hard in the face after orgasm, he could run away confident that he could not be reported. Later, he stopped running off and instead took his victims' wallets, threatening to find them and kill them if they went to the police. He lost count of the number of times he did this before the first murder. He had begun to hear talk around the bars of a "Thursday guy" who was reported to be a sadist, a little out of control, so he decided to change his usual haunts and go to a different part of the city. That's when he met his first murder victim.

It was his face that Tony saw in the nightmares. He was a lovely boy, he said, "with the bluest eyes." He choked up at this and stopped talking. It was not easy to think about, he admitted. I felt nervous about what he might tell me. It is one thing to read about a killing on paper, and quite another to hear about it directly from the killer. As Tony began, he switched to the historic present tense, which confused me at first. I subsequently realized this was common in Spanish, which had been his first language. Later in my career, in my work with trauma survivors and through further study of the nature of traumatic memory, I would find that it was typical for many people (not only violent offenders) to slip into the present tense when describing painful events. The psychological explorer in me finds this fascinating: such a distortion to temporal reality is a way of unconsciously signaling how live their memories are for them, that they are not filed away somewhere in the past, where they belong. I always try to remember these kinds of verbal shifts to reconstruct later, noting down key phrases that stick in the mind.

"We go to his house, and all the way there in the taxi I'm thinking, 'I'm going to do it, I'm going to have him.' I know I can kill this one. He's so young and trusting, and he has such a lovely face, peach fuzz, soft skin. His place is a flat at the top of a building, so we have to climb up two flights of stairs, stumbling and racing each other to get up there so we can fuck. We drink a bit when we get up there and take poppers, then we start to kiss, and I feel this urge to choke him that starts in my groin. He smiles up at me, those eyes of his—and he's trying to look so sexy, and I can't bear that look, those eyes, and that's when I grab him round the throat. He isn't strong. I'm stronger, much stronger, and soon . . . it's done. I look at him and feel disgust. I hit him in the face, then kick him a few times, till I realize he's not moving. He's dead. Then I think I need to get out of there, but I'm afraid someone will find his body and I'll get done. What can I do? Get rid of him, hide him—but how? Throw him in the river or a canal? It's the middle of the night and I don't even know where we are, what part of town. I think of dragging his body down all those stairs, but that'll wake the neighbors for sure. I look around and decide I have to get him into a bag or a suitcase or something, and I ransack the place, find a duffel bag, but even though he's small he won't fit, and what if his body gets stiff? Outside the dawn is coming. I have to hurry. I can see the house backs onto some woods . . ."

He broke off. I knew what he was coming to, and it would not be easy to say in any language or any tense. Tony had decapitated his first victim, sawing his head off with a kitchen knife. The body and head were eventually found near each other, dumped in the woods. There had been much lurid public speculation about the profile of the monstrous mind that had done such a thing and what it all meant, but I was about to discover that the rationale had been quite prosaic. Tony kept his eyes fixed on the floor as he told me that he quickly worked out that the head was the heaviest part of the body, "like a bowling ball," and so "I have to cut it off." "It's hard," he said, and then, under his breath, "takes ages." I waited as he gathered himself, his breathing shallow.

"Once the job's done," he resumed, "it can go in one bag, while the rest of him fits into another bag, and then I lug them both down the stairs, trying not to make a load of noise, to bump into anything or drop him." Only then did he look up at me to check my response, and I remember that I managed to keep my face still, just nodding thoughtfully—not as difficult as it might seem, because I understood that, for Tony, this was a practical part of "the job." Learning to control emotional reactions to what patients say is a basic part of any doctor's training, Medicine 101. Freud likened the work of therapy to surgery, and we wouldn't think much of a surgeon who opened up someone's abdomen and blanched or even ran from the room, crying, "There's cancer everywhere in there!" This is why we have therapy ourselves while we are training, to become aware of things that might get under our psychological skin. Again, we take our feelings about patients, whether negative or positive, out of the room to discuss them with our supervisors. During the session itself, it's my duty to focus on my patients' emotional experiences, not my own.

It did occur to me that the social banality of this particular session with Tony was absurd. Here were two people in a room talking about decapitation, but to anyone passing by and glancing through the glass panel in the door, there would have been no sign that we were having such a bizarre conversation. We might have been chatting about the weather. I saw no point in asking Tony more about the decapitation, a pragmatic solution to a difficult problem. I was mindful too of serial killer Dennis Nilsen's petulant observation that people were more interested in what he had done to men's bodies after death (dismembering them and flushing them away) than the fact that he had killed them. I asked Tony to tell me, when he was ready, what had happened after he disposed of the young man's body. I was deliberately using the past tense, but he persisted with the historic present, in this vein: "Next day I go to work, and it seems to me like a dream. I convince myself it isn't real, you know? And when he's found, and it gets reported on the news, I just pretend to myself it isn't me."

In *Julius Caesar*, Brutus describes that same feeling: "Between the acting of a dreadful thing / And the first motion, all the interim is / like a phantasma or a hideous dream." Shakespeare's eloquent summary is psychologically perfect, and also anticipates modern research which has shown how perpetrators of violence enter into a dreamlike or "dissociated" state during their offense. This makes the detail difficult to recall afterward, and it becomes easier to think, "It wasn't me," or "It didn't happen."

Tony went on, offering a further revelation, still in the present tense: "Everyone is talking about it in the Thursday bar where I go now. I do too—I even volunteer to walk one kid home so he gets there safely, and I feel good about that. But then I think I could do it again anytime, and nobody will know it's me. I'll do it, and it won't matter because it's not real." I nodded, thinking how this kind of denial was such a familiar human impulse, arising from a desire to preserve an image of ourselves as good people. I've heard divorce lawyers say that many clients, during their first meeting, will describe how their marriage broke down because their soon-to-be ex is a villain, while they are blameless. The lawyers nod and make a note, but they know such claims are only the start of the story, and the same could be said in therapy. Denial for Tony ran deep and allowed him to keep an awareness of his bad self out of his consciousness; if his violence were real, it would matter, and that would be unbearable. The fact that he had gone so far as to convince himself that he was protecting a potential victim from harm was pretty remarkable.

Tony went on to tell me about the two other men he had picked up in different bars and killed, disposing of their bodies as best he could. He did not decapitate them, which meant it took some time for the police to connect the first murder to the later ones. Eventually, they caught him after finding a matchbook from his place of work in the last victim's flat. After his initial denials, Tony confessed and pleaded guilty to all three murders. He got three life sentences, with a twenty-year minimum "tariff"—the length of time before he could apply for parole. Today, that would be seen as too lenient, and he would likely get life without any chance of parole.

Not all therapy sessions are made up of big reveals like this. Most days they are unremarkable. We sit, we talk, we listen, two human beings exploring thoughts together. Tony and I didn't return to the murders again, but we did talk more about his nightmares, which were still ongoing. In one of our sessions, he complained bitterly to me that the patient in the room next door had gone and talked to the staff about *him* shouting in the night, which had upset him. He'd confronted the man, accusing him of lying. A row ensued, until his nurse Jamie stepped in and revealed that the other patient was right, it was Tony who was doing the shouting in the night. Tony couldn't believe how unreal this felt. But he also didn't think Jamie would lie. He told me he "couldn't get his head round it," but he didn't argue about it any further. I thought the fact that Tony was able to tolerate his nurse saying something that he found uncomfortable might be an indication that he was finding the therapy helpful. I believed Jamie had sensed this and done the right thing, and I told Tony that I benefited from my own discussions with the nurse. I had the impression that Tony liked to know that Jamie and I were connected, almost like a parental couple who were keeping him in mind.

That interchange between Tony and Jamie provided an opportunity to look at Tony's perceptions when distressed. The mind can switch off when there is too much to take in, I explained to him, and we can all ascribe things that we don't like about ourselves to other people. Building on this idea, I asked him whether he could make out what the man next door said when he cried out in the night. Could he hear any words? "He's shouting for help. Over and over again." It would have been too much for me to have said it to him at this point, but it occurred to me that the man shouting for help might have been a memory fragment of a dying man's last desperate screams. So I asked if it was possible that Tony was the one who needed help, upon waking from the nightmares. His face turned sullen and he wouldn't comment. I couldn't tell if he was ready to give up on blaming somebody else for the shouting in the night. But he didn't disagree with me, so I pursued the idea that "the man next door" was shouting the things that he himself could not express, begging for help on his behalf.

He dropped his face in his hands, muffling his voice. "No . . . I don't want to . . . I can't be so weak." I understood his need not to be vulnerable, I said gently, but on the other hand, as I reminded him, he had asked to see a therapist in the first place. "That's a request for help, isn't it?" He grunted, not denying it. I told him I was mentioning this because I thought it could be a reminder that there was a part of his mind that *was* ready to be vulnerable, that actually wanted to be. At that, he raised his head, and I held eye contact, knowing we'd come to an important turning point. "Tony, I think you're brave enough to look at something really difficult." His voice broke, but he didn't look away. "I'm not brave." I looked into his eyes. "You don't think so? Well, I experience you as brave. It takes courage to think about past violence, to take your mind seriously and talk about things that are upsetting with me. It's only in your nightmares that you're afraid. Here you've shown real courage."

This registered with him, perhaps not immediately but over the weeks that followed, and he stopped complaining about the man shouting in the room next door. Gradually, after many more months of talking about his vulnerability and pain, his nightmares tapered off, and he stopped disrupting the ward at night. The nursing staff were pleased with his progress, as was I. Other members of the clinical team reported that Tony's symptoms of depression had diminished too. I hadn't known where therapy might lead when we'd embarked on this journey together, some eighteen months earlier, so I was pleased that his symptoms had improved. The team felt he was ready to return to prison and serve his sentence, and I agreed. Tony was accepting of this, and we began to prepare for an end to our work.

I recalled how I had once doubted whether there was any point in working with Tony, and how some of my colleagues had too. I certainly hadn't imagined what progress or an ending would look like. This early experience taught me that no matter what their history, if people are able to be curious about their minds, there's a chance that we can make meaning out of disorder. Tony had also learned to deal with painful thoughts and feelings, even when this was challenging, which would help him cope better with others in the future. I felt as satisfied as any doctor does when they offer a patient treatment and things shift for the better. I'd also discovered something about how I could deal with this kind of long-term therapy work, especially when I made mistakes, as with my early clumsiness in using the word "abuse" about Tony's father. It was possible to recover the situation and move on from "upsets"—a lesson that would prove invaluable in the years ahead.

One of our last meetings began on a fine June day, when the angle of the sun prompted me to pull the shade across the window, plunging the room into a half-gloom. I could not have imagined the turn our discussion would take. Tony arrived promptly, even a minute or two early. There was a little silence as we settled in, but by now he was comfortable enough to start speaking whenever he felt ready. Abruptly, he commented that it was Father's Day tomorrow. I knew his father had died some years earlier, and I couldn't think why that might be important. "My dad would have been seventy-two by now. That's no age at all. Dropped dead one day, just like that, no warning." He shook his head. "No warning at all." Tony had told me some time ago about how his father had appeared to be in good health on retirement, only to have a sudden heart attack. It had been a shock to everyone, and the news had come to him belatedly because he'd virtually lost contact with his family. He'd only heard about it weeks after the event. "But a lot of blokes drop dead when they don't have any work to go to anymore, right?" Tony commented without emotion. I hoped he was not connecting this to the end of our work together.

I asked him what the term "Father's Day" brought up for him; was there something different about it this year? He shook his head, and I had a sense he felt frustrated, as if he wished he didn't feel anything. "It's just . . . there was no goodbye. Missed the funeral and everything," he said. He looked tearful as he said it, and I told him I thought that must have been very hard. He nodded, and we sat there together for a time, sharing a respectful silence, as if we were at a funeral together. Eventually I asked, "When did he die?" He thought about that, uncertain. "Must have been . . . early August or so. Just before that ginger lad." I wasn't sure who he meant. He hadn't described any of his victims to me in this way. "Let me work it out . . ." he was saying, eyes to the ceiling, trying to recall the timing. "So I guess it must have been . . . 1988, and the ginger lad . . ."

As he did the calculation, I think we both realized at the same time that he was talking about another murder, someone who came before the lovely blue-eyed boy that he had previously identified as "the first." I suppose I ought to have been startled or alarmed, but I remember feeling quite detached and calm. "Is it possible, Tony, that there was a fourth death? That before the young man with the blue eyes, there was another man, this ginger lad, who died?" I chose my words with care, acutely aware that this conversation might be legally important. I could not use the leading word "murder" because that would be for the jury to decide, if it ever came to court. Tony's defense lawyers could argue that I had influenced their client, coerced him into some false confession.

I felt awed by what was happening, by the way the mind's erratically placed walls and doors can suddenly hide or reveal unbearable acts and feelings. Opening this particular door would have been impossible if Tony had not been able to speak about all that had gone before, I realized. Despite the horror of what he was saying, I felt honored to be his witness at this moment. Tony shook his head back and forth, his distress rising. "I don't know, I don't know . . . I thought I told them about him, but now I think I didn't. Oh God . . ." He had confessed to the other three murders soon after his arrest, so why not this one too? I asked if it was because he didn't know for certain if this "ginger lad" was dead when he left him, which was all I could think of to explain it. "No. He was dead all right. I'd just forgotten it," he said, his eyes meeting mine. "I didn't even know I wanted to talk about this today," he added. "But there it is." We considered if it was possible that he had somehow lost this memory, or whether it had been eclipsed by his father's death and his grief.

Our time was nearly up, and I had to let him know what he

probably knew already: he had said something important that I would have to share with others. Together we needed to think about what came next. "But tell me, how did I forget it all this time?" he asked, seeming genuinely anguished. "How do I explain why I didn't talk about it before?" It was an excellent question, and I thought carefully about how to answer. I suggested that sometimes people have to be ready to remember things, to face what they would prefer not to see. Something else occurred to me just then. "Perhaps this memory was part of the nightmare too? Something terrible, like the Medusa head, that you dared not look at?" Tony nodded in agreement. "And maybe it's also coming to mind now because I'm going back to prison. Like I needed to have my mind clear first." I agreed that was possible. We went over what I'd say to Jamie and the team, and what would probably happen next, including informing the police. When I said he'd also need to speak with a lawyer, he asked, "Can't I just talk about it with you?"

I gazed at him, this man who so wanted to talk and who felt things so deeply. I thought about how removed he was from the image I'd once had of the ruthless and unfeeling serial killer, and how much working with him had taught me about the delicate management of my feelings, something that was essential in my work. I could feel great compassion and respect for his honesty, as I did in that moment, and still hold in mind the terrible trail of destruction that his mind had created and the tragedy of each of the deaths he had caused. "Of course," I told him. "Let's talk."

GABRIEL

"A man was arrested today after a stabbing in a north London café, in an apparently unprovoked assault. His victim is in a critical condition, fighting for his life. Our reporter spoke with Mrs. X, who witnessed the attack on her way to work. 'I was terrified . . . honestly, he came out of nowhere with this huge knife . . . It's dreadful the way they let these deranged immigrants into our country to run around hurting innocent people . . .'" Many people would have switched off the radio there and then, whether repelled by the offense itself or by the knee-jerk racism of the woman's reaction. But I immediately wondered about the man who did the stabbing, and whether he would eventually be admitted to the hospital where I worked, since we tended to see cases from London.

Sure enough, a few years later, I would have the opportunity to learn more about the story behind the news report of this "deranged" person, a man named Gabriel, when he did indeed wind up in Broadmoor. After I took on the referral, and before I went to meet him, I turned to the records department to get a better sense of his story. Unfortunately, they had been sent very little when he was transferred—at least, there was no background information, no family history to give me a clue about his life. I found his admission photo and held it up to the light, peering at the long, thin face and fine features, the hunched shoulders and slight frame. He was frowning, his eyes wary and intense. I thought I read fear there.

The records did at least contain some copies of the medical evidence from the trial, and I was able to review several expert psychiatric reports confirming that Gabriel had been seriously mentally ill at the time of his offense. At his trial, experts for both the defense and the prosecution found evidence of an entrenched paranoid delusional system and distorted reality testing indicative of a psychotic illness. Although most people with this kind of mental illness never harm anyone, in Gabriel's case his symptoms had tragically escalated the risk of him inflicting violence on others.[1] Thankfully, his victim survived the attack and the original charge Gabriel faced was attempted murder, but the Crown Prosecution Service indicated that it was open to a lesser plea. After first insisting he was acting in self-defense, eventually he was persuaded to plead guilty to grievous bodily harm (GBH), and upon conviction the court directed that he should be admitted to a secure hospital for treatment, based on medical advice from psychiatric experts. In an ironic win in the mental health lottery, Gabriel would gain access to the kind of specialized treatment that was unlikely to be available to his victim or the bystanders affected by his offense. This would probably never have been available to him before (or unless) he had committed the crime.

As with many patients detained under mental health legislation, Gabriel's stay in the hospital was deemed "indefinite." It would depend on the progress of his recovery and professional views about whether his risk to others was reduced, with the Home Office overseeing any decision regarding his release (a responsibility that is now in the hands of the Ministry of Justice). Today, the average stay in a secure psychiatric hospital is about five years, but when I met Gabriel, it could be much longer—he might be there for ten years or more. I had just completed my training and had qualified as a consultant forensic psychotherapist, but I was continuing to work as a forensic psychiatrist, mostly evaluating people for court reports and doing research. I was also working in an NHS trauma clinic, so I split my time between there and Broadmoor. It was a valuable juxtaposition in many ways. At the clinic I found it especially useful to be able to treat refugees from different parts of the globe, which would serve me in my work with Gabriel.

In that period of moving back and forth between hospital

and clinic, I also gained new insight into the prevalence of post-traumatic stress disorder (PTSD) in both patient populations. It's part of the myth of violence that the victims are always fearful and ashamed, whereas the perpetrators are angry and callous. My experience is that there are many perpetrators who are ashamed and traumatized by their offense, and many victims who really struggle to manage their understandable feelings of rage and vengefulness. Both victims and perpetrators need help for their psychological pain; as beautifully articulated by the American philosopher/priest Richard Rohr, "If we do not transform our pain, we will most assuredly transmit it."[2]

Among the trial documents was a statement from Gabriel's victim, which provided a point of view I rarely get to see. The bald type seemed to shimmer with the man's anger and confusion. "There I am, minding my own business, waiting for my coffee, when this little black bloke starts shouting a bunch of gibberish at me . . . waving a bloody great knife and then he comes at me for no reason . . ." His statement ended with the assertion that his assailant "must be a fucking nutter." I felt the man's distress weighting every word, the present tense revealing how "live" his terror was to him. It recalled the language of some of my patients at the trauma clinic, whose experiences ran the gamut from survivors of accidents and natural disasters to refugees who were victims of human rights abuses or even torture. I hoped that alongside the medical treatment he would have for his physical wounds, he would also get help for his psychological injuries.

By the time I was asked to see him, Gabriel had spent many months in our intensive care unit for patients who are aggressive to others, meaning the focus is primarily on risk reduction and security. For some of that time he'd had to be in seclusion, the secure hospital's version of "seg" (the segregation unit in prisons, also known as solitary confinement). Social isolation is not recommended for someone who is acutely mentally ill; one judge in a recent US civil rights action described the segregation of prisoners in poor mental health as equivalent to "depriving an asthmatic of air."[3] I've studied this and given legal testimony on it, and I know there are no easy answers; its use in secure contexts is one of many "rock and a hard place" ethical challenges for medical professionals working within the justice system. There is formal oversight of the use (and misuse) of segregation in the UK from independent groups like the Howard League and the Independent Inspectorate of Prisons, and in Europe from the European Committee for the Prevention of Torture. The American Civil Liberties Union and similar organizations are active in the US, where the application of extreme isolation in so-called "supermax" prisons is controversial and the effects of total confinement are much studied.[4]

Eventually, Gabriel was able to move on to a rehabilitation ward, once medication had reduced his general level of paranoia and hostility. But I understood he could still be aggressive and disturbed, interspersed with periods of being depressed and tearful. He held on to a persistent belief that nursing staff were coming into his cell at night and raping him; this had also been a feature of his mental state when he was on remand in prison awaiting his trial, and it had not abated over time, despite medication. This residual paranoia was the reason I was asked to see him.

Even before the sea changes in the NHS, and the subsequent years of austerity and increasing cuts to mental health care services in the UK, there were only two or three consultant psychotherapists on the Broadmoor staff at any one time, alongside a small group of (non-medical) psychologist colleagues. When I met Gabriel, we were serving a population of about six hundred. The grim concept of triage is a familiar one in medicine: if supplies are short, you treat the people who have the most chance of getting better. Back then, two decades ago, it was still relatively unusual for patients with psychotic illnesses to "make the cut" and be offered any psychological therapy. They had long been thought to have too much reality distortion to be able to benefit from it; just as there are people who are too physically unwell to have surgery, a certain amount of psychological well-being is required for the self-reflective process of psychotherapy. Suffering delusional beliefs could also make people like Gabriel too agitated to sit in a room with someone like me for any length of time, much less an hour. Stalled in a kind of permanent fight-or-flight mode, he might be, as Gertrude says of Ophelia in *Hamlet*, "incapable of [his] own distress."

Despite all this, the lead psychiatrist on the team looking after Gabriel wanted to test a theory he had. He knew about my work in the trauma clinic and outlined to me his idea that Gabriel's continuing aggression and suspicion of the nurses at night could be PTSD. Some diagnoses enter everyday discourse because, unlike so many other medical acronyms, they are self-explanatory. We can all understand that living through certain kinds of scary experiences might destabilize your mind. The symptoms of PTSD are well known, from hyperarousal to flashbacks, nightmares, and insomnia; they are a staple of many twentieth-century novels, movies, and TV series. But descriptions of PTSD can be found as far back as Herodotus's account of the Battle of Marathon and Shakespeare's *Henry IV*, when Hotspur's wife speaks of her worry for her husband, when "in thy faint slumbers, I by thee have watch'd and heard thee murmur tales of iron wars." Once known as "shell shock" or "battle fatigue" (and the poetic American Civil War era's "soldier's heart"), the label of PTSD formally entered the medical canon about forty years ago, in response to the chronic symptoms American researchers observed in Vietnam veterans.

With so little of his history available, we had no idea if Gabriel had direct experience of war, but expanding research had shown us that PTSD affected people caught up in many other scenarios, including transport accidents, domestic violence, and terrorism— virtually anything involving fear of loss, death, or injury. Today's statistics indicate that seven out of ten people in the UK are likely to experience PTSD in their lives, but thankfully most will make a full recovery within several months. The bad news is that for the few who do not, treatment of their chronic PTSD is difficult, in part because they face what I think of as a "survivor's dilemma": confronting their feelings can be too terrifying and overwhelming to bear, and yet continued avoidance makes them worse.

We had a new therapist in the hospital who had trained in a promising PTSD treatment called eye movement desensitization and reprocessing (EMDR). I had no training in EMDR, but I knew a little about it. First introduced in the US back in the mid-1990s, it is a technique that charges our memory system with a dual task involving attentional eye movements. The therapist moves a finger back and forth in front of the patient's face, asking them to follow the movement while remembering and describing traumatic images and the feelings they evoke. Today, it has become the treatment of choice for people with PTSD flashbacks, and numerous studies conclude that the results can be impressive.[5]

The EMDR therapist had the usual doubts about working with a psychotic patient, but said they were open to trying the technique with Gabriel, if I could prepare him through therapeutic conversation. I was willing to try. Times and ideas were changing, and I had seen some intriguing new research coming out of Holland that introduced the new idea of a psychosis spectrum. While individuals at the far end might be too unwell to benefit from therapy, others might respond if therapists adjusted the dialogue to keep in mental step with them and meet them where they were. Although it could happen, studies were showing that it was rare for the whole of a person's mind to be psychotically irrational, and therefore it should be possible to reach out to a part of a patient's mind that still had the capacity to reflect.

Before my first session, I tracked down Dave, Gabriel's primary nurse, hoping to find out what *he* thought about the problems his patient had with the night staff. Dave professed himself as baffled as everyone else. "Gabriel's from East Africa, and we thought he might feel some connection with Michael and Joseph because they're from Kenya . . . but he shuts them out and gets hostile if they try to speak with him." I knew him to be a well-meaning and good nurse, but I winced internally at Dave's assumption that his colleagues Michael and Joseph would have anything in common with Gabriel, apart from coming from the same vast continent. But it was an easy assumption to make, and I have to admit that I've made similarly simplistic observations myself over the years. I think any of us can use clunky language at times, even if (or perhaps because) we have completed our mandatory sensitivity training.

I was prompted by Dave's comment to go away and better educate myself about Gabriel's native Eritrea, about which I knew little. His country was incredibly diverse, with seven national languages and as many different religions, and it was full of internal conflicts, as well as intermittent wars with neighboring Ethiopia. I was cautious about reading too much into Gabriel's choice of Michael and Joseph as antagonists. He could be struggling with a mistrust of authority figures in general—which might include me. "How's he doing today?" I asked Dave, trying not to sound anxious. "You're in luck," he said. "He's in a good mood, seems willing to see you. Just don't ask about the hat."

So, of course, the first thing I noticed about Gabriel was the hat, a soft brown beanie pulled low over his ears, which he wore with the usual patient uniform of baggy T-shirt and tracksuit bottoms. Hats are not encouraged in the hospital as they can be a hiding place for weapons or contraband, and they can also be symbols of allegiance, sporting or political, which might provoke controversy. I was surprised that he was allowed to keep it on, but I did as I was told, trying to suppress a *Fawlty Towers*-style thought of "Don't mention the hat!" My curiosity about it could wait.

We met in the corridor outside the nursing station. I introduced myself, showing him my name badge, before unlocking the door to our meeting room and ushering him in ahead of me. I had been given one of the rooms nearest to the nursing station, and it had reinforced glass panels in the door. That can be a distraction for patients, but if Gabriel could see the nurses and they could look in on us, he might feel more comfortable—as would I. In addition to Dave's being on duty, I was glad to see that one of the health care assistants, Trevor, was keeping a watchful eye. He was a big round bear of a man, popular with staff and patients alike, and his presence was always reassuring.

Once we took our seats, I confirmed that Gabriel understood who I was and why I was there, and explained the usual ground rules. In response to simple questions, he muttered something which might have been "Yeah." He had a surprisingly deep voice, I thought, in contrast with his slim build. I knew that his first language was Tigrinya, the most widely spoken language in his home country, and that although he'd been living in the UK for the whole of his adult life, his English was not fluent. This was another layer of difficulty to surmount: it's always hard to offer reflective space to people whose first language is not the same as my own, and in my experience, therapy cannot be done through an interpreter. It's a fact that few staff in prisons and secure hospitals are fluent in a second language—I include myself in this—and even if staffing has become somewhat more diverse over time, unfortunately there have never been the resources to hire bilingual experts on an as-needed basis. In a flawed system, I try to do what is possible within the limitations and work to change the things that I can. I would speak as slowly and clearly as possible, and hoped we could find a way forward.

Gabriel readily agreed when I began by asking if I might call him by his first name, which is never something I take for granted. Next, I inquired if he had ever met a therapist before, and got only a blank look. I realized he might not recognize the word, and it occurred to me that he might not know what therapy was. I tried again. Did he have any experience of talking about his life with a doctor? "Yeah," came the throaty reply—which could mean anything or nothing. I hadn't phrased that well. "Are you okay with us meeting today, Gabriel?" He thought for a moment, wrinkling his brow as if it were a trick question. "S'noo," he offered. After a confused pause, I realized that he meant, "It's new." Underneath that comment might have lain a little pleasure at the novelty of this encounter, which was something. We spent the rest of the time on banalities, with me asking how he was finding life at the hospital, phrasing questions in such a way that he could answer "no" or "yeah" as he wished. I didn't see any point in forcing him to say more if he wasn't ready. It was a long hour, and I left feeling doubtful—but I also knew that, as ever, I needed to sit with my uncertainty and keep an open mind, as I hoped Gabriel would too.

The next half-dozen sessions did not give me much optimism that Gabriel would ever be able to receive therapy of any kind, let alone EMDR. At the most basic level, he lacked the verbal range. His English vocabulary seemed to extend to perhaps one or two hundred words, repeated with dreary monotony, with the ubiquitous "you know" punctuating short sentences, and shrugs or grimaces doing a lot of the conversational heavy lifting.

Our sessions continued much like the first one: an awkwardness and some minimal exchanges, mainly about daily life, which tends to be a staple of early therapy. He avoided talking about feelings at all costs, blocking any attempts to try to draw him out on things that he liked or disliked about the hospital. The most emotional observation I got out of him was that he didn't like the food. At the time, I probably attributed this to the language barrier, or even to anxiety on his part; later, I read about a personality construct with the clinical name *alexithymia* (literally, a lack of words for emotions), often associated with autism and other disorders, which might have been relevant. I'd also discover that there are many patients who just need a lot of time to be able to get to the point where their feelings can be explored, and regrettably, we can't always offer that.

I heard little about his past. We established that he was thirty-seven years old and had mostly lived in London since he came to the UK. North London? Yeah. Had he worked? Yeah. What type of work? This and that. Sometimes odd jobs in restaurants; sometimes helping some guys in the street markets. His English comprehension appeared to be much better than his ability to articulate ideas, which I'm sure is common in second-language speakers.

Often he used curse words, mainly "fuck" and "shit," but not directly "at" anything, and certainly not aggressively aimed at me. It was like dealing with someone who has picked up a few words of a new language, including some fruity slang, and then uses them indiscriminately as adjectives: "the fucking table," "the bastard chair." Sometimes I felt he was edgy, even hostile in response to my questions, but he did show up to meet me each week, and generally on time. He always wore that same brown beanie hat, tugged low over his ears, no matter the temperature on the ward or the time of day.

I began to think it might not be a safe assumption to base our course of treatment on presumed trauma. His past was "another country," one that he might never want to revisit. I thought about his criminal history, as listed at his trial: all the cautions, arrests, and convictions he had for repeated petty crimes and minor acts of violence prior to his final, near-fatal assault on the man in the café. There might be something in there, but it was really just a catalogue, terse and unrevealing. After many weeks, a social worker colleague told me that some further records she'd applied for had finally arrived, which gave us a few more morsels of information dating back to his arrival in Britain two decades earlier. It appeared that he had originally come to the UK as a young asylum-seeker, as had many of the people from war zones whom I was seeing in the trauma clinic. Trauma might be seen as inherent to their experience; after all, they had to have a well-founded fear of persecution in order to get asylum. But the trauma clinic experience taught me not to assume anything about the meaning of this in terms of a refugee's identity, and I saw many times how some people were made more resilient and were fortified by their ability to survive. They were the first to remind me that it was paramount not to generalize about what it was to be either a trauma survivor or a refugee. At one point, I even had various individuals in group therapy at the clinic come to me to request one-on-one treatment because they felt they had nothing in common with the other people, aside from their immigration status.

Gabriel's notes revealed nothing specific about what had prompted him to flee his homeland, nor what he felt about it. Nothing was recorded about his family either; all we knew about his asylum application was that he'd arrived on his own, with the support of a missionary group. I saw that he had been given leave to remain in the UK, probably because he was just seventeen at the time. Sadly, if the same young boy from a war-torn country tried to claim asylum here today, I imagine he would be refused; our current government's "hostile environment" policy is pretty pitiless.

One thing that was clear, even from the scant record, was that Gabriel didn't settle into life in the UK easily or happily. A placement was found for him in a foster home, but he repeatedly ran away. Once he turned eighteen, he lived on the streets and began to abuse drugs and alcohol, supporting those habits with theft and burglary. He was reported to be in possession of knives more than once. That wasn't out of the ordinary for a homeless person who might need to defend himself, but I thought it could also be an early indicator of paranoia. I was interested to read that the police had taken him for psychiatric assessment on several occasions, concerned that he was mentally unwell. But each time his behavior was put down to drug use, and once he was detoxed and had served a short sentence, he was sent back out on the streets. He had been involved in minor episodes of violence on and off, usually scuffles with other homeless people, until the day in the café, when he committed what is known in the jargon as his "index offense"—i.e., the crime that led to his detention. It is not unusual for prisoners and patients to refer to this offense as "my index."

When I arrived on the ward for our seventh session, Trevor was on duty, and he didn't look happy. He said Gabriel had been up in the night, shouting at the staff again. But now he was a little more settled, and Trevor hoped we could go ahead with our meeting as planned. He went off to fetch him, while I set up the room. When Gabriel arrived a few minutes later, I was in my seat. I smiled up at him, gesturing to his usual chair. "How are you today?" As I spoke, I heard my voice bouncing across the dead air between us, a little too chirpy and upbeat, colliding uncomfortably with his apparently dour mood. He didn't reply but slumped down, cross-ing his arms and drawing his brows together in an exaggerated frown, the familiar hat pulled low over his forehead.

I wasn't especially concerned—the sullen posture was famil-iar enough from him, and indeed from many of my patients. I watched his sneaker-shod foot kicking irritably at the floor tile—"any minute now," I thought, "he'll call it a 'fucking tile.'" But instead he said nothing. I told him Trevor had mentioned that he'd had a lousy night. Gabriel nodded and glared out of the window, brooding. Then he mumbled something rapid under his breath. I managed to catch a few phrases: "Bastards won't leave—how do I sleep—stop it, I said, leave me alone!" Quite a lot of words for him to come out with in one go, and perhaps that's why I then made an error. I wanted to encourage him to say more and thought it would help to focus on his lack of sleep, so I put to him the most banal question, requiring only a "no" or a "yeah': "Did you man-age to get any sleep at all?"

At that, his body language transformed. He snapped up straight in his chair, hands balling into tight fists, his voice resonating in the small space. "How can I? Fuckers want to fuck me." I said nothing, despite the shock of his words, and he rolled on: "If I sleep, they DO IT like in prison. Rape me, RAPE me. They want to make me a WOman!" I still tried not to react, keeping my face impassive and nodding, hoping to show only that I comprehended what he was saying. He'd really worked himself up. I was hit in the forehead with some flying spittle as he hissed, "You know it. You a woman! You can be raped any time, any minute. DANGER! We both in danger! These people! People treat me like dirt! Get in me—get inside . . . make me not a MAN . . ." His fist pounded the table, and I think I flinched. Then he raised his right hand, and I sensed he was going to strike me, but no, he was pointing his index finger, furiously indicating something outside the door, and I followed his gaze to the nursing station. "Fuckers, fucking nurses . . ." As he raged, his eyes bulged and his words became less intelligible, as if they were stuck in his throat, choking him.

I was aware of feeling frightened, but I could see that he was distressed and needed to express his emotions. I tried to bring the emotional temperature in the room down. "Gabriel," I said softly, "is there anything I can do to help?" He leapt up out of his chair and began pacing to and fro, growing more and more frantic, with more shouting and spitting, a torrent of words spilling out. I thought I heard something about being "fucked up the ass," and the words "night" and "nurse" repeated again and again, like a furious mantra. This was a reprise of familiar accusations, his delusions of men breaking into his room and raping him. "No more! No more! Enough of this shit!" In the moment, I thought I should stand up too, meeting him on his level, but it was a bad move. Maybe he thought I was trying to stop him or block him from leaving—and he shoved me hard in the middle of my chest, causing me to topple backward onto the floor. My yelp of surprise brought the staff running.

The throbbing, shrill tones of the alarm bell echoed down the ward, just as Gabriel burst out of the interview room, casting about for something to wield as a weapon. He went to pick up a chair, but they are special heavy ones that don't readily move, for just this contingency. In frustration, he grabbed some magazines and papers from a nearby counter and hurled them into the air, raining them down on the crowd of staff who had arrived in response to the bell. He was wrestled to the floor by five or six people; they are highly trained for such eventualities, and it took only seconds.

I dusted myself off and held back so that I was away from the restraint zone and out of Gabriel's line of sight. I could see Trevor kneeling at his head, speaking softly to him. The alarm bell had stopped, and all was hushed now, so quiet I could make out some of the comforting words Trevor was using, the repeated "Okay, it's okay, you're safe, you're okay, Gabriel." The other members of staff held his legs and arms until he stopped raging and thrashing, and when he settled enough, they took him away "in holds," his arms pinned to his sides. I saw that the few other patients who were on the ward at the time quickly melted back into their rooms or were ushered away by one of the nurses. Although rare in a rehabilitation ward, these things happen, but such incidents can still be unsettling for everyone. For patients, depending on their own experience, reactions may vary from anxiety to anger to lack of interest; for staff, it will be of paramount concern not to let the episode cause an escalation in tension that might spread and complicate life on the ward.

"Gwen, you okay?" The nurses were anxious, fluttering around me, bringing me water and checking I wasn't bruised or bleeding. I told them I was fine—and I really was. Mostly I felt angry with myself for not being able to help Gabriel, and I was also worried about what this incident might mean for our work together. It could be taken as evidence that Gabriel was, as some had predicted, just "too mentally disturbed for psychotherapy." In addition, he might now be seen as higher risk because he had attacked a doctor, which is pretty unusual anywhere in the health service, but especially rare in Broadmoor. The most at-risk staff are probably the ward nurses, because they are a constant presence, but the majority of our patients never attempt to harm anyone who is caring for them.

The incident was nobody's fault, but fears of accusation and blame were heavy in the air when the staff met to discuss the incident before they went off duty. Notes had to be taken and forms filled out; a formal follow-up was required. Gabriel had come into the room already upset by something, I said. My sense was that he had been sleep-deprived, agitated and fearful, and that he didn't assault me as such; I was simply an obstacle when he wanted to leave the room. Trevor was rueful and apologetic, saying he should have anticipated a problem that day and we should have canceled therapy—he knew his patient wasn't at his best. I couldn't let him take on that responsibility. I had wanted to go ahead with our session, as had Gabriel, and to my mind there had been no obvious risk.

I asked the team if anything in particular had happened with Gabriel the night before, something out of the ordinary. They didn't think so; nothing had been reported or logged. I didn't for a moment believe that anyone had actually tried to hurt him, but I wanted to know if there was some word or action that had triggered a memory of another night, or another time. Again, I felt frustrated at how little we still knew about Gabriel's mind or history, but I was determined not to give up. Later, I would wish I had clarified which nurses had been on duty the night before, and would feel as though I had missed a clue.

Debate continued the next day about whether the therapy was too much for Gabriel to handle. The team psychologist suggested that Gabriel was not ready for psychodynamic psychotherapy, with its emphasis on reflection and relationships. It might be that he needed a different type of treatment. There are several types of talk therapies, each with a particular emphasis and application; all of them have value and efficacy. I practice psychodynamic therapy, an approach with its roots in psychoanalysis; as the work I have described thus far suggests, it is mostly focused on increasing self-knowledge. This comes through helping people recognize the meaning of their language or actions using the relationship with their therapist. I argued that I wanted to continue this work with Gabriel, adding that it might be harmful to him if our work was terminated abruptly. If we went ahead, we would signal that his anger was understood and might have meaning. Why take an outburst of anger as evidence that therapy wasn't right for him, when outbursts of anger were part of the problem we were addressing?

I knew by now that "upsets" like this (and they come up again in other cases I will describe) can also be turning points, leading to a discovery of new feelings and ideas that are essential to progress. I still had hopes we might eventually fulfill the original idea of readying Gabriel for EMDR. I could sense the pessimism about this, palpable in the room, but I looked to the consultant psychiatrist for support, and to my relief he said, "Let's stick to the plan." We resolved that I would continue with the therapy for the time being, with increased supervision from, and liaison with, the ward staff. Gabriel's medication would be increased at night to help him sleep, and I would only have a session with him if he was feeling settled on the day of our appointment.

I returned to see him the next week, and the next and the next. The sessions were slow and frustrating, and there were days when I thought maybe others were right and this man was just not ready. Gabriel could only tell me that he felt ashamed that he had pushed me and kept apologizing for it in a way that was frankly distracting because it kept us focused on the event without actually reflecting on why it had happened. I tried to get him to think about what could have got him into such an angry and fearful state of mind. Did he have any idea what I may have said or done that had made him erupt? "Nah," he said, looking stricken.

After some weeks, the increased medication and possibly some good nights' sleep appeared to have settled him. He was able to convey that his distress when he lashed out that day was not with me but instead had come from his "night fear." His accusations of rape by the night staff were, I noticed, morphing into complaints about being spied on. He mentioned Michael and Joseph, the two African colleagues that Dave had talked about with me early on, and mimed how they would press their faces to the glass in the door of his room to check him on their rounds, at all hours of the night. He thought this was "fucking with him" in some way, although the staff explained to him that such visual checks were required for safety. He told me that he knew their interest in him was "evil," but when I asked him to elaborate, helping him by using the simplest "yes or no" questions I could formulate, he couldn't. There was something there that was too hard for him to communicate or for me to understand.

As Christmas approached, our conversation took an unusual

turn. It was mid-December, the last session before the holiday break; I would not see him again until January. We had taken our seats and were settling in when I heard the sound of singing. Some of the ward staff were practicing for a caroling session that they were doing later to raise money for a mental health charity. I'd been saying something bland about the darkness drawing in early lately, when Gabriel put his finger to his lips. "Sssh . . ." I shut up and listened. Faintly, through the wall, came the sweet sound of voices combined in a carol. "All hail said he," they sang, "thou lowly maiden Mary, most highly favored lady . . ." before stopping short for someone to recover from a sudden coughing fit.

"Right, again, once more from the top," called a male voice, rising above the others—that was Trevor. The choir began anew. "The angel Gabriel from heaven came, his wings as drifted snow . . ." At that, Gabriel broke into a smile that actually merited the adjective "beatific." "S'me!" he said, triumphant. "S'me!" "Oh, of course," I said. "Your name . . . a name with meaning." That touched him, I could see. "Yeah. Strong," he responded quickly, placing his hand over his heart. "God is strong in me." Next door the choir were singing another verse; they were on to Bethlehem and Mary now. A clear female voice rang out with the line "most highly favored lady." Encouraged by Gabriel's good mood, I ventured an obvious observation. "A song about mother and son, isn't it?" "Yeah," he said. "Mother Mary."

And then, to my amazement, he added, "I miss my mother." This sentiment was so fluent and so appropriately sad; any one of us might miss our far-off mother in the holiday season. This was his first-ever mention of his family to me or anyone on the staff, as far as I knew. We didn't even know if his mother was still living, let alone his father. The minimal information I had been able to gather thus far suggested that young Gabriel might have been orphaned by war when he left Eritrea to make a new life, but was that actually the case? I would not ask him straight out, because I wanted him to enlighten me, but he lapsed into silence, head bent so that I was looking straight at the top of his worn beanie hat. A few threads of wool stood on end at the crown, like filaments from a burned-out bulb.

From my limited research into Eritrea, I knew that the country had a significant Christian population. "Do you know that carol? Did you sing that at Christmastime, back home?" "Nah," he said. "My mother—an angel voice." The image of an angel bending toward a young woman to give her the good news of a son formed in my inner vision, an angel who tells Mary, "Do not be afraid." I asked Gabriel if his mother sang. He gave a quick nod but didn't say anything, and I didn't want to push it. I was able to confirm that the church was where he had met the missionaries who helped him travel to the UK, but then he fell silent again. I felt frustrated, as if I had found a window onto something important that turned out to be nailed shut.

"What was Christmas Day like for you, with your mother . . . and other family?" He looked up, meeting my eyes. "Fear." I waited in silence, and he managed a little more. "My mother. My father . . . my sisters. Everyone has fear. No one sings after the soldiers come." I assumed he was referring to the Islamic militia I'd read about, who might have tried to shut down churches, but I didn't ask. I would allow him to lead me wherever he wanted to go; I was there to follow. Given how little we had talked about his early life, this was such a remarkable exchange that I did not dare do anything but breathe, nod, and pray he continued. I also realized that our allotted hour was nearly over, which was bad timing—especially since we were going to be separated after this over the Christmas break.

The choir next door began to disperse. We listened to the scraping of chairs and chatter in the corridor outside, as I thought about how I could end this session. I considered the link between the absence of his mother and my absence from him and our work together for the next fortnight, but I decided not to go into that; I might come back to it in the new year. The carol had probably done enough emotional work for Gabriel for the day. I just thanked him for talking to me about his family and asked him if he could keep our conversation in mind so that we could return to it in the new year. As we parted, I wished him a happy Christmas. "Happy Christmas for you, Dr. Gwen." A nod, a smile, a proper goodbye—it was progress. As I walked away, I held close the gift he'd given me; we never know what may cause someone to open up in therapy, and nobody should be discounted for treatment.

We met again in the first week of January. Waiting for him in the meeting room, I watched as a thin dusting of snow covered the paths and lawns outside the window. Out of the corner of my eye I caught sight of the brown beanie hat—Gabriel was at the nurses' station, his familiar baritone greeting a staff member. To my ear, he was upbeat, but I couldn't gauge his mood by sight—his face was impassive when he walked in. Before either of us said a word in greeting, he pulled out a photo and set it on the small table, right in the center, then took his chair opposite me and folded his arms across his chest, awaiting a response.

I was careful not to assume anything and asked if it was okay for me to look at it. He gestured for me to go ahead. The photograph was faded and crumpled with age. I wanted to touch it, to smooth it out with my hand, but felt I should not. Within a white border stood a handsome couple, a man and a woman who might have been any age between thirty and fifty, and whom I assumed to be African, possibly his parents. My eye was drawn to the woman's hair, plaited in an elaborate arrangement across the top and around the sides of her head, then falling loose at her shoulders. Their dress was a mixture of Western and traditional: wide sashes of cotton cloth, decorated in intricate patterns, wrapped around their waists, and both in plain T-shirts. The man seemed to have a bandage or cast on his right calf, and he held a musical instrument in his left hand. They appeared to be standing on a city street, with cars and tall palm trees visible in the background.

Instead of immediately asking about the people or the location, I asked, "Is that a guitar?" Gabriel frowned, perhaps a little baffled as to why I had commented on that detail. "Kirar," he said. "S'like a guitar." I nodded thoughtfully and studied the photo a moment longer. "Can you say who they are, Gabriel? This seems important to you." With exquisite care, he picked it up and tucked it into the pocket of the hoodie he was wearing, then confirmed what I had guessed: they were his parents. When I asked where the photo was taken, he told me Asmara, the capital of "Ertra," as he pronounced it. "Are you from Asmara?" I asked. "Nah," he said curtly, not meeting my eye.

After a bit, he continued. Halting and searching for words, he was able to explain that the photo was taken not long after they left their home village on the coast, "after the soldiers came." The first part of that revelation felt easier to discuss. "Leaving home— that's hard," I said, and he bobbed his head in fervent agreement. His eyes were shining. During the next hour, I learned more than I could ever have thought possible; for the first time, we were fully emotionally engaged. Using a combination of mime and his English, and prompted by occasional questions from me for clarification, Gabriel was able to communicate his story, despite the language barrier.

First, he told me how brave his father had been in getting them out of danger. It sounded like the man had acted swiftly in the face of shocking violence. A few days before Christmas, Gabriel said, when he had just turned fourteen, the soldiers came from Ethiopia, arriving in their village at dawn. Screams woke them, and Gabriel ran outside, his father just behind him. Their neighbor and his wife were outside their house. I wasn't clear about whether they were related in some way to Gabriel's family, but I didn't want to interrupt him to find out. The man was dead, lying in the dirt, his throat cut, "all his blood coming out," and the woman was kneeling in front of two soldiers, begging for mercy.

One of the soldiers brought the blade of a large knife down on her head and it split open "like a melon," Gabriel said. His father grabbed him and pushed him into the undergrowth, and then they ran—here Gabriel whistled and gestured with his hand to indicate something whooshing past his ear, maybe a bullet, then another and another. His father fought off the soldiers, who nearly captured them, by the sound of it. They managed to get away just as the fields around them erupted into flames. "Fire in the sky," he told me, eyes raised to the ceiling. "Fire up to there." As he recounted this dreadful tale, I didn't move, still transfixed by that image of the woman and the melon. Such a terrible, horrifying thing.

The family left behind their farm, losing all they had. Gabriel's father had sustained a deep wound on his leg where a soldier had tried to slash at him with his big knife. Gabriel drew the weapon for me in the air, describing an impressive blade with his long fingers, then grasping the invisible handle in both hands and hacking at the space between us as if to clear a wide swath through a cornfield. At first, I thought he must be exaggerating the size of the thing; then I imagined how huge a knife, or possibly a machete, might seem to a small boy in a state of terror.

Somehow they were able to join his mother and sisters; how they did that wasn't clear to me either, but I gathered that they all made it to the city, where people from their church gave them aid and shelter. They heard that there were no other survivors of the attack on their village and the surrounding area. I said something inadequate about loss, about the magnitude of it, and he nodded solemnly, holding eye contact for several seconds. "And then?" I asked.

They made a life in Asmara, but they struggled and didn't have enough to eat. After a few years, "church people" offered to get Gabriel out of the country, perhaps with his mother and little sisters. But she wouldn't leave without his father. He didn't explain how it came to be that he made the trip on his own, soon after he turned sixteen. The idea may have been that he would earn money abroad and send it home to help them, a common dream of the economic migrant. I perceived Gabriel more properly as a refugee from violence, running from rather than to anything. I wished he could tell me more, like how he traveled through North Africa and across Europe, and how long his journey took, but I didn't want to be in interrogator mode. I had found over time that it's really not necessary to know every detail of people's pasts in order to treat them. I was grateful and humbled to have as much as he'd been able to give me.

I did ask if he'd ever been in contact with his family since he arrived in the UK. "Two times, maybe three or so. Long time ago." Some kind people had helped him to make phone calls back to Asmara not long after he first got to London, but in those days before cell phones it was difficult. When he did get through, he was told his father had gone back to the village some months after Gabriel had left, to try to salvage what he could from their home, but soldiers found him and killed him. His mother stayed on in the city with his little sisters, working in the church, he thought, but he couldn't be sure because so many years had gone by and he had stopped calling them. He didn't spell it out for me, but I understood that he felt terribly ashamed when he ended up on the streets and in trouble with drugs and the police; he hadn't wanted to continue the contact.

As this narrative emerged, finding its shape through fluttering hand gestures and delivered in simple English that was remarkably free of expletives, I thought about the immensity of what was happening in the room. This was the psychotic man who had delusions about strange persecutions by the night staff, the furious patient who had pushed me to the floor in a rage just a few months earlier. Despite his life's many ruptures, this same man had taken a chance by trusting me with his story.

Perhaps this was the first time that he had been able to share so much with another person. It was possible that before this day, other professionals he had encountered had tried to draw him out—missionaries, social workers, and the like—but he had been too unwell. They had probably not had the same time and space to create an alliance with him, and had seen only the foreignness and the paranoia. I didn't blame them; after all, I'd had a first-hand glimpse of the "deranged" man who had terrified people in a north London café when he pushed me over that day. In order to get to this place of trust and attention, he'd had to go out and commit an act of near-fatal violence; this sorry irony is something I will return to again and again in the stories that follow. I considered myself lucky that I'd had the chance to restart therapy with Gabriel after that "attack" on me and go deeper with him, not as if nothing had happened, but as though everything he did mattered. I felt a sense of privilege to be sitting with him.

The words of a colleague of mine came to mind, a man who speaks of the "strange and terrible beauty" of our work and of the honor it is to bear witness to our patients. Gabriel was not the anonymous "nutter" his victim had described; he was a man whose name had special meaning, who was strong. He had been a boy with a mother, a father, and two little sisters, with a home and a past and hopes for a future. I explained carefully to him that I would like to share what he had told me with his clinical team, to make all of us better able to help him, and with his approval I did so at our next team meeting.

Everyone was visibly moved, especially Trevor, who mused aloud whether there was any chance that the mother was still alive. What if we could find her somehow? He looked around the room for encouragement. The social worker nodded: they could look into it. I'd known them to be successful in tracing family members, having seen it with other patients from other countries, yet I felt I had to share my genuine uncertainty about this. I said it could help Gabriel in his recovery, but renewed contact or a failure to find his family could also be so painful that it would undo his progress and trigger his psychosis. Ultimately, it would have to be Gabriel's call; this was not something that we could decide for him. As a team, we decided that Trevor and the social worker should pursue it with him.

I have to own up to some anxiety when I heard he had agreed. The wheels ground into motion, creaking through various institutional processes and agencies, with slow responses from Eritrea. While we were waiting for news, Gabriel and I continued to meet. When we didn't hear anything, he began to fret, telling me that finding her was probably "impossible"—a new word for him. I reminded him of the time we had heard that Christmas hymn together, and the pride he took in the strong angel he was named for. He stared at me as if he didn't remember what I was talking about, but it seemed to calm him a little.

Sometimes we just sat in silence together or had conversations that were as banal as they had been in the early days, talking about the lunch menu or the weather. It may seem surprising that after such a profound shift in one session we could lapse like this, but as all of the examples in this book show, the truth of the therapy process is that it ebbs and flows, and gains are usually followed by long, mundane plateaus. We continued to be hampered by language constraints too, but over time it seemed to me that Gabriel's

English was improving, and he was more coherent than before. I'm sure this was because as he felt more secure, he became less hostile and paranoid.

I thought he might now be capable of some reflection on his journey into violence, and I gently led him into a conversation about this by suggesting that he bring images of what he feared into our meetings, perhaps torn from magazines. I've worked with some wonderful art therapists who have used this technique, and while I wasn't specifically trained in this type of therapy, I thought it could be a useful avenue for Gabriel to go down, partly because it surmounted the language barrier. He willingly did so, which allowed us to talk about his fear as an image and how that felt in his body. We used visual ideas to explore the different ways that people experience fear. He would draw a lightning bolt to the head, or a body with a dark scribble on the throat, stomach, or heart.

After that I felt able to explore with him his dislike of the African night nurses and suggested that they might unwittingly remind him of the soldiers who had terrorized him as a boy. It was a bit of a leap to make and I wasn't sure if Gabriel fully understood the idea of this kind of projection, but the team did report that his complaints about the two night nurses were less frequent in the weeks that followed our discussion, and everyone hoped that if he were able to make contact with his mother soon, we would see more substantial progress.

As winter turned into spring, we all became excited when our social worker colleagues announced that they had found her, having made contact with the same Christian group that had helped Gabriel come to Britain long ago. A long-distance call was arranged between mother and son. Trevor and Dave would sit with him to provide support and feedback.

In a movie—perhaps the Broadmoor version of *It's a Wonderful Life*—this would be the moment when the string section took their cue and raised their bows, a choir of angels singing out as Gabriel and his mother were reunited before a shimmering tree. But Broadmoor is the antithesis of Hollywood, and that's not how it went at all. Gabriel's consultant called me the next day to say that our patient had been deeply distressed by the phone call. The line hadn't been great, but the real problem was that he couldn't understand his mother; it was as though he had lost his ability to follow her local dialect. I felt for him, trapped in a linguistic no-man's-land, and my heart sank.

Apparently, Gabriel's mother was terribly upset about his being ill, which was all she'd been told in advance of the telephone call. Gabriel indicated to Dave and Trevor that he couldn't tell her the truth about his time in prison and his struggles with violence, and certainly not about the attack on the man in the café or the fact that he was locked up in a secure hospital. Broadmoor is a difficult enough place to describe to the English, so how was he to find the words and surmount the shame he felt in order to reveal the truth of his situation to her in far-off Eritrea? He only confirmed to his mother that yes, he was in a hospital. Then she barraged him with questions. Did he have cancer? Was he in pain? Before long, he ended the conversation.

In the first twenty-four hours afterward, he reverted to being paranoid and hostile, accusing the two African night nurses of poisoning his mother against him by contacting her before the call and telling her lies about him. He became psychotic, railing that "that old woman" with the quavering voice could not have been his mother, who had a voice "beautiful like a bell." He decided the nurses he hated had bewitched her. Over the next few days his paranoia gave way to tears, and he began weeping and wailing incoherently.

Everyone was disturbed by this turn of events, professionals and the other patients alike. I think we all—me included—felt painfully deprived of the dream that a mother's love might bring some peace, if not a magic cure. All doctors—and, indeed, serious professionals in any field—have to live with a certain amount of disappointment and frustration during the course of their work, and Gabriel was one of my teachers in this regard. He was instrumental in helping me to understand that I had to take such setbacks in my stride and accept that they are as transitory as our successes. Like the hero of Kipling's poem "If," I needed to try and treat those two imposters triumph and disaster just the same.

Our next few sessions after that disappointing call were not comfortable to sit through. He would spend the whole session crying quietly, telling me how hurtful it was that his mother seemed like a stranger and how sad he felt about his father being dead. What a transformation from the early days of our work together, I thought, when he could not even articulate what he felt about daily life in the hospital. As I had experienced with other patients, I became a fellow mourner. His pain got into my mind and brought silent tears that wet my cheeks. I have a therapist colleague who uses a beautiful phrase—"judicious self-disclosure"—as a way to speak about the value of choosing to share our human emotional response with a patient. Such connection is the essence of therapy, but it has to be different from the sharing a professional will do with friends and family, because the mutuality is different. With a patient, the therapist is sharing something real about themselves in order to help the patient accept something real. It requires mindful control, which is why most therapists spend a lengthy period in therapy themselves. We can then appreciate the difference between our minds and the minds of others from the patient's perspective, as well as the boundary between disclosure and self-exposure. When he first noticed my tears, Gabriel shook his head furiously, saying, "You don't cry, you don't cry, Doctor!" He was worried that he had hurt me in some way, and I could see he was anxious that this was similar to the time he pushed me. I explained that wasn't the case, and that therapists want to take pain away and feel sad when we can't do that for someone. "Do you understand, Gabriel?" I could see that he did.

In the weeks that followed, the acuteness of his grief receded, and Gabriel became open with me again. He could talk to me about how disturbing the call with his mother had been and why. As his ideas about the staff and their poison and witchcraft diminished, something new emerged. Gabriel wanted to ask me if I thought his mother might have the same fear that he did. Recalling the images we had looked at together, and the way we'd visualized fear in the body, he thought she may have felt her fear in her throat. He asked me if that could be what made her voice sound different. I said I didn't know, but I suggested that perhaps we could try to arrange for him to talk to someone else from the Eritrean community—I was thinking about contacting nonprofits or his original church group, since I knew we didn't have that resource available in the NHS. Perhaps there was someone who could help explain what his mother might have experienced since he had left. If we could find the right interlocutor, they might even assist him with the dialect issue on the phone "next time" . . . I trailed off, knowing my colleagues wouldn't want me to suggest he have another call with his mother anytime soon. I thought that it might be something Gabriel would be able to revisit someday, when he felt ready. The period of mourning had been painful for him, but it had grounded him in emotional reality: his grief, unlike his fear, was real and justified.

I started to consider whether he could begin EMDR therapy, but others on the team looked dubious when I suggested it, because the process involved holding frightening images in mind and going over and over the events he'd described to me. Although he'd proved that he could speak about these things, EMDR still might not be right for him; it could be too stressful. People were feeling bruised by the disappointment of that contact with his mother and were upset that an intervention we had all supported had caused him such distress. I explained how my experience of Gabriel during our "lamentation sessions" suggested to me that his mind had changed at a deep level. Instead of fleeing from past trauma by reliving his memories in the present and locating his terror in strangers, he had allowed himself to grieve for his lost father, his lost home, and his lost life as an ordinary human. I thought that a slow, gentle course of EMDR, with the right support, might give him more belief in his capacity to be sane, which would be a valuable outcome. The contact with his mother had been disturbing to Gabriel, it was true, but in more recent months he had not lashed out at anyone verbally or physically. Trevor and Dave, who experienced daily how Gabriel had benefited from therapy, also had some positive feedback, saying that the two night nurses, Michael and Joseph, had reported a much better interaction too.

When we next met, I explained EMDR to Gabriel in the plainest terms I could muster. I told him everyone on the team was aware that he had shown colossal courage and that we had all noticed a positive change in him. What did he think? I thought about the melon splitting, the fire in the sky, and his lost father, standing by his mother in the sunshine with his musical instrument. Could Gabriel bear to look inside his own mind and work with those images? He reached under his beanie and scratched his head, and then, to my utter astonishment, pulled his hat off—the beanie that I had not been allowed to ask about at first and which I had effectively forgotten about all this time because it was out of bounds. Across his brown scalp and through his black hair ran a big white scar, looped like a rope across his ear, the tip of which was missing. By then I may well have seen or heard some reference to this from a member of staff, but I'd always respected Gabriel's wish not to speak about it with me and to wear his hat. I'm sure I was always curious about it, but I was gradually becoming able to let things happen in their own time—and even if I had known that the scar existed, it wasn't for me to ask him about it. I was far more interested in why and when he might choose to show it to me.

When he did, in that moment I understood that he was filling in an important gap in his self-narrative for me, indicating a new level of trust: his neighbors and his father were not the only ones who had suffered at the soldiers' hands. But he had survived. Here was a manifest reminder that fear and trauma have to be transformed, or they will stay in the mind like an unsheathed knife, a real and deadly blade moving in unreal time, transmitting pain to others. For once, I was the one without words. I kept my eyes on Gabriel, waiting to hear what he was going to say next. He twisted his hat in his hands, then told me that he felt strong, like his name. He thought he could do what I'd suggested. "I think so too, Gabriel," I said with a smile. And I meant it. It was time. But I had to ask him one more thing: "I wonder what it was like for you to take your hat off for me just now? It's the first time you've done that." He shrugged. "I was cold before."

He had a long road ahead, but I had faith that EMDR might ease his symptoms and could even make it possible for him to progress to a medium-security unit, where people who do not pose a "grave and immediate danger" to the public are treated. As it turned out, he stayed on in the hospital for years and became a kind of elder, seeking to support new admissions, especially younger black men. While the EMDR may well have worked to release him from the pain of his past trauma, he seemed to be stuck at Broadmoor because there were no spaces in the medium-security units, which were—and still are—always oversubscribed. I used to see him around now and then, long after our therapy ended. He would always greet me with a wave, and I noticed he'd given up wearing his beanie, most days.

KEZIA

I loathe being late at any time but especially when I have a big day ahead. A new case was preoccupying me as I drove fruitlessly around the hospital lot searching for a parking space. I was full-time at Broadmoor now, having qualified as a forensic psychotherapist a few years earlier. My role in the rehabilitation ward involved working with between fifteen and twenty male patients with varying mental health needs, but I'd just been asked to see someone on the female ward, a young woman called Kezia. There were far more men than women in Broadmoor, reflecting the fact that our prison population is overwhelmingly male and many more men than women are violent. I did not often get called upon to work with women there.

During my days in the trauma clinic, I'd become interested in whether exposure to trauma might be a risk factor for violence in female perpetrators. I'd published one or two papers on this theme, and Kezia's case sounded as though it might resonate with some of the ideas I'd been exploring. But from what I could gather, her situation was complicated, for the staff as well as the patient. Officially, supervision is mandatory only during training, but I'd made a point of speaking to a colleague in advance, putting in place some support from them if I was to see Kezia regularly.

I slid my car into a spot at least ten minutes' walk from the staff entrance, just as the heavens opened for a heavy downpour. I realized I didn't have an umbrella and would have to make a run for it. As I went through security, the image I presented was not an elegant or a dry one, and I was grateful when one of the staff took the time to get me a bunch of paper towels. He did his level best to keep a straight face as he checked my ID, and let me through with a cheery "Lovely day for it, Doctor!"

I made my way to the admin building, swabbing at my wet hair while juggling keys and bags to wrestle with the series of gates and doors leading to my office. After checking my diary and messages, I caught the last part of the morning staff review, which alerts us to any significant events from the night before and gives the current state of play in different areas of the hospital. I was just in time to catch the tail end of a discussion about "a spoon lost on the admission ward," which might sound amusing, unless you know that a spoon in the wrong hands and the wrong state of mind can become a weapon. Grabbing a notebook and pen, I headed off to the women's wards to see my new patient.

Today, Broadmoor is an all-male facility, but at that time there were still a hundred or so female patients. A move had begun to decommission some high-security services and create more medium- and low-security psychiatric units for both males and females around the country, which would be provided by both the NHS and the private sector. I'd worked in one of the first of these, in south London, before I came to Broadmoor. Due to greater need, the initial wave of new facilities had been for men. Now medium-security female units were being phased in as well, and the plan was that all the women held in Broadmoor, many of whom had been there long-term, would gradually be transferred out, so that within a few years our women's service would close. Kezia was meant to be part of the first group to move on, but just at the point when she was considered ready, a concern had arisen about her original motives for offending, and how that might affect her future risk. Her clinical team thought someone from our psychotherapy service should assess her to see whether some therapy sessions might help.

I arrived on the women's ward with a few minutes to spare, and as usual I went to check in with the nurse in charge of the shift. I was glad to see it was Mary on duty; we knew each other, and she gave me a friendly wave as I signed in on the wall chart. She was "old Broadmoor," a psychiatric nurse whose father, mother, and extended family had all worked there and who knew the place like a groundskeeper knows their garden. She had a phone jammed between her shoulder and ear, finishing a call as she pushed a folder toward me—Kezia's medical notes, where everyone on the team would write something about their contact with her. The entries didn't tell me much about her state of mind, mainly providing brief glimpses of the mundanity of life on the ward: "Kezia ate a good dinner"; "Kezia went to education this afternoon"; "Kezia was compliant with her medication."

I waited for Mary to come off the phone, wanting to ask her for her view of my new patient; we who helicopter in and out of life on the ward depend on and greatly appreciate the insights of our nursing colleagues, who are "on the front lines." But Mary didn't have much for me, shrugging as she admitted, "She's a bit hard to read . . . A model patient, you know." I made a face, and we both laughed at the hospital shorthand: the model patient is the one you watch out for most. I thought she might also be reminding me not to take this at face value. "I wouldn't have thought she needs therapy myself," Mary was saying, her tone deliberately bland. "But then she's not my patient. Jean-Paul would know more." She flicked her eyes over to a colleague standing in the doorway, a tall, slim young man I'd not met before who was busy chatting with two older patients. I planned to catch up with him later. Now it was time to meet Kezia.

She was waiting for me in the corridor, and I smiled and held out my hand as I walked up to her. She smiled back, immediately making good eye contact. I introduced myself and led her to the interview room I'd booked. The chairs were not uncomfortable, and though the room was small, the window looked out over the trees to the hills beyond and the ceiling was high, giving a feeling of space. I'd seen her admission photograph, taken around the time of her trial ten years earlier, when she was in her early twenties. To me, it brought to mind a school photo of a squirming child forced briefly to sit still, with hair combed neatly and white blouse buttoned high at the collar. Now a wild tangle of tufts and curls formed an uneven black halo around Kezia's head, and a jolly cartoon unicorn decorated her faded T-shirt. Her shapeless leggings were wrinkled and stained, and she wore bright pink fluffy slippers on her feet. She had the dazed appearance of someone who had just rolled out of bed, but it was immediately interesting to me that she had been on time, ready and willing to attend our meeting. It might mean that she was agreeable to the idea of working with someone like me and understood why I had come.

Kezia had been admitted to the hospital ten years ago, shortly after her arrest on a potential murder charge involving the death of a male care worker, Mark, who was working in the rehabilitation facility for people with mental illness where she was living at the time. She had a history of paranoid schizophrenia, with vivid auditory and visual hallucinations. When the police arrived, she told them that Mark was a demon and was "trying to possess her brain," so she'd had to kill him. As they took her into custody, Kezia insisted she could still hear the demon's voice taunting her. She lashed out and kept shouting at some unseen figure, until the police hastily arranged for her to be assessed by a local psychiatrist, who referred her to Broadmoor. There she had remained as she awaited trial, and she never left.

At her trial, the psychiatrists who gave evidence had been unanimous that Kezia was acutely mentally ill at the time of the killing. Eyewitnesses spoke of her disturbed mental state, and evidence of recurring bouts of inpatient treatment and medication was presented. She pleaded guilty and was convicted of manslaughter, an offense which in English law is differentiated from murder in terms of the intention to kill. Kezia's intention to kill was thought to be diminished by her mental illness at the time of the offense, and so she was convicted of a slightly less serious crime, similar to the idea of second- or third-degree murder in the US. In English law, such a defense can only be raised in murder cases, and judges have discretion over the sentence passed. Many people like Kezia do go to prison and serve long sentences there, but because there was good evidence that she was mentally ill at the time of the offense, the judge opted to send her to a secure hospital instead, following the recommendation of expert witnesses.

The psychiatric formulation (the medical explanation of her case) was quite straightforward. Kezia's fatal violence was driven by the paranoid delusions that were a recognized symptom of her severe mental illness. She had not had a sane motive to kill Mark; it was her illness that was to blame for the killing, not Kezia. The psychiatrists who had looked after her over the years agreed on this narrative. They assured her she was not to blame, and if she kept taking her medication, her mental illness would not recur and she would not be dangerous to others. By all accounts, she was compliant and accepting of this explanation and had never been at all difficult or rude. When a place became available, the clinical team applied to the Home Office for permission to transfer Kezia out of the hospital to one of the new medium-security units. In time, it was possible that she might make further steps in her rehabilitation and even return to community life.

Then Jean-Paul sounded a note of alarm. He had not been at the hospital for long, having come from working in general psychiatric services, but he had quickly formed a good rapport with Kezia and became her primary nurse. The primary nurse is an important supporter of and advocate for their patients, and Jean-Paul had initially been positive about her proposed transfer. However, at a team review of her case, he outlined a concern that Kezia was becoming too attached to him. He was getting the impression that she felt jealous if he spent time with the other female patients on the ward, and this had prompted him to ask Kezia for more information about her relationship with Mark, her victim, who had also been her care worker. Not all nurses would do this, but it's certainly not forbidden or discouraged. I imagined Jean-Paul was curious and eager to help her.

He reported to the team that Kezia had indicated to him that she had been in love with Mark, and possibly jealous of him as well. It made him feel uneasy to think that jealous impulse could be activated again if she became as attached to him or any other male care worker. What if she might actually be "bad, not mad"? Borrowed from a description of Lord Byron ("mad, bad and dangerous to know"), this is somewhat clichéd shorthand for a major academic debate in my field. It is the kind of dualistic thinking we find in relation to other complex philosophical questions: for example, the well-worn nature or nurture question in mental health or discussions about sex and gender. I think such binary arguments dodge complexity and seem to be an attempt to prevent our thinking about what it takes to live together in a group, in terms of our culture, our habitat, our norms. I am reminded of a wise observation, often credited to Carl Jung, that "thinking is hard, that's why most people judge." I knew the temptation. Like Jean-Paul, I had come into the profession with a lot of learned theory and youthful assurance, giving rise to a jagged kind of judgment that had to be gradually sanded down over time. Working with Kezia was an important marker on that journey.

The referral letter I had read had been frank about the problem Jean-Paul's report had caused within the team: some people were inclined to dismiss the nurse's anxiety, but others were concerned that Kezia might present a risk that couldn't be managed with medication. It could be that they'd overlooked something important for the last decade, and that this might even lead to a challenge to her original conviction and another trial. The psychiatrist coordinating her care (the responsible clinician, or "RC" in UK hospital jargon) told me he was skeptical, but the anxiety was enough to make him put the brakes on Kezia's transfer and ask for a psychotherapy assessment.

I had my doubts, based on some of the research I had been doing.[1] Far more than with men, there appeared to be a societal need to explain away female violence as the result of trauma, even though most violent men have histories of trauma too, and despite the fact that most traumatized women (and there are a lot of them) are never violent. I also questioned whether Kezia could have hidden her jealousy for so many years, although her RC had mentioned to me that it had taken considerable time to stabilize her mental state after admission, and it was possible she had just been too unwell for anyone to spot this sooner. It might also be the case that she had never discussed her feelings about Mark—or anything else—before now because she'd never been given the opportunity. As I've indicated, due to a prevailing idea at the time that trauma was the principal reason for their violence, few female offenders were ever invited to engage in talk therapy, especially if they were mentally unwell. It was unsurprising to me to find that Kezia had not been offered any since her arrival. While this could also be put down to a lack of resources and the rarity of her offense, I was beginning to think women's violence was generally seen as a topic to be avoided, even in a hospital like Broadmoor; this was partly what motivated my research into gender bias and violence early in my career. I hadn't heard much about it while I was training, although I had seen some women who scared me. In one instance, while on a placement in a clinic in the community, a woman had threatened a male therapist during a session. When I heard shouts from his office, I ran along the corridor to check what was happening. I rounded the corner to discover that he had barricaded himself in his office, while the patient, whom I can only describe as "growling" with fury, was gouging out chunks of his wooden door with a sharp object. With a speed fueled by cowardice, I leapt into a hall cupboard and locked myself in. Bleakly comic in hindsight, the situation was resolved when the patient gave up and left, disappearing down the stairs in a flurry of expletives, with no harm done and without any police or legal involvement. But I was left with a curiosity about this woman's rage and cruelty; if she'd been male, she would have been arrested and probably imprisoned, which made me wonder if women's capacity for cruelty and violence was a no-go area in our culture. This memory has stayed with me in a way I think it would not have if the raging patient had been male, because male violence seems so familiar. The other intriguing question is whether I would have intervened if I'd been a man, rather than throwing myself into a cupboard. I can't know the answer to that.

Kezia's diagnosis was also a factor in her lack of experience with talk therapy. When she was first treated for paranoid schizophrenia as a teenager, back in the early 1990s, the focus of treatment was on medication, not talking therapies. This was partly related to the widespread belief in those days that people with psychosis couldn't use therapy, as I've touched on in the case of Gabriel, and to try it was generally seen as a waste of scant resources. Unfortunately, racial discrimination was probably also a factor; historically, much less therapy has been offered by mental health services in the UK to people of color than to their white counterparts. I'm glad to say that the situation is somewhat improved today, but there is still a long way to go. This is a deep-rooted and systemic problem, part and parcel of wider institutional racism. People of color continue to be underrepresented as therapy patients and professionals both in the community and in secure settings.[2]

This case was further complicated by the ethical difficulty of my being asked to try and resolve an anxiety in the minds of the clinical team rather than in the patient's mind, a situation I hadn't often encountered at that time, though it would happen many times over in the future. I was uneasy about embarking on a course of therapy that might change the way in which Kezia was seen, and I would need to think carefully as I was going forward. This was a major reason why I'd arranged for supervision. When I'd been circling the parking lot that morning, the quixotic thought had occurred to me that I was being asked to play detective, a kind of mash-up of therapist and Sherlock Holmes, boldly taking a magnifying glass into someone's mind—as if that were even possible.

"I got your letter," she said. Her voice was soft and low, south London with just a hint of the Caribbean. She held out the appointment letter I'd sent, which looked like it had been read many times over, folded and refolded. I started to comment, when she opened her mouth to speak again. "Sorry, sorry," she said. I told her to go ahead. "Nothing, no—you talk," she mumbled, more shy than impolite. I launched into my usual speech, thanking her for agreeing to meet me and setting out the parameters for our work. I had the sense of her attending closely, head bobbing as if she understood every word, but the gaze of her brown eyes was unfocused. I had to ask, did she know why she'd been referred to me for therapy? She nodded eagerly, the good student who knew the right answer. "They want me to talk about what I did . . . but it's such a long time ago. I have to put it behind me and move on." I echoed this back, to let her know I had heard her, but also to make sure I understood her meaning. "You've got to put it behind you?" "Put it behind me, move on, yes," she said. "But they want me to talk about it first. It was ten years ago, you know. Almost exactly." I recalled the date of her offense, having just read about it, and realized it was indeed the anniversary that week. She cast her eyes down, and I followed her gaze. Her hands were in her lap, cradled under her stomach as if it were a large cat, which looked like a form of self-soothing. I reassured her that we didn't have to talk about her offense that day. She lifted her head, confused. "But, Doctor, I think they want me to." She was so eager to please, which made me think again about Mary's enigmatic comment that she was a model patient.

Maybe she could tell me what she'd talked about with her other doctors, I suggested. She replied in much the same way as before: "I was mentally ill and that made me do what I did, and they said I was not guilty because of my illness but I should take my meds and I would be better, so I can put it all behind me and move on." She stopped, then added, "Is that enough? I think they want me to talk about Mark, don't they?" I thought her mention of him was interesting, but I steered her away for now. In training, I'd learned by trial and error—and via a lot of feedback from my supervisors—that it was counterproductive to get into the topic of someone's offense too early, even if they raised it. It was important to build a rapport first, so I invited Kezia to talk to me about life in the hospital and her interests off the ward.

She told me she went to classes in the hospital education center and to occupational therapy, and spoke of some pictures she'd framed to sell in the hospital shop. She also liked to go to chapel regularly and sometimes met with the chaplain, which reminded me that I'd heard about her strong religious faith and her family's evangelical Christian background. Early on in their careers psychiatrists are trained to be aware of and sensitive to the diversity of beliefs in cultures, because it is crucial to the process of trying to work out whether a person's thoughts or beliefs are "normal" or evidence of mental illness. Faith beliefs are a good example of the kind of mental experience that psychiatrists have to assess and consider. Academics, philosophers, and pundits may argue about their validity, but in a psychiatric sense, faiths are not delusions, because they are based on reason and an awareness of doubt, as well as being culturally coherent, whereas delusions are rigid and culturally alien.

I asked if she could take me back to the beginning. "Of what? My crime?" No, I told her, I meant after she was born, the beginning of her life. "Ohhh . . ." She lit up with a big wide smile, more than happy to talk about her early childhood in Jamaica. Born in her grandmother's house, in a small village far from the capital, she lived there with her mother and two younger siblings until Mum left them, when Kezia was six years old, to go and find work in the UK. The children stayed in the care of Gran, whom Kezia clearly adored. Her eyes shone as she talked of the games they would play, and how they went running around in the sun with no shoes on and swam in the sea with giant turtles. She said her best memories were of attending church with Gran, where there was wonderful singing. To my surprise, unprompted she closed her eyes and half recited, half sang a fragment of a favorite hymn, from Psalm 23: "He leads me beside still waters / He restores my soul."

My thoughts went to her delusions about demonic possession, and whether she had been exposed to other kinds of religious thought beyond the Christian church she described. I knew a little about what that might include; I'd come across patients who had talked about their beliefs in obeah and voodoo, but I didn't want to make any assumptions. Again, I was working on keeping an open mind, holding myself "in the Bardo." Keats describes the quality of thought this requires as "negative capability," a mental stillness that hovers in doubt and doesn't settle on obvious answers. This would be a lifetime's challenge for me, a skill that had to be rehearsed and relearned in my therapeutic practice many times over. Here it was important to pause and think about what the demons Kezia had thought were possessing Mark meant to *her*, not to me. They might turn out to be symbolically important in her life. By this time, I had seen a lot of delusional patients in the course of my work, but ideas of possession like this were not common. More often, people suffered from ideas of grandeur or inflated self-belief ("I can kill you with one blow"; "I'm a top spy for MI5"; "I can read your mind, I know what you're thinking"), or their delusions were paranoid and they believed that other people meant them harm or that they were under surveillance. I had learned that delusions were never just plucked from the air and that they tended to arise out of individual beliefs and experience, as we saw with Gabriel, whose paranoid delusions reflected his fears and unprocessed traumatic memories.[3]

Kezia was so animated that I simply let her carry on, smiling and nodding my encouragement, without interruption. I waited for her to come to what I knew was the next chapter of her life, beginning with her mother returning to the island when Kezia was ten years old to take everyone with her to live in the UK. There was no mention of a father figure at any point, and I didn't press her, hoping that that information might emerge naturally. When she got to the point where she arrived in London, she stopped, as if there was no more to say. Her face fell.

"Did it seem very gray here, after Jamaica?" I prompted. She gestured to the rain-streaked window and the dull sky beyond, as if to say, "What do you think?" She'd never been so cold or wet as she was that first winter. "It was like a different planet!" We both laughed at her tone, and she went on to tell me about school, how difficult she found her studies but how she had hoped to train as a nurse once she was grown up. The family went to church in their new neighborhood, where her mother found a boyfriend. He was one of many, Kezia said. The picture she painted was of a life with no one steady male presence, just a series of unpleasant men, some of whom were violent to her mother and the children. Social services got involved a few times, but the children weren't removed from the family home.

When she was eighteen, she learned that her beloved Gran had died. As she told me this, her voice caught, and I felt her grief like another presence in the room, settling as a kind of coldness over us, a deep woe. She struggled to continue. "Then my sickness came. I was sent to doctors and nurses and hospital, and then they gave me medicines, but I hated them. I got so fat. I wanted to be out, to go to college. I promised Gran I would go." Her voice cracked with dismay and sorrow. I could only comment that it sounded painful. I thought—but did not say—that this was a lot to contend with, at a time when most young people are full of dreams of what they might do in life. Instead, she had lost not only her grandmother but her grip on reality.

Just then, I became conscious that I was suddenly feeling sleepy. That wasn't my usual experience in sessions, but maybe there was something about the rhythm and timber of Kezia's voice. I shook myself a little, swallowing a yawn, hoping she hadn't noticed. It was nearly time for the session to end, and I wanted to discuss the way forward. I put it to her that we could meet again the following week if she wished, and she agreed, asking me bluntly if that's when we would start talking about "her crime." I assured her we would get to that, but first I wanted to hear more about her life beforehand. We could decide together when she was ready to go further, and I promised I wouldn't just spring it on her. She rubbed her hands on her thighs anxiously and stood up, as if we'd sealed a deal. "I just want to put it behind me and move on." We were back to where she'd started. "I get that, Kezia, I really do."

Before our next session, I made time to meet with Jean-Paul. I asked if he could help me with any more details about what Kezia had said that made him think she'd been in love with Mark, the man she'd killed. Could he recall the actual words she'd used, verbatim? He hedged a bit, saying this was more of a feeling he had, based on comments she'd made to him. For example, she'd told him about a song which she said always made her think of Mark, a love song. He also spoke about his concern that she might develop feelings for him and described to me an angry outburst when she found him talking with another patient on the ward.

Later, I would consider with my supervisor the importance of jealousy as a motive for killing. This is not an emotion that's alien to us; most people know that disturbing mix of rage, fear, and grief, although few will ever kill as a result, or even countenance doing so. Jealousy has long been a favorite motive in tragic narratives, both real and fictional, and Jean-Paul was drawing on that tradition. My job was to see if that explanation was in any sense true for Kezia.

I remember once while I was in training discussing a similar case with a group of forensic psychiatrists—all of whom were male, as was often the case back then. Someone referred to "Othello syndrome"[4] or "morbid jealousy" as a rationale for our male patient's violence. In *Othello*, Shakespeare demonstrates how a good man is overcome by a "green-eyed monster"; jealousy as a fantastical and powerful force which generates his fatal violence. I commented that I wasn't convinced that jealousy provided a complete explanation for our patient's fatal violence toward his wife, given that there are many jealous men who don't express themselves in this way. To my surprise, one of the most senior of the men responded testily, "Only a woman would dismiss a man's jealousy." That shut me up, as it was meant to, but later I wrote to him to try and explain that my objection was based on psychological and legal arguments, not my sex. I still think that's correct, but I also appreciate that there may be something I don't fully fathom about masculinity, not having lived it myself.

The Othello defense is almost always made by men, but then again, they do most of the killing. Among the small fraction of the UK's total prison population that is female (around 5 percent, although this figure is on the rise), the majority are serving short sentences for nonviolent crime. Only 5 percent of all homicides in the UK are committed by women, a figure that is similar around the world, as UN and other global studies consistently demonstrate.[5] There is no consensus as to the reason for this wide difference between the sexes, but it's probably multifactorial. It is possible a male's Y chromosome increases the risk of violence, but this does not explain why the majority of people with Y chromosomes are never violent. Some theorists have argued (more plausibly in my view) that male role expectations mean that the threshold for the use of violence is lowered, so that it becomes "normal" for real men. A similar argument has been made for women: that it takes more for a woman to kill because it's somehow unnatural in terms of feminine stereotypes and social norms. It is also suggested that the maternal and caring function of women in our culture might be protective against violence, making them more pro-social, a term which describes behaviors seen as helpful to other people, including sharing with, cooperating with, and comforting them.

Ascribing mental illness as a motive when women commit murder may be the easiest response in a society that is ambivalent about women's capacity for violence and wants to both condemn and excuse it in a way that doesn't happen for men. It struck me that the psychiatrists who had examined Kezia after her arrest had probably focused on her obvious symptoms of mental illness, and not so much on her psychological experiences as a young woman who'd migrated from another country and culture. They may also have focused on mental illness because Kezia had been violent before when she was unwell: I'd learned that at the age of nineteen, she had physically attacked her mother during a psychotic episode, leading to an urgent admission to a local psychiatric unit. Her mother was unhurt but frightened and told the medical team that she was not willing to have Kezia return home to live with the family when she was released. This meant that Kezia was eventually housed in the rehabilitation home where Mark worked. I wanted to know much more about all of this, but I knew we had groundwork to do first.

Over the next six months, she and I met regularly, gradually moving into a more reflective mode of conversation, where I would not ask questions but instead let her start our session with whatever was important to her that day. We talked more about her past, about her friendships and hobbies growing up in Jamaica, and the ups and downs of her family relationships. She commented that nobody had ever wanted to know about this side of her life before. I was never bored, but I did notice that the sudden strange sleepiness that had affected me in our first session would return sometimes and I always had to be on guard, ready to stifle a yawn or pinch myself. I realized this occurred whenever Kezia lapsed into talking about grief or loss, and repeated her familiar litany about "putting it all behind her" and how she had to "pick up the pieces and move on." As if hypnotized by her words, I would feel a profound weariness rising within me. I can only describe it as a sensation of being "knocked out," which I fought off and hid from Kezia as best I could. I would have to think about this with my supervisor.

I was asked to join the latest case review for Kezia. The team wanted some feedback, or maybe some answers. Did I have any yet? Before agreeing, I felt I needed to talk to Kezia about what had happened with Mark. At our next session, I reminded her that we both knew Jean-Paul had instigated the debate that had brought us together, and that he had suggested a new explanation for her offense. I reminded her of our first meeting, and asked if we could return to the link between her mental illness and the crime. "I think it was hard for you to talk about it then, wasn't it? Would it be okay to do that now?" She agreed, but then asked, "Where do I start?" I suggested she could begin at the point where she first met Mark. As she started to talk, her account merged with the reports and witness statements I'd absorbed, and the events began to live in my mind's eye.

After she assaulted her mother and wasn't allowed to return home from the local hospital, Kezia had spent a miserable year "stuck in there" while an alternative placement was sought. Eventually, when a hostel bed became available, Mark visited her in the hospital, coming by a few weeks before her transfer to introduce himself and explain that he would be her key worker (or case manager). He was also of Afro-Caribbean heritage—his father was Jamaican. He answered her questions and talked to her about life in the hostel, making her feel welcome. On the day of her release, he helped gather up her things and drove her to her new home. They had a good relationship from the start. He was a man of strong faith, and he talked to her about a forgiving God, a concept alien to her experience, but one that was comforting to hear. "He made me feel home," she told me, and I thought her slip of the tongue might be important. In therapy, words matter, regardless of how mundane they may seem. We can all relate to an experience of saying something we don't intend—or, as the old joke goes, "A Freudian slip is when you say one thing and mean your mother." I thought Kezia may have said exactly what she meant. In that slip might lie the meaning of home for her, whether it signified that Mark represented Jamaica, a fantasy of a father, or some more abstract concept of safety and love.

It was difficult to ascertain what happened next between Kezia and Mark, or if something changed in the weeks after she moved in. She did not add much to what I already knew. She had been well when she left the hospital with Mark, even if she still felt guilty and hurt about her mother's rejection. She joined in with activities and settled into her new room. She told me she took her medication every day, even though in the wake of her arrest some people claimed that this might not have been the case. I sighed a little, as I always do when I hear this familiar cliché about people being "off their meds," as if that handily explains everything. In one of my private-eye forays to the hospital records office in search of more insight, I had also come across some photocopies of police reports, which featured among them Mark's handwritten notes confirming that she was compliant with her meds. I found it moving to see this kind man's large, round handwriting on the page, commenting that Kezia was "stable but a little low" as the weekend approached and he went off duty.

At the end of a previous session, Kezia and I had been talking about how people tend not to use the word "goodbye" when they part company—"including you, Dr. Gwen," she said. "People will say, 'See you,' or 'Until next time,' or sometimes just 'Later' or 'Bye,' when they ought to say the whole word. 'Goodbye.' Did you know it means 'God be with you'?" I had made a mental note of this because it seemed so important to her, and now I reminded her about it as we got closer to talking about her crime. She said she had seen Mark on the Friday afternoon before the homicide, which took place the following Monday. "That was the last time you spoke before you killed him?" Kezia winced at that, but I trusted that she knew by now that I didn't mean for my words to hurt her. Using such direct language at the right moment can help people to speak openly about their offense, because it shows that I am ready to hear about it. I was thinking of the bicycle lock model of risk factors for violence, curious as to what the final "number" was that clicked into place for Kezia on the day she killed Mark. Was it something in their last goodbye? It might have been a tiny lever that dislodged a fatal cascade.

She sat completely still, her lips pressed tight, head bent, perhaps mustering her courage. I noticed that her appearance had changed quite a bit since we began working together. She was dressed in a clean tracksuit and her hair was now arranged in neat cornrows. I told her I knew it was difficult to think about Mark's death, but putting it into words might make it easier to understand. "I don't think I want to understand more." She spoke so softly I had to lean in to hear her. "I know it happened because I'm a bad person." She had never voiced this sentiment before, and I echoed it, thinking it was significant: "A bad person?" All along, she had appeared to accept the official judgment that she had done what she did because of her illness. This idea of fault or agency seemed like a new thought.

When she didn't expand on her comment, I returned to my original question and asked her if Mark had said goodbye to her. Had he used that specific word? "No! 'So long,' he said. 'So long.' He repeated it twice." She told me that those two words and the way his voice sounded when he said them had made her feel desperately afraid. She suddenly realized that there was a hidden meaning in his goodbye: it was a reference to how long she might have left to live. Mark was giving her a coded message that he was possessed by a demon who was going to kill her, very soon. As she talked about the terror of this moment, her face flushed. "I stayed in my room all that weekend and said his words over and over. So long. So. Long. So long. I was pacing the floor, almost wearing a path in the carpet, and I couldn't sleep. My heart felt like it was going to jump right out of my chest. The minute Mark walked back into the building, I was 'not long' for this world. I knew I was going to die."

She agonized over what she should do about it, and that's when she had the idea to kill him. "I thought it was the right thing," she told me. "It felt like I had no choice." I waited for her to say more, then prompted her gently, "And you couldn't tell anyone?" My question sounded lame to my ears. She shook her head and started to cry, but collected herself soon enough, wiping furiously at her eyes. She was ready. She began to describe the day of the homicide.

"Monday morning came, finally. I heard the door slam, and I heard Mark's voice down below, calling out as he came in from outside. So I peeked out from my room on the landing. He was going through to the kitchen, and I knew he was getting a knife. He would stab me to death as soon as I went in there. I had to get away. I took off my shoes so I didn't make noise on the stairs. I could see the front door, just a few feet from me. The sun was coming through the glass panes, in pink and green and yellow squares. I thought I could get out, run down the front steps and into the street, away from the danger. He wouldn't dare kill me out there. Then Mark called out my name, asking me if I wanted a cup of tea. I had to face him. But I could never outrun a demon man. I figured the only way to do it was to surprise him, so I went into the kitchen and ran toward him, grabbing a knife from the counter, then another. I went for the demon's eyes and throat, and then I stabbed its evil heart." She stopped there, winded as if she'd just run a mile quickly, and slumped in her chair, putting her hands over her face. I let her sit like that for as long as she needed to.

The shocking tragedy here, for me, was the juxtaposition of those bizarre delusions and coded messages with such familiar human responses as fear and exaggerated thinking. I'm sure most of us can recall instances when anxiety and insecurity based on fear made us invent stories about someone we cared for—the partner who gets a text from a strange number and therefore must be having a clandestine affair, or the child who is late home and must have been abducted or mugged. Those instincts combined with Kezia's psychosis to terrible effect. It was a catastrophe, in both senses of the word: a sudden turn (or overturning) and an awful denouement.

I knew what followed from the witness statements at trial, including police testimony that was vivid in its detail. At around nine o'clock on a wintry Monday morning, the police and ambulance services were called to the hostel. The petrified staff and residents were huddled in a little gaggle outside in the cold, preferring to brave the elements rather than witness whatever lay within. The police entered the house with caution, stepping around the bloodstained prints of those who had run from the crime scene beyond. A young woman poked her head out of one of the bedrooms that lined the corridor, her name badge identifying her as a staff member. She pointed toward the kitchen. "In there." Behind her, a couple of other pale faces peeked out: two elderly women and a middle-aged man, residents she was trying to protect and comfort. "Blood everywhere!" the man croaked.

The double doors to the kitchen were ajar, and when the police pushed through, they were greeted by a grim tableau. A big man aged around thirty, black, dressed in jeans and a T-shirt, lay on his back in front of the stove in a spreading stain of blood, his sightless eyes raised to the ceiling. Kneeling beside him was Kezia, streaked in blood but evidently unhurt. She was rocking back and forth and chanting, "I've done the wrong thing, I've done the wrong thing." A kitchen knife, its long blade red to the hilt, lay beside her, and when a female officer persuaded Kezia to rise, a smaller knife was found half hidden under the body. Mark had sustained more than a dozen knife wounds and was dead before the paramedics arrived. I could feel Kezia's anguish and imagined her crouched there, surrounded by uniforms, lost somewhere beyond reason. Truly a nightmarish scene.

Hostel staff and residents reported that Kezia was shouting as she struck at Mark again and again. She was locked in a bitter argument with an invisible opponent, using phrases like "Come out, come out" and "In the name of Jesus." Mark had tried to back away, and others attempted to intervene, but she was "like someone possessed," as one resident had it, "unstoppable." A description of her in custody in the immediate aftermath read: "Suspect made no sense—raving about demons, God punishing her, going to hell etc. etc." Ironically, this suggested to me that within her own reality, she had become the thing she most feared: a terrifying monster who kills.

There were plenty of psychiatric assessments to read: one made when she arrived at the hospital, as well as those prepared for her trial and sentencing. Colleagues who first saw her on her arrival in Broadmoor commented on how acutely ill she was, how she had talked of visual hallucinations, of shining demon eyes in Mark's face and her belief that she was in terrible danger unless she could "get it out of him." I was doubtful she would remember any of this, but I asked, "Do you recall what you said, what you felt about yourself, when you first came here?" She met my gaze. "I was bad. A bad person. I ought to be punished. I ought to have died." I did not try to reassure her, but I did gently point out that the court's verdict was that her illness was the cause. I reminded her again that she had told me as much when we first met.

"I know," she said. "But I can't—I just—I have to put it behind me and move on . . ." She had her arms crossed, hugging herself as she rocked back and forth, repeating "put it behind me and move on . . ." like a mantra. It was then that I felt the sleepiness return, really overwhelming me now, as though my consciousness had been blanketed by a heavy, suffocating force. I fought and lost, and I feel sure I was asleep for at least a minute. "Are you all right, Dr. Gwen?" Kezia tapped on my shoulder. She was peering at me with some concern. Was it my imagination or was her expression critical? Honesty is always the best policy at such awkward moments because it demonstrates a commitment to look at everything that happens in the room. I told her that I didn't know what had come over me then, but it felt as if my mind had switched off for a minute.

"I wish I could switch mine off too," she said. "I don't like having thoughts about what I did to Mark." "You're afraid to think of it?" I asked, my mind going to Macbeth and his haunted line, "I am afraid to think what I have done." "Yes," she said. "If I think about it, I'll know the truth. I'm a bad person. It was not my sickness, it was me doing evil." What did she mean by evil? I had to ask. She looked a little confused. "Well, Jean-Paul . . . he thought maybe I killed Mark because I had feelings for him. I mean . . . boyfriend kind of feelings. And if I did, then that's evil, that's the devil in me for sure. Isn't it?" So much was interesting in that thought, but I wanted to explore the notion of "boyfriend feelings" first. I asked if she thought Jean-Paul had been correct. She frowned. "I don't think so. I've never had a boyfriend, though, so I really don't know."

That comment stunned me with its simple sadness, though I think I was able to keep my face neutral. I was acutely awake now, aware that a new thought was forming in Kezia's mind, something I needed to pay attention to and unpack with her. She went on, a little haltingly but determined. "I thought if Mark . . . I mean, Mum would never tell me about my dad, so I was thinking maybe . . . he might have looked like Mark. Or what if Mark maybe even had the same father, back in Jamaica, and we were related?" A familial attachment, rather than a romantic one. I pressed the point. "Do you think you were jealous of Mark?" She thought about that and then said simply, "I was sad when he went away." "Went away?"

I echoed, thinking she was referring to his death. "At the weekends . . . He went off home at the weekends and there was nobody to talk to."

Another possible meaning for her attachment to Mark was starting to emerge. Her sense of rejection by him when he went home to his family at weekends had stimulated an older memory of being left behind as a child when her mother went to the UK, coupled with other painful "leavings"—the loss of her homeland a few years later, the loss of her grandmother and the aching loss of a father figure she'd never known, whom she wanted to imagine as a kindly Jamaican man like Mark. The psychological pain of separation, migration, and bereavement can be agonizing, but these aspects of her life may have been overlooked or at least underweighted when Kezia first became mentally ill.[6] The periodic loss of her mind (breaking with reality) due to her illness added an extra psychological load: for her, leaving and being left meant both love's removal and mental chaos.

At some point, her internal fear of being left alone became an external one of being attacked. She had been struggling with terror for who knows how long. What an overpowering burden this must have been. For the last few minutes of that session we sat together without speaking, which can be as important as any dialogue. It was a companionable silence, as if we had endured and survived something together, which I suppose we had. When I left her that day, we both said, "Goodbye," being formal and careful with the word, as if we were exchanging a gift.

In my supervision I had a lot to discuss, starting with my baffling loss of consciousness. It wasn't something my colleague had direct experience of either, and I can say that in the thirty years since, I think it has happened to me with only one other patient, a man whom I knew had a history of depression and suicidal ideation. It is unusual for therapists to become sleepy in sessions; generally, it's not boring or soporific work. If it does happen, we are trained not to ignore it, like any other sensation that might arise. I was counseled to interrogate the feeling as I might any other emotion that came up in sessions.

In the weeks following Mark's death, Kezia had on more than

one occasion expressed a wish to die, and this led my supervisor and me to think about whether the suicidal thoughts in her mind might be too awful for the "model patient" to allow into her consciousness. We began to formulate the idea that she had projected those feelings into me. When therapists mirror and identify with their patient's experience like this, it is called "projective identification," meaning the therapist's mind is resonating with a patient's displaced feelings. At a superficial level, this is similar to the idea of an infectious mood. When we are trying to empathically connect with our patients, some of the more atypical aspects of their mental experiences may be transferred. In conversation with my supervisor, I found myself saying that I felt like I was "drowning" as I struggled to make sense of Kezia's mind. After some discussion, we both recognized that this could be a response to suicidality in my patient. Kezia's conscious mind might be trying to drown out her liveliness, and with it her pain, like a "big sleep," to use Raymond Chandler's striking euphemism for death.

In our next session I tried to explain something of this to Kezia, but when I couldn't get my point across, I came right out and asked if she had ever felt suicidal, which she promptly denied. I was mindful of her evangelical Christian background: she may have been raised to think of suicide as a terrible sin, which might make it doubly hard for her to talk about it. But now that I had aired the subject, I noticed that there was a change of atmosphere in the room, as if I had surfaced into fresher air. In future sessions, I would still fall asleep from time to time, and Kezia would wake me up. She would always ask me what I thought it was that she didn't want to think about that day. It seemed she had not only grasped the idea of projective identification, but she quite liked it. Eventually, I would return to the theme of suicide, and we were able to talk more about it. My brief unconscious episodes faded away, and together we explored the metaphor of "dropping off," as if from a cliff of consciousness, and discussed whether both she and I were in less danger of that now. We agreed that if the idea of suicide was out in the open as something we could both think about, then perhaps I could stay awake and she could stay alive. It was such a valuable lesson for me about the subtle and surprising ways human beings can project and share strong emotions, especially painful ones of grief or loss.

As the eleventh anniversary of her offense came around, Kezia and I reflected on the emotional importance of the event together. She was tearful in these sessions, and I felt tearful too, but I didn't think this was a projection on my part, only a natural human resonance with the tragedy of what had happened in her life. The work I do often makes me sad. I doubt I've worked with many patients with whom I've not experienced some kind of sorrow, especially when we've got to know each other over time, in long-term therapy. There aren't any rules for therapists about how to handle this, other than to make a judgment specific to the patient and to bear in mind that trust must be established before certain kinds of communication are possible. I had enough experience by the time I worked with Kezia to know that sharing grief in treatment can occasionally be helpful, but knowing quite when to do so is part of the art of the work, which is new every day.

Ultimately, all I do in therapy is in service of the patient and the work; it's not mutual or about me. This means that sometimes, letting my sorrow be seen is important to the patient; more than empathy, it is a form of witnessing and respecting their lament, what they've been through. I might also say, as I did that day to Kezia, that I am conscious of how sad I feel listening to them. With her, I added, "I can see why this is distressing for you," which led us into a deeper discussion about the meaning of feelings. I asked her about the demon she imagined had taken possession of Mark and threatened her life, and how she felt about it now. She told me she thought it was maybe located inside her, not Mark, like a "normal demon." "A normal demon?" I asked. "Yes, like . . . grief or anger or sadness . . ." She sighed. "You know . . . the kind we all have."

I felt I was ready to report back to the clinical team. Our work together had convinced me that the original understanding of Kezia's offense was sound: that she had been mentally unwell when she killed Mark and that her actions were motivated by her delusions rather than jealousy. I stressed that it was also important to realize that Kezia's violence was influenced by her unresolved feelings of loss. In future, it would be important for those working with her to think in a careful and nuanced way about her need for close relationships and how they related to her survival. She was so sensitive to loss that any sense of rejection or feeling of abandonment might cause her suicidal feelings to return, even if she managed to mask them under her placid, "model patient" exterior. This could make her risky to herself and others.

I thought all this made perfect sense, but I could see that some of the people in the review session looked bemused. I had the impression they felt I was overthinking things, even if they were being nice about it. Someone asked if I thought we could still move her on to the medium-security unit. Yes, I said, but it was important that professionals working with her there be encouraged to look beyond the labels of "schizophrenia" and "psychosis" and "homicide" to see her grief, which she might still need help to think about and work through. I was surprised not to see Jean-Paul at this meeting, as Kezia's primary nurse, but Mary told me he had gone. He'd decided "Broadmoor wasn't his kind of place," she said. "Too stressful." She gave a disdainful sniff at her colleague's lack of persistence, as if he'd failed a test of loyalty. I wasn't all that surprised; by now I knew this kind of turnover wasn't unusual for mental health workers, who have long had higher rates of burnout than any other medical staff in the NHS, who in turn have significantly higher rates than workers in other white-collar professions. This was once reflected in their compensation, but austerity cuts have put an end to that.

That wasn't quite the end. Kezia's transfer process would take nearly another year, so I offered to keep seeing her, not least because I was concerned that leaving Broadmoor might be another big loss for her, after so many years there. In a sense it had been her most secure home, or her "stone mother," which is a twentieth-century idea about long-term residential care. We continued to talk about the long-term effects of loss and grief on a person's mind, and how sometimes we have to lament for what we have done and what is lost in order to start afresh. At our last session, Kezia gave me a card she had made for me and cried when we said goodbye. This time I made an effort not to do the same but to share with her my respect for her hard work and my hope for her future.

It was nearly a year later before I had reason to return to the female ward to see another patient. The plans for closure of the women's service were advancing by then, and I asked Mary, still a permanent fixture in the ward office, if she knew how some of the women who had already moved on were doing in their new home, including Kezia. "I went up to one of her case reviews in the new unit. She's doing fine. Just fine. In fact, she asked after you. Told me you used to fall asleep in her sessions sometimes . . . is that true?" I ruefully confessed. "Not quite the model therapist, are you?" she teased. "You're right," I told her, but maybe it was for the best. To be a model anything is a little too lifeless.

MARCUS

The man sitting opposite me leaned forward and stabbed the air between us with his index finger. "The first chance I get, I'm going to kill myself. Got it?" I wondered what response he wanted— that I would beg him not to do it or urge him to reconsider? "I mean it. First chance I get, that's it!" Again, I couldn't tell what he thought I should say or do with this information, and I wasn't sure myself. So I went for this: "Can you say why?" His eyes widened and he snorted in disbelief, as if he had never heard a dumber question. "Why? Seriously, woman. I'll be pushing sixty when I come out. If I live that long. I'll be an old man. Ugh." He shuddered theatrically at the very idea.

This was my first meeting with Marcus, and though new patients will generally address me as "Doctor," I noted that he had called me "woman." It was almost an epithet, which might say something about his idea of me or about what all women meant to him. I was even more curious as to why the idea of old age was so terrible to him. He made it sound as if it were a fate worse than the years he faced in prison, or even death. I let the horror of his older self settle a bit. I wasn't surprised that the silence stretched on for a while—many people in therapy are muted after something disturbing or fearful is raised. He had a new thought. "And I do feel bad about what I did, you know. About Julia."

We were sitting in one of the nicer meeting rooms in the admissions ward, facing the well-tended gardens. Through the window behind him, I could see the high perimeter fence, jutting out beyond the trees. It was mid-morning, when most patients were off the ward doing occupational therapy or taking exercise. I'd picked a time when we could get a quiet room where we would not be disturbed or distracted, although there was always the background noise of the television in the common area nearby. Marcus had recently been transferred from prison to our care at Broadmoor Hospital because of concerns about his suicide risk. I was not meeting him as his therapist. By this time, in the mid-2000s, I was looking after a ward as one of the senior psychiatrists on the hospital's staff, overseeing a team of people, including mental health nurses and therapists. I continued to see a few of my one-on-one therapy patients, but the majority of my time was now spent supporting staff in their work, acting as their supervisor and sounding board, an important function and something I continue to do to this day. My role in Marcus's case was as his "RC," or responsible clinician; in legal terms, this meant I would be acting as coordinator of his treatment while he was detained in the hospital. I would have some dedicated individual time with him, but other team members would be doing the day-to-day work and providing feedback in regular case conferences.

On admission to Broadmoor, Marcus had just turned forty and was one year into a life sentence for the murder of Julia, a young woman who had been the receptionist at his workplace. He was married, she was single; they'd had a brief affair that had ended amicably, and they had remained friendly. On her last night alive, Julia had invited Marcus to her apartment for a drink after work. According to him, after sharing some wine and chips and chatting for a while, she revealed that she'd begun online dating. In response, he'd strangled her to death with his necktie. Afterward, he drove home to his unsuspecting wife, and then got up the next morning and went to the police station, where he confessed to his offense, telling them that Julia had "made me jealous." As I've discussed in regard to Kezia, jealousy has long been accepted in our society as a motive for "crimes of passion," and it's notable how often it is volunteered as a rationale when people are arrested for violence. It is also well known that intimate partner homicide (IPH) is the most common type of relational murder, and numerous studies have shown that women are the main victims, although their abusers are not a homogenous group.[1] IPH also has the highest risk of subsequent suicide, so Marcus was not atypical in that regard either.[2] But I thought there was much more for our team to discover about why he felt Julia had to die and why he was now expressing a wish to kill himself.

At this time in my career, I was getting deeply into reading and writing about early childhood attachments, and was working on a book about it with a German colleague.[3] Attachment theory is a psychological model that built upon Freud's ideas about the significance of early childhood, and it was developed by John Bowlby, a British psychiatrist working with emotionally disturbed children in the 1950s. He suggested that humans, like other primates, are motivated to attach to others across their life span, and developing a secure attachment bond in childhood is important for later mental health. Subsequent studies using this theory would show that insecurity in that early attachment is a risk factor for a range of psychological problems, including mood regulation, psychosomatic disorders, and difficulties in forming close relationships with family, partners, and even health care professionals.[4]

It was not until the 1990s, when I was in training, that empirical research into this subject really took off. It had not been on the curriculum when I was a trainee, but now ideas based on attachment theory were being more widely discussed among my colleagues. I made it a focus of my research after I qualified, studying the links between childhood trauma, insecure attachment, and poor mental health in later life. It also became more and more apparent to me that there was an explicit link between attachment experience and the linguistic ability to tell a true story of yourself. I'd seen examples of this before, but Marcus would provide new insight—all the more so because he did not immediately appear to have any difficulty in talking about himself.

Around the time I met him, I had also become a mother, which gave my thinking about the attachment bond between parents and children a further "lived" dimension for me. Like the arts, working in my field requires an involvement of heart and mind that means the personal and the professional are never separate, something that can be a difficulty and an advantage in equal measure.

The Venn diagram of "Gwen" (mother, wife, daughter, friend) and "Dr. Adshead" always has some overlap, although, like the mind, it is always transforming and re-forming.

In our first case conference, my team of colleagues had talked of how Marcus's situation was particularly puzzling because he had no previous history of violence before he took Julia's life. Killing another person by strangulation has to happen at close quarters, whether it involves pulling tightly on a piece of cloth around their neck or squeezing hard with one's hands, both of which require considerable strength and determination. The man sitting opposite me seemed to have both, and it occurred to me that this might also mean that he was able and likely to take his own life. I took in his stance: shoulders back, spine straight, palms on his knees, feet planted on the floor, seeming both grounded and ready to move. It was the posture of a man claiming his space and asserting his masculinity. With his thick dark hair, blue eyes, and youthful appearance, I could see why women might find him attractive.

As I usually do on a first encounter, I asked him where his story started and how we came to be meeting. Everyone's approach to that seemingly bland opening question is different, and the choice they make about where to start their narrative is revealing. I noted that Marcus seemed pleased to be asked, and I thought perhaps it was a welcome distraction from talking about suicide. His body language changed. No longer staring at me, he gazed at the ceiling, clasping his hands behind his head and relaxing into his seat. "Where shall I start?" he said. It was clearly a rhetorical question. "I'm in financial services," he began, "pensions, investment funds, bonds. Know what I mean?" I nodded briefly, sensing that he wasn't really interested in whether I did or not. It was clear he wasn't going to start with his birth or early childhood. The narrative that followed contained many clichés of a self-made, special person: he was "first in the family to go to university," "a bit of a rough diamond," "the odd man out." He claimed he had set up a thriving business by the time he was thirty.

All the while, he spoke spontaneously and easily, making eye contact and occasionally using hand gestures, most eloquently when describing the size of a deal or the scale of his various businesses' rapid growth. He emphasized several times over the phenomenal success he'd had, telling me how he'd been profiled in the press and invited on the speaker circuit alongside captains of industry twice his age. If all this was true, it would make him an unusual offender, because to be that successful in business, you usually need pro-social aspects to your personality, traits like empathy and conscientiousness. I made a mental note to compare the details of his account with whatever documentation I could access about him. Even small discrepancies can be illuminating, and false self-narratives increase our risk to ourselves and others.

As he went on and on, like a singer listing his greatest hits, I recall thinking that most really successful people don't do this; they don't need to. It was almost as if Marcus was trying to convince himself that all this was true. Suddenly, he changed the subject. He sat for a moment, looking at me through slightly narrowed eyes, as if gauging what I thought of him so far, then commented, "I hear you're very good, by the way." I didn't for a moment think that he'd heard such a thing, and I made no response to his flattery, but I was interested that he wanted to say it. In the context of his self-aggrandizing professional narrative, he might feel he had to claim "the best" for himself; there was something entitled there.

He'd said quite a lot since our session began. I had hoped he might go back further in time, to his school years, if not his early childhood, but he shifted to the present day and wanted to complain about it. He listed for me all that he had lost and what he missed from his old life, especially his business empire, but also his wife, his freedom, his possessions . . . He mentioned several cars he'd owned, smiling fondly as he spoke of his favorite, a sports car of some kind which was "a real beauty."

By this time, I was starting to feel a bit nonplussed. In contrast to what I'd understood from the referral that had brought him to our care, Marcus did not appear depressed or suicidal in the least. It was possible he was building a "wall of words" around himself, as people sometimes do to buttress themselves against deep distress so that they don't become overwhelmed. After all, he was just a short way into a life sentence, and coming to terms with that is akin to getting a terminal cancer diagnosis. You lose the time you thought you had to live out your life, and it takes real effort to find a new way forward, like feeling your way in a dark room, lost without a light.

"How do you come to be here in hospital?" I asked, when he finally paused. He rolled his eyes. "You know all that, they must have briefed you." I told him I'd like to hear it from him. There was something in his stubborn gaze, a flare of anger I sensed, as he rewound to his first statement of the day. "Because I tried to kill myself in prison, and I'm still going to do it, first chance I get." I nodded calmly. "And what has prevented you from doing that before now?" I don't think he was expecting that question, and he had to consider his reply for a minute. "The truth is" — I wondered what was coming, thinking that Marcus's truth might be different from other people's — "the only reason that I haven't done it so far is that the prison officers were watching me day and night." There was no hint of distress or paranoia in his voice; he seemed proud, like an actor who had commanded a loyal audience. "So I'll do it here instead. First chance I get. I'll do it." I gave an "I see" sort of response, which definitely wasn't what he wanted. He looked deflated, as if he needed more from me. There was something vulnerable about his manner, a fragility, I thought, despite his alpha male presentation.

I'd spoken to my colleagues in the prison who had requested his move to the hospital, and they admitted that although they had stymied Marcus's attempts to kill himself, they thought he was serious about it. They described one incident when he managed to get hold of a broken CD and dared them to stop him from cutting his throat with the sharp edge. It was unsurprising that they had sent him to us; he must have taxed them to the limit, and I knew they had already had three suicides in that prison in the last twelve months. I could see exactly why they didn't want him there. His suicide risk was now the responsibility of the hospital.

I used the remainder of our session to explain our team's setup to Marcus. The goal was to work together to treat him for depression, aiming to reduce his suicide risk and get him back to prison to continue serving his sentence. He scoffed at the idea that he'd ever leave the hospital alive and asserted that any efforts to stop him from taking his life were bound to fail. Before he left, he did ask me how many people were on "Team Marcus," and I sensed his satisfaction that a whole group of highly trained professionals—not just me, a lone woman—would be focused on his needs. I knew that just because I couldn't immediately see signs of his depression, that didn't mean he was faking it. By law, he must have been seen by two psychiatrists to qualify for his transfer, and I had no reason to think they'd been misled. It is much harder to deceive mental health professionals than people think.

After that initial session, I put Marcus on a course of antidepressants and regular therapy sessions, which would explore his personality and relationships and might help us understand what his plans for suicide meant to him. I told the team that we needed to keep him under constant watch, whether awake or asleep. I can still remember the details and faces of two men I assessed as a young trainee who were successful at killing themselves, and I worry to this day that I failed them somehow. At the time, my colleagues had rallied around me and been supportive. My supervisor had assured me that in one case there was no way anyone would have had an inkling—the man seemed fine to everyone who met with him; and in the other the patient's anger had masked a deep despair. Everyone in my job fears this eventuality, and I didn't want it to happen again; we could not risk a human error that allowed Marcus to achieve his aim.

"Doesn't look all that suicidal to me," grumped one of the seasoned health care assistants on the ward a few weeks later. There's often a disconnect between body and brain, of course, but if someone does not respond to antidepressants, or any other kind of medical intervention for that matter, it can mean they aren't in need of them. Marcus had only complained bitterly about the side effects. He'd also been utterly uncooperative with everyone, from his therapist to the nurses, just as he'd been in prison. The team were dubious about whether he was really depressed, or even distressed. "He just wants to make us anxious all the time," said one perceptive junior nurse. I thought she was right. Marcus was apparently not interested in understanding his suicidality, but still keen to threaten and show off about it, just in case we weren't getting the message. There was one memorable occasion when, during the communal lunchtime, he tried ramming food and paper napkins down his throat in full view of other patients, who were highly disturbed by this display. Another time he tried to strangle himself with a twisted strand of toilet paper in front of a staff nurse, in a disturbing parody of the way he killed Julia.

His antics were gradually alienating everyone on the ward, although the staff would do their best to manage their responses. Our training, peer support, and supervision all help when we're faced with someone as trying as Marcus, but the people on the front lines are only human, and it is especially challenging for the more junior staff. There were many tetchy exchanges and difficult moments. Having someone on constant suicide watch for days on end can disrupt the smooth functioning of a ward, as multiple staff are taken up with that individual's full-time care. It makes them less available for other patients and treatment activities, and it is not unusual for the person on suicide watch to attract resentment from other patients. This was exacerbated by Marcus's constant negativity; he complained about the nurses, the food, other patients, and how we were failing to help him. I was told by a colleague that he had appeared one morning at the ward office in a terrible temper and demanded to see "the manager." He wanted to report that the night nurse assigned to watch him the night before had dozed off for a moment. The nurse had to be disciplined, he said, for his total incompetence. "I might have died while he slept!"

I myself witnessed how he would march around the unit with his put-upon nursing escort, proclaiming to anyone within earshot that he wasn't used to being stuck with such uneducated and uncultured people. He complained that he had nothing in common with any of the other patients, clearly missing the irony that the only reason he was there was because he had, like them, been seriously violent to others. He was provocative in other ways, butting into private conversations to demand attention; more than once, this led to threats and attempts at assault from angry fellow patients.

It felt as though we were all looking after a large, malign baby with no awareness of others' needs or feelings. Within the clinical team, we began to wonder if Marcus was more narcissistic than we had realized. The concept of narcissism in psychiatry is a complex one, referring not to an illness as such, but to a kind of personality style in which people present as entitled, exploitative, and grandiose. It draws on the myth of Narcissus, a beautiful young man who rejected his admirers and fell in love with his own image when he saw it mirrored in the surface of a lake. The tragedy of Narcissus is that as he tried to get closer to the person he desired, he failed to recognize himself and so fell in the water and drowned. In real life, people with narcissistic personalities struggle with relationships and tend to die early. Occasionally they will seek treatment, but it is rarely successful because therapy requires trust and vulnerability, and a narcissistic person uses grandiosity and entitlement to suppress feelings of need. Controlling and belittling others brings them superficial relief, even if it means alienating people who might be able to help. That sounded a lot like Marcus.

Narcissistic personality disorder is a popular diagnosis these days, especially for men in powerful roles. I'd suggest this is partly because accounts of pathological narcissism seem awfully like our current cultural concept of healthy masculinity. There are debates in my field about whether all narcissism is bad, and if it isn't, where we might draw the line between normal and abnormal, or possibly malignant, forms. It's clear that all adolescents go through a narcissistic phase, for example; I remember that period in my own life, manifesting itself in truly terrible poetry about the bleakness and beauty of the world which no one but me could fathom. Thankfully, most of us come out the other side of this process unscathed (with bad poetry unpublished). Those people left with an enduring dash of narcissism in adulthood can be dynamic and charismatic, and it may help them in motivating and inspiring teams. I noticed that quality in Marcus during patient community meetings on the ward, where he began to lead discussions about demands for better conditions; it was another forum for performance. To my surprise, a few professionals who visited from other wards and were unaware of the details of his case told us that they found him to be charming and thought we were a bit hard on him. I did notice that none of these people were male, a fact that had more relevance later, when I found out more about his true history.

Marcus continued resisting attempts to help him and complaining and interfering on the admissions ward, to the point where staff grew worried about the risk of his being assaulted by fellow patients. We decided to move him to a rehabilitation ward, where the other patients had less acute mental health problems and were making progress in their recovery. This meant they would be off the ward for much of the time, taking part in occupational therapy and other activities. They might still find Marcus infuriating when they had to be around him, but at least they would be less likely to hit him. His therapist kept patiently trying to engage him in some reflection on his feelings, and I spent time chasing down colleagues at the prison who had sent him to us, as well as contacting his lawyers, hoping to find out if they knew anything more about his past that might help us to gain a better understanding.

It became clear that he was an unreliable narrator of his own life. He'd been to university but didn't graduate, dropping out after a year. He'd run businesses, yes, but none of them was successful, and he was mired in debt and litigation. He didn't have criminal convictions for violence, but he had previously served two short sentences for fraud. I also learned that he had an old conviction for criminal harassment (which included behavior the law would now define as stalking) relating to a girl he had dated in his twenties.

His deceits extended to his family life. In addition to his wife and Julia, Marcus had simultaneously been involved in at least two other long-term romantic relationships. The first that his wife of ten years knew about all this was when the police arrived at her door to inform her that her husband was under arrest for murder. She met the women when they came to the trial to give evidence about Marcus, and they were equally shocked and distressed to meet her. Both of these "other women" testified in court that they never knew Marcus was married, nor were they aware of the reality of either his financial or his professional situation. Each one had believed Marcus when he explained that his frequent absences were due to important business abroad—quite a tribute to his skills of denial and control.

And yet I knew from talking to my prison colleagues that his wife had continued to make regular phone calls and visits to him in prison after his conviction, sticking by him when the others did not. He told our therapy team that he construed her loyalty as evidence of his being an excellent husband, in spite of his collection of other women—let alone the affair with and murder of Julia. I was powerfully reminded of the narrator of the Browning poem "My Last Duchess."[5] The narrator, the duke, is about to acquire a new bride, whom he describes as "my object." He also describes calmly how he had his late wife killed because she smiled and thanked other men in the same way that she smiled and thanked him; she did not treat him as "special." I could easily imagine Marcus using the same language.

So far, he'd said little about the killing of Julia. I read more about the circumstances of her death in the court documents, bearing in mind that the only living witness was Marcus himself. Computer records did support his account that she had been online dating and had shown him her profile on the night of the murder, when he said she taunted him about her "other men." I tried to imagine what her reasons would be for doing this, if what he said was true. Was it to wound him? To show off? Or to prove they were just friends? When I'm working with people who have hurt or killed others, I have to think about the victims and their view of things, almost as much as I do about the perpetrator. It's important for me to consider how they saw or heard the person I am now working with, and I try to stay mindful that they too had a story to tell, though their voice has been silenced.

Thinking about the victim also reminds me of the risk the person posed to them then, and might still pose now. I never thought that Marcus would be violent toward me while he was a patient; the risk seemed linked to his attachments to women he attracted. This did not include me, but I realized that it could in theory apply to others around him, thinking of those women colleagues who had visited the ward and commented about how likeable he was. It is important to grasp that most murders depend on the perpetrator's particular relationship with the victim, and outside of that relationship the danger is minimal. Contrary to irresponsible media reports, people who have killed are not generally dangerous to everyone. But in this case, a risk remained that Marcus might try and con any women he encountered into liking him, if he saw them as a potential addition to his collection of admirers.

I thought of how he might have disarmed his victim, Julia, whom I imagined as slim and dark-haired, for some reason, though I'd never seen a photo of her. I wondered about her last evening with Marcus. There must have been a point when she realized that something was different. Did his expression change? His voice? When she first felt his necktie slip around her neck, did she think that he was joking? The police reports noted that the laptop was found on the floor, the screen cracked, as if it too had been assaulted. Did he hammer it with his fist or sweep it off the table?

The nearest Marcus had come to that moment in therapy was to express his outrage that Julia had showed him the dating site at all. "She didn't think of me for a minute!" he had told a colleague in one of his therapy sessions. "How was I supposed to feel when she did that?" He looked genuinely puzzled when they pointed out that given his marriage and other girlfriends at the time, it appeared he had one rule for Julia and another for himself. "She invited me to her flat! She made me feel small!" he blustered. When asked if he thought that excused his response, he was, for once, unable to muster a glib reply. He was not so out of touch with reality that he could reply in the affirmative, even if he wasn't able to articulate a no. Instead, he reverted to a familiar complaint. "Our discussion of this is totally pointless," he said. "You people are doing nothing to help me, and I might as well kill myself." But when asked what kind of help he wanted, he could not answer.

The next time I met with him, I tried to ask him a little more about that night with Julia. We had been talking about all the plans he'd made for his life, from a young age, during one of his usual litanies about how much he'd lost and sacrificed, and how all that planning had been wasted. I commented that it felt like planning was important to him, and he agreed, saying it was essential in his line of work. He liked to plan, but what was the point now, when life stretched out so emptily ahead of him? He really needed to just end it all . . . Before he could slip back into that groove, I interrupted him, asking if he had made a plan to kill Julia when he arranged to go to her flat that night. I wondered if the question might anger him or if it was too much to ask, but he looked amazed, almost shocked by the idea. He insisted that his crime was unpremeditated, that it never would have happened if she hadn't provoked him like that. This is a cruelly familiar line of reasoning in domestic violence cases. The blame is put squarely on the victim, who is generally female. If only she hadn't done this or that, everything would have been rosy. Marcus admitted to me he had actually been hoping that Julia would sleep with him that night, for old times' sake, and had told his wife not to expect him back home till late.

How was he feeling when she opened her laptop to show him her dating profile? He said he was angry and saw it as her boasting about meeting other men, "rubbing it in." The way he framed it made me wonder if she had been the one to end their brief romance and was therefore—in Marcus's perception—rubbing salt in that wound. He recalled her sitting at the table scrolling through the internet dating site, asking him what he thought of this or that prospective suitor, and he got the feeling that she was laughing at him somehow, shaming him. That was interesting, but I didn't want to interrupt because now he was into the story, his words coming fast. "I had to make her stop," he told me. "I had to stop her talking." The mode of death made sense to me then: by strangling her, he had literally stopped her voice and her laughter. I was reminded too of how many of his own failed attempts at suicide had involved his throat, his mouth, or choking. If we were tired of hearing his endless complaints, perhaps some part of him was as well; suicide might be the only way he could silence his own voice.

Marcus moved in his chair, so that he was half turned away from me and looking out of the window. I followed his gaze but there was nothing to see, only a row of bare trees beyond the fence, stark and black against a pale winter sky. Slowly, he told me how he'd "watched the light go out in her eyes" as he twisted the necktie around Julia's neck. In a neutral tone, he said it reminded him of a time when he was a boy and his dog had caught a pheasant, bringing it to him in its death throes. He was quite surprised, he commented, at the similarity between the two experiences, that extinguishing of life and light.

I believed that Julia had never seen this coming, and now I wondered if Marcus hadn't either; if he was being honest when he said how he had not planned to kill her but had been ambushed by his anger. I have heard many times over how that derailment of reality, that crash into fatal violence, can begin with what might sound like such a trivial action, the final number in that mental "bicycle lock" combination clicking into place. Here it seemed as if it was something as random as a wave of Julia's hand, a little laugh heard as teasing or dismissive. I have seen again and again in my work how what seems like nothing is in fact huge, how a tiny moment has a terrible butterfly effect that triggers disaster.

This kind of dissociation from reality may help to explain why progress in therapy with people who have committed violent crimes takes so much longer than with those who have not. To get to that one revealing moment with Marcus, my team and I had to endure many long months of complaints, tantrums, and those endless repeated threats of suicide, which we could not ignore. And soon after he told me about the homicide, he made another attempt on his own life, this time by using clothing to try and fashion a noose with which to hang himself in his room. It was time for a new approach. When we next met, I invited him to think about whether it made sense for him to continue in the hospital any longer. I wasn't bluffing; if he wouldn't engage, returning to prison had to be a genuine option for him. After all, he had not responded to medical treatment, and as he had said to us so many times, we weren't helping to ease his suicidality.

I added that I was worried he was alienating everyone around him, which made it hard for us to sustain a therapeutic relationship. Only that morning, one of the younger female health assistants on the ward, Amanda, had come to speak with me about him, shaken and distressed by his behavior. It was part of my role as the RC to be there for staff who needed help in staying compassionate, which they can only do if they speak out about and own their critical thoughts. I knew Amanda to be a kind and not easily ruffled young woman, and listened carefully as she explained that she had not allowed "that asshole" to leave the dining room for his occupational therapy appointment because he had not cleared his breakfast plate, as was usual practice for all patients. Marcus had been incredibly rude in his response, calling her names and telling her she was unqualified and uneducated, and he would make sure she was disciplined, if not fired, for her behavior. He didn't quite say "Do you know who I am?" but he might as well have.

I reassured her that she'd done the right thing and wasn't about to be fired. I checked that she hadn't actually called him an asshole, which would have been a boundary violation that I would have had to report. I've seen and heard much worse; it's not common but it does happen, and helping staff to do better is part of my job. We sat and talked for a while about her concern and about how these kinds of negative feelings toward patients are not "facts" about us or the patients. They tell us something about the patients' minds as well as our own, and only become a problem if we act on them. We always need to think about what the communication might mean for the other person. Sometimes people are unlikeable because they don't like themselves, a truism that extends well beyond forensic settings.

I was glad that I'd had this conversation with Amanda. When I went over the incident later with Marcus, he was rude about her in just the way she described, and I felt a surge of contempt for his selfishness and his lack of care or ability, especially relative to what I knew about Amanda's diligence and compassion. In our next team meeting, I would tell his therapist how I'd wanted to snap at him, "How dare you? You have no right to criticize anyone after what you've done!" I had felt superior and entitled to attack him, to make him feel small, just as he probably had with Amanda— and with Julia. I wondered aloud to my colleagues whether he was feeling as helpless as they were. I would learn many times over as my career went on that it is always a greater act of compassion to empathize with someone you don't like. It became clear that my feeling of contempt could be a resonance with Marcus's contempt for his own vulnerability and despair in the face of his life sentence.

In the room with him I simply commented that it was interesting that he seemed to want to humiliate and punish a young woman, and I asked if it was possible this conflict with Amanda might have a link to his offense. At this, he dropped his head and twisted his hands together, looking defeated—a new posture for him. "Why do you always keep on about it?" His voice was so low I had to lean in closer to hear. I reminded him of where we were and that he had confessed to and been convicted of Julia's murder. He shrugged, as if that didn't matter. I went on. "But it seems this truth is difficult for you to look at, as if it's easier for you to be hard on those who are trying to help you do that." He lifted his head then, his voice angry and bitter. "They—you people—you really don't care if I kill myself. No one cares." I let that rest a moment, and then I saw that he was crying. Colleagues had told me he'd cried before in front of them, in a noisy and demonstrative way, but this was silent weeping, his shoulders shuddering, his cheeks wet. I made no attempt to stop him by offering words of comfort or tissues.

It was a long ten minutes before he stopped. He looked up at me and said, "I needed that, I think." I met his gaze and said, "It's so important to get what you need, when you need it, sometimes." He smiled at that, but it was a genuine smile, free of the mocking condescension I'd seen from him in the past. Then he said something quite unexpected: "All I wanted was to be beautiful." I was so taken aback by the statement that I had no idea what to say. I once had a patient who told me, apropos of nothing at all, that she had been "considering how the world is like a grapefruit." Sometimes we just have to allow the incongruity of a word or idea and wait for it to make sense—or not.

Marcus was trying to tell me more, but he was struggling to find words, all his former fluency gone. "I do know . . . I have to go back to prison . . . do my time and . . . I just don't know . . . I can't imagine life when I come out, you know, I'll be bald, I'll be fat, unfit, nobody will look at me. It's not fair . . ." He came to a halt. "Not fair?" I echoed. "I just never thought . . . a thing, something like this, could happen to me. I mean . . . I know I've done wrong but I'm not a bad person . . . and now I can never put this right." I was conscious that we had been talking for nearly an hour, an emotionally taxing one for Marcus. He probably needed a break, and I needed to go and think about what he'd said and talk to the staff and his therapist. For the first time, he thanked me as he was leaving, and when he got to the door he turned back, offering what is known among my colleagues as a "door-handle moment"—a final thought that might be quite revealing. He said he'd just had an idea about the support workers, staff like Amanda. "They aren't so bad really. It's just they're young and have their lives, right?" I only just suppressed my astonishment that he could notice another person's experience and agreed that he was probably right.

After that, I set aside the idea of sending him back to prison just yet. I needed to further explore what he meant by that striking comment about wanting to be beautiful. It raised questions about his early attachments in childhood, but I knew we lacked that kind of personal history.

Over time, after much fruitless calling around and dead ends, our team did manage to obtain his early medical records, which I reviewed with interest. They told us he'd been diagnosed with depression at a young age, sufficient to be kept out of school on more than one occasion. He and his family had been referred to what was then called "child guidance" and is now known as Child and Adolescent Mental Health Services (CAMHS). Some therapy notes from the few sessions he had back then indicated an emotional bleakness to the family dynamic. He had a silent father who seemed absent and a mother who was preoccupied with three younger siblings. I was interested to see that he'd been adopted at the age of one; then, a few years later, his adoptive mother had been able to conceive with the help of fertility treatment and went on to give birth to her biological children, twin boys and a daughter.

Early separation from or loss of parents is a common cause of insecure attachment, and adoption is one version of this. It is quite common: at least a third of the population have experienced some version of insecure attachment with their parents or caregivers in early childhood. We did not have any details about Marcus's adoption, but I had to consider the possibility that he'd been removed from his birth parents because of abuse and neglect. If so, as I knew from my study of attachment, it would have had a significant developmental impact, especially if Marcus's adoptive parents had also failed to give him the parental care he needed. They may not have been bad people; they may have been overwhelmed with the demands of their expanded family, or Marcus may have been as challenging as a toddler as he was in adulthood. The notes from the child guidance clinic suggested that his parents refused to take part in family therapy for long. After a handful of sessions his mother had apparently said she didn't have enough time to continue with it, and his father had been uncooperative and even dismissive throughout the process. Marcus had been left emotionally stranded.

I also noticed that from a young age he'd had lots of treatments and consultations for minor medical problems. It looked like his mother did pay attention to him when he was physically ill. During his first recorded experience with depression, she had repeatedly brought Marcus to the GP after he complained of pain in his back, stomach, and neck. This phenomenon of unexplained bodily pain is common in people who struggle to express emotion and aligns with the theory that all emotions begin in the body. I have seen how people with established risk factors for violence manifest painful feelings in the body, but they can also turn to causing other people pain because they are unable to articulate their own. It is only through action that they can express themselves.

It is not that we thought Marcus's adoption and issues with his parents had caused his later violence; these certainly aren't "bicycle lock" risk factors, since we know that of the millions of people with similar childhood experiences, few will ever go on to harm anyone, and certainly not to kill. But there was probably something in his early life that might give us an insight into the meaning of his violence for him, and everyone felt frustrated by all the unfilled blanks. Again, there is no central filing system tying together police or medical records, social services history, and so forth. For all the "sleuthing" I might do, I knew that, unlike a detective in fiction, I wasn't going to end up with all the information I needed. Above all, I wished I could find out in what context

Marcus had first understood the idea of beauty, with its link to love and desirability. I doubted I would ever know.

We talked in our team about whether his murder of Julia might be linked to unresolved anger over a dual rejection by the first women in his life, his two mothers. There has been extensive research into rejection and its relationship to hostility, and how this can extend from childhood into adult life.[6] Marcus's anger had been like the proverbial dormant volcano, until it erupted with Julia. She was probably not his target, but just the wrong woman at the wrong time. Her act of showing him her "other men" online may have been perceived by Marcus as Julia laughing *at* him, while also rejecting him. But this still didn't unlock what he'd meant by that wistful idea that he only wanted "to be beautiful."

Ten years later, I would be reminded of Marcus and that wish of his, when a high-profile news story broke which would illuminate his case for me in a new way. In 2014, there had been another spree shooting across the Atlantic, as shocking and dismaying to me as all the others that had come before it. In the sleepy college town of Isla Vista, in Southern California, Elliot Rodger, a twenty-year-old student with a history of depression, murdered his roommates, then jumped into his car and drove through the sunny streets with a small armory of weapons he'd acquired, firing indiscriminately from his car window, killing and injuring random strangers. Rodger videoed himself throughout, talking his audience through the massacre. When the police closed in, he posted the video online and then turned the gun on himself. Later, a long autobiographical screed was also found on the internet, as well as many other videos, which he had taken the time to publish before the deaths he planned for others and himself.[7] Both the manifesto and his videos had a central theme: he was entitled to take revenge on a world where women were allowed to reject his wish for closeness and sex. Much like Marcus had taken no responsibility for Julia's murder because she made him jealous, so Rodger took no responsibility for his actions and declared "they" had forced him into involuntary celibacy and violence.

It's rare that one has the opportunity to read the views of a multiple homicide perpetrator, written in their own words, so I took the time to go through Rodger's 150-page manifesto. It was dreadful to read, hopeless and mind-numbing in its tedious detail and repetition, but it powerfully reminded me of Marcus's incessant complaints. They had bored into the space between him and his caregivers, leaving us powerless to help him, while he smarted from a sense of grievance. For both of these men, women were not real people in their own right but supporting players in a dreary drama. I found in Rodger's writing (and in his many videos, which showed a variety of different looks, including changes of hair color) a repeated yearning to be attractive. It occurred to me that he was echoing Marcus's wish "to be beautiful."

After that revelation had come from Marcus, slowly things began to change. He became less arrogant with the staff and other patients, and less querulous; his suicidal threats decreased in frequency. In time, he was able to come back to his "beautiful" comment and explore it further in therapy. He spoke about how he became overweight after he started school and was teased for it by his siblings and schoolmates. He grew increasingly depressed over his appearance, feeling unwanted and unloved, and it occurred to him that his birth mother must have given him up for adoption because she did not like what she saw when she looked at him as a baby, and did not want to see how he might develop. This was as searing as it was irrational to hear, and I could only tell him that I understood how that feeling must have been painful for him. As he reached adulthood, Marcus said he adapted his appearance, working out and changing his diet until he felt he was pleasing to women. He devised a strategy of lying to them about who he really was; it had been important to keep a string of women on the go, he said, in case one should lose affection for him and he needed another. This was his way to feel in control, so that he could never be abandoned.

Ironically, as Marcus began to accept and speak about the reality of his past, for the first time in our care he developed obvious symptoms of clinical depression, including tearfulness, low mood, insomnia, and weight loss. He withdrew from activities and barely spoke to others, answering only that he was "fine" when asked. He was not overtly suicidal, as he had once been, but I remembered the suicidal man, long ago when I was in training, who had also maintained that he was "fine"—up to the point where he took his own life. I thought silence from Marcus was more ominous than any ostentatious threats, and it reignited a worry about his suicide risk. It took another six months and the help of medication and more therapy before he would slowly emerge from his depression.

We had given him a chance to resolve his inner conflict by caring for him, allowing him to talk about his needs and his anger toward people who had failed him early in his life, and encouraging him to grow up enough to fully grasp the reality not only of his experience, but of other people's thoughts and feelings. This enabled him to take responsibility for his choices and recognize that it was his job to stay alive and do his time, or as he put it, to "pay his dues" for taking Julia's life. Eventually, he told me that he now felt he had a chance to take a new approach to life, and we talked about how sometimes it is necessary to be stripped down in order to rebuild. A placement was found for him in a prison not far from where his wife lived. I was told that by then she had decided to divorce him, but she wanted to continue to offer her support and visit him regularly. This generosity of heart had a powerful effect on Marcus, and he was able to show a real appreciation of her loyalty, accepting it as a gift instead of taking it as an entitlement. He returned to prison, and to my knowledge he has not been referred again to secure psychiatric care. I hope it is of some comfort for Julia's family to know that he is facing up to and serving out his sentence, as he should.

A thoughtful colleague of mine, Professor Shadd Maruna, has described this creative process of change after tragic events as "making good."[8] I recognize it can be difficult for people like Marcus to ask for or even access this kind of psychological help until it is too late, but I wish the overweight, distressed, and isolated teenager's thoughts about his need to be beautiful had been heard much earlier in life. I do recall reading that Elliot Rodger had multiple therapists and interventions in his youth, yet he was still undeterred from his fatal violence; there are no easy answers or certain solutions when a mind is disordered. It is possible that as a young man, Marcus might also have been incapable of being curious about his mind or unable to trust others, and he might not have accepted or been helped by therapy. I was glad I'd had the opportunity of working with him as an adult, to witness the way he became willing to open his mind in order to start healing past hurts. Everyone has that option, both inside and outside of forensic settings, though many will not take it. It is true that Marcus had tested the limits of my tolerance and even provoked me enough to mirror his hostility, and everyone on our team had grown weary as he held us hostage to his repetitive and self-aggrandizing performance of despair. But we had come through it to arrive at something better, and seen, not for the first or the last time, that it is only through a staunch belief in the possibilities of every human heart that we move forward, even if we go haltingly and sometimes stumble.

CHARLOTTE

All prisons are noisy, but when I go to work in a female prison, I'm greeted by a richer acoustic than the usual clang of percussive gates and jangling keys turning endless locks, mixed with that low bass hum of constant human movement on metal staircases and cement flooring. The atmosphere is a cross between a girls' school and an aviary filled with raucous tropical birds calling out to each other as they hover singly and in groups in common areas of the geometric cell blocks, some of them chirping "Miss! Miss!" at me as I go by.

A new government had come into power in the UK in 2010, in the wake of the global economic crisis, and there was dramatic change afoot in the NHS and all public services, including massive cuts to mental health care. A painful external review process had begun at Broadmoor, which would ultimately lead to a change of gear for me. I continued to work in forensic services within the NHS, but I left the hospital and began working in the community with the probation service, as well as in prisons. At the women's facility, I joined a health care inreach team (a specialist NHS mental health team who work in prisons). Our work included assessing prisoners to ensure that those who were mentally ill and needed treatment were identified early, and those who were in distress received some kind of support. At the time that I met Charlotte, I was taking part in a specific initiative to try to support those women whose mental health problems had led to extended stays in prison.

At that time, the number of women in prison in England and

Wales stood at 4,320, out of a total prison population of around 84,000. By 2019, according to a report by the Prison Reform Trust,[1] that number would double to nearly 8,000 women (although there would still be about 80,000 men)—a very lopsided gender ratio, and one that is broadly similar around the world. The individual populations of our female prisons number in the hundreds rather than the thousands, with more than 80 percent of inmates serving sentences of less than twelve months for nonviolent crimes, chiefly theft. The fact that they are assessed as less risky means female prisons in the UK are not nearly as restrictive as those for men. As opposed to the overcrowded male system, which is dominated by several Victorian-built monoliths with antiquated facilities, the women's prisons I've worked in are modern builds, with some amenities that might be surprising. As I made my way to my first appointment of the day, I heard the rattle and clink of cups as I passed the staff café, mixed with the varied tones of lively chatter between the prisoners who worked there. Further down the corridor, I caught laughter and argument accompanying the buzz of hairdryers in the prisoners' beauty salon. I always marveled at the elaborate styling and manicuring that went on in there and felt rather disheveled by contrast.

I worked my way through the complex, checking my notes for the right wing and cell number, and occasionally calling to someone ahead of me to "Hold the gate!" or "Wait for me!" to save on some of the laborious locking and unlocking that punctuates all movement through a prison. I prefer not to see people in their cells if I can help it, but there were no available meeting rooms that day, so having checked with the staff that it was safe, I had decided it was better than not meeting at all. It was morning and most of the cells in this area were unlocked, with many of them empty as people went out to eat, work, or exercise. The door to the cell I approached was firmly shut. I knocked and waited, checking my watch to make sure I wasn't too early, but I was right on time for our appointment and I hoped she was expecting me.

The woman who opened the door was a portrait in gray. She frowned, greeting me with a blunt "Who are you?" Her hair, which might once have been a vibrant auburn, was faded, frizzy and shot with wiry white strands. Her eyes were a watery blue, her skin sallow. Her face looked untouched by sun or wind, signifying a life spent indoors. Her loose trousers and sweatshirt were equally drab, and I felt my clothes were jewel-bright by contrast. I try to dress for work so that I look unremarkable and therefore harmless, but I suspect I don't always get it right, not least because I can't know what lens other people may look through. "Charlie?" I'd been told that was her preferred name. "I'm Dr. Adshead. I sent you a message to say I was coming?"

"What do you want?" she said, her voice as flat and colorless as her appearance. I explained that I was working with people who were in prison past their recommended release date, and I hoped we might have a chat. When she was nineteen, Charlie had been sentenced to life for murder, with a tariff, or minimum sentence, of ten years; today, with judges imposing longer and longer tariffs, that might have been fifteen. But by the time I met her, she had spent thirty years inside. The notion of overstaying one's time in prison may sound odd, but as I've touched on in other cases, a life sentence doesn't have to mean being in prison for life. People can apply to be released once they have served the tariff imposed by the judge, provided they are no longer seen as a risk to the public, although they can be recalled to prison at any time if necessary. This had been true for Charlie, whose antisocial behavior in the community while on parole had seen her sent back inside three times over. It's expensive to keep people incarcerated, and over the last decade increased efforts have been made to break this logjam, including additional resources to fund mental health teams like the one I was working in at the time.

I had no idea what she would say. I've been met with a lot of hostile responses to the offer of therapy in prison, ranging from "I don't want to talk to a fucking shrink" to "What are you going to do to fix me then?" I could engage with those kinds of responses; the worst was to be met with silence. I asked her if we could talk for a bit. She shrugged and turned away, leaving the door ajar. Hardly a warm welcome, but I'd take it. I stepped inside. Like most prison cells, it was small, maybe eight feet square, with a bed bolted to one wall and a shelf serving as a desk opposite. There was a window with a view of a bit of cloudy sky, and a half-screened toilet area—"in-cell sanitation" is the norm in newer prisons and in newer men's facilities and most women's prisons. I noted that the space looked tidy because it was lacking all the mess of pictures and objects that indicated personality, family ties, or other interests. There was a stack of books on the desk, and I squinted to try and make out their titles, without success. Many women have nothing in their room, not even a single book, so I was interested to see what she was reading.

Charlie hunched on the edge of her bed saying nothing, allowing me to fuss about with the only chair, talking to myself with that cheery self-talk that professionals tend to use to fill a silence. "Right, well, where shall I go . . . just here? That all right with you? There we are, that's it . . ." I could see that Charlie looked disconnected, almost absent, and I tried to make eye contact as I launched into an explanation of our project and its aim of helping women like her break out of what appeared to be a pattern of returning to prison. "So," I said, offering a favorite question of mine that rules out a yes-or-no answer, "what do you think about that idea?"

"About what?" She sounded tired and bored, and I felt annoyed. At the same time, I recognized that my reaction probably reflected her own irritation that I was there, uninvited. We were both middle-aged, but for a moment looking at her I was reminded of myself at fourteen or so, sitting in just that posture, hunched on my bed with arms folded and head down, full of ennui and attitude when asked to do something I didn't want to do. Boys do this too, but there's a special kind of contempt that has been perfected by adolescent girls. As we sat there in a silence made all the more awkward by being at such close quarters, I noticed that one of her mismatched socks had a hole in the toe. It struck me as a tiny but insolent commentary, a refusal to mend.

I could have asked her to tell me more about herself that day, but I decided against it. Experience had shown me that it was best to establish a rapport first, especially when someone had not yet agreed to work with me. I had been given a précis of her original offense in the referral from the prison's mental health unit: she had been part of a gang-perpetrated homicide in the late 1980s which sounded pretty horrible. I've discussed how unusual homicide is in our society, and "joint enterprise homicide," when several people collaborate to kill someone, is particularly rare, especially when the victim is a stranger to those involved. The fact that this group was so young—all of them under twenty—and included females made it even more of an anomaly.

Eddie was a homeless man in his sixties living rough on the streets in Charlie's neighborhood. He would always beg for food and cigarettes while intoxicated. Sometimes the police would move him on, but like a lost cat he would always find his way back to his favorite spot in the local public park. I'm sure we've all seen many Eddies, growling or chuckling on a bench, smelling of urine and beer. They do no harm to anyone, but mothers steer their children out of these men's path and people avoid their gaze as they hurry by. One summer's day, Charlie's group were in the park, lying on the grass in the sun, evading school or work, drinking and taking drugs. As twilight came, they moved off in search of food and came across Eddie at the edge of the park, relieving himself in a sheltered spot out of sight of the main road. As they approached, a few of the boys and girls jeered and started to harass him, calling him names and throwing beer cans at him. He tried to run away but stumbled and fell. In that moment the group pounced. As I read the police reports of the beating, of the broken bottles and stones they used to hurt him, along with their fists and feet, I pictured a whirling Hydra, terrifying in its many-headed force and malicious energy. Eddie was no Hercules and offered little defense.

Later, Charlie was identified as having blocked Eddie's escape as he managed to struggle to his feet, head bleeding and begging for mercy, according to a passing jogger who testified at the trial. She and another girl had shoved the old man back on the ground, where his head struck the asphalt with an ugly crack. The autopsy put the cause of death as "internal injuries sustained by multiple contusions to the head and abdomen and a hemorrhage in the frontal lobe." The gang scattered into the night, by all accounts laughing and whooping as they ran, but were soon rounded up by police. Eyewitness testimony and forensic evidence made the criminal case straightforward.

After their conviction for joint enterprise murder (when two or more people are charged with equal responsibility for the crime) the other codefendants were sent to various juvenile prisons, since some were as young as fifteen. When they reached eighteen, they would be moved to the adult system. They all received life sentences, with an average minimum of ten to fifteen years. I'd been informed that the others had long since been released into the community, and only Charlie was still inside. I thought I'd begin there, by asking if she knew this, and why it was so. She just gave a little "couldn't care less" shrug. I would try something else. "Charlie, I know how unusual it is to kill a stranger. I've worked with other people who've done this." That caught her attention, and she peered up at me from behind her frizzy fringe. "Why?" "Good, we're conversing now," I thought, "that's a start."

"Anyone who ends someone else's life also changes their own life forever," I said. I'd heard many people say in therapy that they had never thought of themselves as someone who could or would kill anyone, and how it can make you a stranger to yourself. I added that I had seen how people who had killed needed help to start thinking about the unthinkable, and how important it could be for them to articulate those feelings. Unlike many other big events in life, there is no how-to manual for life after homicide, no sources of information or guidance to follow. It wasn't surprising, therefore, that some people found it incredibly hard to figure out what to do, how to make progress or how to handle a new, alien identity as a convicted murderer. Therapy gave them some tools to do that.

Charlie followed every word I said, but when I finished, she blurted, "I don't want to go over all that shit again. It makes me upset, you know." She shifted her position on the bed so that her back rested against the cell's gray wall, her legs jutting out, dirty-sock holes facing me. I had a brief thought that in some cultures, showing someone the soles of your feet is considered highly offensive. But in this case, I suspected she just needed to put more space between us. "There's nothing for me out there, you know," she mumbled. "And I took a life, so why should I have one?"

This was a singular and intriguing comment, implying a metaphor of life as an object of value. I hadn't generated that idea for her, and I was heartened that she had offered it. It was a potential sign that she had words for her experience—the first step in the verbal dance of therapy. Despite her outward signs of reluctance, Charlie might just want to engage. Before I left, she confirmed she would meet me again and even smiled briefly when I responded with an over-hearty "Excellent!"—as if we'd done something momentous together. I guessed she was thinking of me as a nice enough idiot, and there were worse ways to pass the time. I paused at her cell door, indicating her book collection. "I see you're a reader." I pointed to one of the books, a fat hardback, asking what it was. She turned the spine around to remind herself. "*A Suitable Boy*—by some Indian bloke." "Ah," I said, intrigued by her choice, and as I glanced back from the doorway I saw she was leafing through the pages as if curious about what I thought it revealed.

I wasn't making any particular assumption about that book, but everything has meaning and the objects we choose to have in our personal spaces are always a kind of communication; they aren't called "interiors" for nothing. Novelists tend to use metaphor, which is a literary form of "transference," as my mentor Murray Cox liked to remind us when we were trainees; it is always significant when a patient uses a metaphor in therapeutic discourse. And as children's author E. B. White said, reading is a sign of an alert mind, which is crucial for effective therapy.

I made my way down to the prison's probation unit, which held offenders' records, to ask for Charlie's file, including the trial reports. I felt a rising curiosity about this woman, and I wanted to discover more. But as I read through the documentation, my heart sank. Her depressingly familiar life story left me feeling helpless and angry. Charlie had been in local authority care on and off from the age of seven, when she was first removed from her drug-addicted mother's home by social services, due to physical abuse and neglect. She did not thrive in foster care and was verbally abused by one foster parent, then rejected by the next. Presumably because no one else wanted her, she was returned at the age of ten to her mother's care, where she was faced with a new stepfather and two older stepbrothers. Home 2.0 was no improvement. The adults fought, attacking each other and the children, and the brothers bullied and harassed their weaker sibling. As she approached puberty, their abuse developed a sexual component. One social worker's note stated that Charlie had complained that her brothers would "grab her all the time," touching her breasts and genitals.

School may have seemed a comparative haven to her. Although she could be loud and aggressive at times, both in class and in extracurricular programs, she did well at English and art. She told one teacher she hoped to work with disabled children when she grew up. As she moved into her teens, she struggled with exams and homework, and got into physical fights with other students. She was finally suspended from school and ran away from home at the age of fifteen, taking to the streets with other children like her. They were not officially a "gang" in the criminal sense, more of a unified organism moving in the same direction—mostly away from authority. A therapist at the time noted how much Charlie seemed to enjoy the paradoxical combination of identity and belonging she got from the group, and the anonymity of moving in a pack, writing, "She says she felt braver as part of a group."

Belonging is a precious thing if you've never experienced it at home, and the sometimes abusive pressure in a gang to stay loyal and join in with criminal activity is a low price to pay. The trouble is that at such a young age, when people are still forming a sense of their independent selves, boundaries can blur between their identity and that of the group. If you're not sure where you end and others begin, it can be hard to know exactly where the boundary of reality is too. In later life, or indeed in prison, this lack of selfhood and individual thinking can have dire consequences. Disinhibiting drugs and alcohol exaggerate these feelings, as does the adrenaline involved in some gang situations. I noticed that Charlie had also told her previous therapist that she "had a rush" when the group went out and successfully shoplifted or stole a car for joyriding.

She had spoken to social workers at some point about how

protective she felt toward younger girls who joined the group, acting like a big sister and giving them advice about avoiding sexual assault on the street. Unfortunately, she had not been able to protect herself. Not long after she turned sixteen, she went to score some drugs from a local dealer on behalf of the group, and the man—who was twice her age—overpowered her and raped her. Charlie was so enraged that she took an unusual step: she marched down to the local police station and reported him. Rape has, unfortunately, long been one of the most underreported crimes, and Charlie's response was all the more surprising in this case because she was regularly at odds with the law.

Charlie's complaint went no further. The rape had occurred some thirty years earlier, and I believe that reforms to rape investigations and prosecutions would make that less likely now. The only result was that she was taken back into a care home, where she stayed until she was eighteen. She settled well into the facility and managed to present with some positive attitudes, talking with support staff there about her ambitions to work with disabled people or perhaps do something to help animals. But she was also cautioned by police several times during this period for minor offenses, including criminal damage and petty theft, and she was regularly taking drugs and abusing alcohol.

It would be easy to see her life as one long period of small advances hampered by repeated disappointments and obstructions, a kind of Snakes and Ladders game she always lost. When her eighteenth birthday came around, she lost her care placement, which meant that she left a secure environment while still vulnerable and unprepared for the adult world. Although Charlie knew it was coming, on the day she had to go she refused to say goodbye to anyone and on her way out smashed all the glass out of the front door of the most stable home she'd ever known.

This was not her first or last destructive outburst. They continued throughout her time in prison and were seen as more evidence of her "failure to progress." Before our next meeting, I heard she had done it again. This time she had wrecked her cell, creating as much havoc as she could in that small and barren space. In a sudden tantrum, she had thrown her few possessions around the room, tearing pages out of books and breaking things, and when prison officers rushed in to restrain her, she screamed and fought, saying she wished she were dead. All of this was apparently triggered by something minor, a frustration that would have been familiar to her and which she had apparently tolerated without a problem many times before: a member of staff had told her she would have to wait for approval of a request slip to visit the prison library.

I had to think about whether her initial meeting with me had stirred up something in Charlie's mind that had brought on this episode. She had been settled enough when I left her that day, but I knew the emotional significance of any human communication can take time to make itself felt. This is true for all of us, but it may be intensified in the minds of people like Charlie who have spent long periods negating or avoiding their emotions. The mind has so many layers of function it is impossible to know when a certain comment might go off like a depth charge; maybe some paranoia was ignited by my passing comment on her books, or she might have been disturbed by the fact that I had talked about her offense without sufficient preparation. I considered also whether having to wait for gratification (going to the library) had contributed to her violence. I called her offender manager to ask for more information about her last failed parole and discovered it was an almost exact replica of the current situation; apparently the recall to prison had been precipitated by a row with a member of staff in the halfway house where she was living who had stopped her from going out without the appropriate written permission. It sounded like there was a pattern there.

After her tantrum, I heard that Charlie had not been moved to a new cell, as was standard practice. She had begged to stay where she was, and because she had done no great damage, this was agreed. She was disciplined with a warning, however, and because of her suicide threats, she had to go on the ACCT book—shorthand for a protocol of assessment, care, custody, and treatment. This meant her carrying at all times a bright orange file containing her notes, visible as a sign to staff and other prisoners that she had tried or threatened to kill herself. I am sure this was a good idea on one level, as part of the "belt and braces" approach designed by the prison bureaucracy to keep people safe, but I felt certain Charlie must have hated it. Not only could "being on the book" mean taunts and bullying, but that orange beacon singled her out as different, and it was clear to me that Charlie wanted nothing more than to fade into the background, remaining gray and anonymous.

I was right. She was infuriated by the ACCT file, leaving it behind in the dining room and other places around the prison "by accident" more than once, and repeatedly asking to be "taken off the book." She argued that she had never been suicidal in the past and had only talked of wanting to kill herself in the heat of the moment.

Prisons and mental health services always take the tragedy of suicide seriously and cannot ignore suicidal threats, as I've described in the case of Marcus. With Charlie, the staff were especially sensitive because only a month earlier, a male inmate in a nearby prison who had made a similar threat but not been put on the book had hanged himself, generating a storm of hostile media coverage. Suicide has been designated as a "never event" in some mental health services, meaning it must never happen, a diktat implying that professionals will be held to account if a patient or prisoner does end their own life. This is unrealistic. Although caregivers may be rightly criticized for errors, some failures of care are systemic, not individual; for example, a doctor may not have the right equipment or training to manage a situation. The self-directed cruelty and despair that drive suicide are as risky as a blood clot or a dying heart muscle; when they are too advanced, there is no hope of medical professionals averting death. It is understood that cardiac surgeons may not be able to preserve life in all cases of heart surgery; by the same token, not all persons intent on suicide can have their lives saved by psychiatrists.

This is yet another example of the fundamentally different perceptions held in our society about mental and physical health services. It is ironic that the only way to maintain a mental health service (both in the community and in prisons) that did not have to bear this risk would be if we stopped offering help to depressed and at-risk people. Some NHS trusts have decided to do just that, to avoid dealing with the difficult legal and social outcomes of having a suicide on their books. This means that when someone is most in need of treatment or a listening ear, they may not be able to access it. The result is achingly predictable.

A few weeks later, Charlie and I would have our first proper session, in a small office on the wing normally used by "the Listeners"—prisoner volunteers who operate like the Samaritans, a volunteer group, to offer support to peers in distress. It was not an especially hospitable or pleasant space, dingy and cramped, with no window. A small glass panel in the door let in a little light and allowed others to look in as they passed by. The room was an odd shape, a sort of thin pentagon, so it was difficult to sit as I would have liked, with a wide space between the facing chairs. As in her cell, we sat opposite each other at awkwardly close quarters. Charlie shoved the hated orange file on the floor under her chair as soon as she sat down, which seemed to me a revealing gesture of how much she didn't want to talk about her vulnerability. I made a mental note not to let her forget to retrieve it when she left.

Charlie was wearing an ill-fitting tracksuit this time, the swoosh trademark on the left leg a cruel irony for a woman who hadn't swooshed anywhere in years, her body grown heavy and slack from institutional food and little movement. There was almost no vestige of the skinny girl who was in the photograph I'd seen when I accessed more information about her after our first encounter. Something in that picture—her wide eyes and raised chin signaling a mix of defiance and vulnerability—brought to mind the mug shot of Myra Hindley, an infamous criminal from 1960s Britain who was involved in a grisly series of child murders. A striking image of the sullen young Hindley, with a mop of bleached blonde hair and heavy eye makeup, staring diffidently into the camera, was featured widely in the media coverage at the time of her arrest. I never met her, but I had seen later pictures of her as an older woman in prison. Much like Charlie, by that time she seemed nondescript, unremarkable in every way, but her public identity was bound to that mug shot, fixed in amber.

I quickly understood that Charlie was not in a good mood. She seemed almost unaware of my presence as she launched into a bitter tirade about the orange file, which was "fucking ridiculous." Then she rattled on, wanting to tell me all about the officer she had fought with, her manner and her diction suggesting I might experience this just as she had. "Stopping me from *reading*. Genius idea, yeah? Such a shit, isn't he, has to control everyone, make himself feel like the Big Man—fuck him, right?"

I kept my face neutral, which is how I felt. Despite some stereotypical media portrayals and the reality that custodial institutions can attract people who like to bully others, in my experience most prison officers are humane folk who want to do a good job and feel frustrated when they can't. As when any small group controls a larger one, prison can be a frightening environment for them at times, and their work is hard. It has been made even more difficult by recent staffing cuts within the service, which are estimated at 30 percent over the last decade, despite the rising prison population. In the last five years alone, assaults on staff in prisons have tripled.[2] Most prisons are built in blocks with wings that are then divided into spurs, each housing as many as twenty-five prisoners, usually with just one officer per spur. They have to deal with the mentally ill, the mean, the mendacious, the terrified, the distressed, and the self-destructive—sometimes all in one person. This takes a certain amount of tenacity and faith in humankind, I think. I was moved when an officer I met recently commented that it was his view that "inside every violent prisoner there's a good man dying to get out."

I've had to work closely alongside a lot of prison officers, in both female and male prisons, over the years and have found them to be the usual mix of good people and idiots found in any institutional hierarchy, or any walk of life for that matter. Often they are just folk who needed to find work locally, many of them young and lacking in training. Prisoners have described to me their various relationships with officers, ranging from a toxic parent-child dynamic to mutual respect and cooperation. Retention of staff is a problem, with one recent survey reporting that a third of prison officers have less than two years' experience. I put it to Charlie whether the officer she had tangled with might have seen himself as following prison rules—was that a possibility? This was an effort on my part to see if she could mentalize, if she had that capacity to recognize what might be going on in another person's mind, as well as her own, or to "think about thinking." Most of us take this ability for granted, but some people find it difficult, giving rise to problematic behavior.

I expected my comments about the officer might provoke an aggressive response, but instead Charlie surprised me. "I know," she sighed, and relaxed back in her chair. This was heartening; something about my standing up for another person's perspective had contained her anger, and there was a noticeable lessening of tension in the room. "I lost it with him. Don't know what got into me," Charlie was saying. A familiar phrase, and whenever I hear it from anyone, I think the same thing: whatever it is hasn't just got in; it was probably lodged there already. But we would go further into this in the course of our work together, I hoped.

Her complaints carried on for most of the session, moving from the "bastard" officer to the library's "crap selection" of books, with me nodding all the while. Only near the end did I comment that so far it felt as if we'd been talking about things that were external to her, rather than what was going on in her head, in her internal world. She was taken aback and had to think about that for a minute, but then she agreed, telling me that she knew she had to figure out how to manage her angry thoughts. "What does anger feel like to you?" I asked. Without missing a beat, she said, "Hot—it feels like dragon's breath when it comes." It was such an evocative turn of phrase. I knew that would go in my notes and I'd give careful thought to it later. Who were her dragons? Were they within or without?

The following week, Charlie arrived on time for our appointment, but she had retreated into herself again and presented as depressed and withdrawn, her gaze on her slippered feet. There was a long silence after she sat down, which I broke eventually by guessing that she wasn't talking to me this time because she felt uncomfortable. Was that it? She shot me a look. "This is stupid. Shrinks never do any good." I thought she was testing me; no one uses the term "shrinks" as a compliment, and I don't know any psychiatrist who doesn't feel dismissed or belittled by it. I've no idea where it derives from, but the association with shrunken human heads used as trophies is not a comfortable one. Charlie's choice of the word made me consider whether she saw psychiatrists as the enemy. I stored that thought away with the dragon; it really wasn't my job to defend my profession, and anyway, I wanted to acknowledge her experience that the previous psychiatrists she had seen had "done her no good." I tried to do this by asking if her comment about shrinks was a sign of hopelessness. Her eyes narrowed. "Why should I have any fucking hope? Is that what you expect from me?" I was interested that she was guessing at what I was thinking. "I know what you want, you people . . . it's for me to have remorse, right? Sorry, but I don't. I was much younger back then . . . when it happened. I'm not the same person now, and I don't feel sad about it. Sorry. Sod off. I'm not going to fake it."

This was complex. She was bright enough and had been in the system long enough to know that forensic and prison professionals do take an expression of remorse as a sign of a diminished risk of future offending, and "prisoner expresses remorse" will appear on a checklist for parole evaluations, as an indicator of lower risk. It is a nice idea, if it were true. The problem is, there's little evidence for it, or rather, it appears from the available data that a feeling of remorse is one of the least important elements in successful risk reduction. This was initially surprising to me, but over time I've witnessed how much more relevant positive factors are, such as a pro-social attitude, investment in getting care and help, and a genuine understanding that a change of mind is necessary in order to have a change of life in the future. In my experience, regret is easier for offenders to access. It is less personal and emotionally punchy than remorse. It may also be more functional because it can act as a motivator for new choices; it is also a verb that implies change, and taking action to change is essential to a new way of thinking and behaving.

I had never mentioned the word "remorse" to her, and I found it interesting that she was attributing thoughts to me that were her own. It was possible that at some level she wanted to feel remorse because she knew she ought to. It could also be that her anger was driven by an anxiety that I was seeing her only as the Charlie of the past, the teenage kid in a faded mug shot, and not as the mature woman that she was now. Her idea that remorse might have an expiry date was also fascinating and I wanted to return to it later, but for now, I validated her line of thinking. "Okay, that's clear to me. Remorse is not real for you, and you want to be honest about that. What about regret? Do you have regrets?"

"Of course!" She was still angry, but not at me, I thought. "I don't know how it all happened." And suddenly, she was taking me to the night of the murder. I was with her in the park as night fell, and with her as she recalled running after the others, racing across the grass in bare feet, stoned and hungry, following their lead. She described in vivid language how she was "swept up" in the gang's unanimous surge of anger and disgust at the old tramp, joining in as everyone went after him. Someone was grabbing his booze, pulling his sleeping bag out of his grip as he begged them to stop—and then she and an older girl, someone she looked up to, pushed him to the ground. She heard an awful sound as his head hit the gravel and she saw some blood leaking out of his ear, but she told me it all felt disconnected from her, "like I was looking at a photograph or something." She gazed past me as she relived this, her eyes unfocused, her face impassive. "He just lay there, you know . . . sort of twitching a bit, and then . . . he was dead. And I was part of it, and I do regret that. But you can't go back. You can never go back. Never ever, not ever." Her repetition reminded me of Lear cradling poor Cordelia in his arms, his agonized lament of "never, never, never, never, never . . ." defining heartbreak with perfect simplicity. He was facing the same devastating truth that Charlie was articulating now: death cannot be undone.

I felt that we were beginning to explore the chaos of Charlie's inner world. I observed that she oscillated between a view that she had to use violence to influence events and emotions, and feelings of compliant helplessness and despair. This vacillation is a familiar feature in patients I've seen who have been exposed to high levels of childhood trauma and adversity, and I've come to see those extremes of violence and passivity as two different and useful personas—a word derived from the ancient Greek for "stage mask." The mask metaphor is such a useful one for thinking about how the mind works in social situations, as we take on or set aside different qualities, depending on certain emotional cues. It is no surprise that in his plays Shakespeare memorably describes life as a stage, with all the "strutting and fretting" men and women "merely players."

It occurred to me that the persona of Violent Charlie reflected a Just World hypothesis, an idea devised in the 1960s by American psychologist Melvin Lerner. From his extensive research, he found that humans were broadly disposed to think that beneficiaries merit their blessings and victims their suffering; or, put simply, good things happen to good people and bad things happen to bad people. This "just deserts" way of thinking is still prevalent today. It may even explain why some victims become perpetrators, a recurrent theme in forensic work, as we've seen. Charlie and others like her internalize their experiences of abuse and trauma to create a belief that if they are excluded from a world where good things happen, then the associated senses of loss, rejection, and envy become toxic drivers for more "badness." They may also feel a need to exert ever more control over others to protect themselves from the badness of their lives and the punishment that the "good people" will hand down.

Her other persona, Passive Charlie, believed that everyone around her had greater power and agency than she did. In this state of mind, she didn't have to take responsibility for anything. "I still don't know how it happened," she had said, just before giving me a precise account of how the murder of Eddie had unfolded. If, as she'd put it, she was just "swept along" and nothing she did was her choice, she could avoid difficult feelings. It was the gang, it was an older girl, it wasn't real to her, it was "like a photograph." I understood how that narrative had helped her to keep shame at bay, which may have been the only way she could bear to go on living. I began to think the suicide threat she had made to the prison officer had not been idle, but so far she had suppressed those feelings by telling herself a story that kept her safe.

We continued to meet together for some months, and she was

increasingly able to talk about her feelings and the past. Her moods would still swing from week to week, but I became better able to assess which mask she was wearing and discuss it with her as soon as she entered the meeting room. We talked about some other stories from her life, and I was interested too in any fictional stories she had read and liked. In one session, I reminded her of our first encounter in her cell, when I'd asked her about the Vikram Seth novel. Did she know why she'd picked that one to read? But she was Passive Charlie that day, and she shrugged, unwilling even to take responsibility for her choice of reading material. It was then that I suggested she might want to look at William Golding's *Lord of the Flies*. The novel had an obvious resonance which could be upsetting for her, I knew, as it described a band of boys who commit a murder together, but I had a feeling it might be relevant to our work.

Charlie didn't comment on my suggestion, and I didn't push it. Our next session began with her in energetic mode, as she told me with some relish a story from the wing that morning about another prisoner who had got into a screaming row with one of the staff and lost all her privileges as a result. She chuckled as she mimicked the woman's helpless fury when she found out what trouble she was in, wailing melodramatically, "You can't do this to me!" I didn't smile or comment, and an awkward silence fell. "What?" Charlie demanded. "You're laughing," I commented, "but you're also describing something that might be painful or scary, aren't you?" Charlie's face reddened and she averted her gaze. "I know." "What did you see when you were watching this happen today, Charlie?" She let out a deep breath, and then met my eyes. "That's what other people see, isn't it? They see *me* like that, don't they? When I'm all stroppy with the officers, and it isn't funny, right?" She was determined to work through this new thought, and I let her run with it, intrigued to see the way her mind was processing it. "I was watching her, you know, throwing stuff and howling and trying to kick him, and I was thinking, 'What are you like? You're a grown woman having a bloody tantrum!' And then I thought, 'If you're having a tantrum . . . you must be a kid. A little bratty kid.' And then . . ." She trailed off. "And then?" I nudged.

"And then I thought, the thought came to my head that . . . I'm not a kid either. I mean, look at me. I'm nearly fifty now, right?" She stood up, pushing her chair back, unable to keep still, as if the idea that she was an adult was electrifying. "My real name is Charlotte, you know, but I've been called Charlie since I was a kid. That's not a grown-up name, is it? And that officer I had the fight with that day, when I smashed my cell? He calls me Charlie too. Worse, he says 'Charlie-girl,' like 'Take it easy, Charlie-girl.' I think that got right inside my chest."

"And let the dragon out?" I said. The dragon metaphor she had used early on had become a code to mean we were working on something important. "You know that book you told me to read, that book about those kids on the island? So those boys, there were no grown-ups around to control them, and that was the problem. It got me thinking, maybe if I was a grown-up . . . I mean, I *am* one! And if I can control myself when I get mad, you know, instead of losing it, like that silly bitch this morning . . . like a fucking child."

This was a bit of a breakthrough, and I wanted to know if she could expand on it. I asked her what could help her to control herself, so she could feel more grown up—could she think of anything? She didn't miss a beat. "I could call myself my actual name, couldn't I? Charlotte, not Charlie. And tell everyone else to do it. That would help, right?" This hadn't occurred to me, but it showed real insight. I smiled broadly, offering that I could do that too. In a lovely moment of clarity, she shook her head vehemently. "No, no, not you. I want to be both Charlie and Charlotte in here. Is that okay?" "Of course," I said, very moved. "That will be just fine."

We came back to *Lord of the Flies* again in later sessions, and she volunteered that she'd found it quite painful to read. She became tearful when we talked about the excitement the boys in the story felt about killing, and that allowed her to speak more about the "rush" she had experienced when she and the gang had gone after Eddie. The emotional truth of the novel was helping her articulate something like regret, while it offered her a way to express how impossible it had felt back then to defy the will of her peers, without being destroyed herself.

I had thought of *Lord of the Flies* in relation to Charlie—or Charlotte—after our first meeting, when I'd seen that she was a reader. Before I'd offered the suggestion, I had debated with myself for some time about whether to risk the upset that this might cause her. Now I was glad. The great Polish poet Wisława Szymborska wrote about poetry as "a redemptive handrail," a beautiful idea which, for me, applies to all great writing and story-telling. It was remarkable to watch Charlotte have the same experience.

She turned to the nickname of a main character in the novel, Piggy, which clearly bothered her. "Why did the writer do that," she demanded of me, "why didn't he have a real name? That was fucking stupid, what was he thinking of?" At first, I was perplexed by what seemed like an inordinate criticism, but as she went on about it, I caught a glimpse of something raw in her anger. On impulse I asked her, "How did you come to be called Charlie? When did that start?" Tears sprang to her eyes, and she had to compose herself before she could answer. She'd always been Charlotte, she told me, when she was a little girl, but then her stepbrothers began teasing her with the nickname Charlie as she entered puberty. They would say she wasn't a real girl, that she had no tits, that she looked like a boy and should have a boy's name ... "And then they started grabbing at me ..." She stumbled and stopped there, clearly uncomfortable. I had a powerful sense that she was reverting to Passive Charlie before my eyes, and when I asked if she wanted to say more, she just said gruffly, "That's it, I've been Charlie ever since," with one of her little shrugs. "But you have a choice about that now," I told her. I needed her to see that nobody could give her agency, she had to take it. She looked up at me, startled, and admitted that what I'd said was true. She'd already made the choice to reclaim her given name.

"What's in a name?" indeed. The language we use to describe ourselves, including how we wish to be known, is always significant, and it is a topic I return to often in my work. Her childhood associations of "Charlie" had kept her in a traumatic place, where she was at the mercy of others and had no choice but to comply or lash out. Over time, there would be another language change. She gradually reduced her use of cursing as an all-purpose communicator of feeling and began to choose her words more carefully, trying to think of the right way to put something before she spoke. One day, we were talking again about the murder of Eddie, and I encouraged her to try and describe her emotions for me in whatever terms she chose—there was no right or wrong answer. After some thought, she volunteered that she thought his murder had "blackened her heart." Grim though that idea was, the way she expressed it was auspicious. She did not offer the more familiar "it broke my heart," which as a cliché might have lacked honesty. Instead, she had generated this metaphor of internal rot to convey her feelings, prima facie evidence of an engaged mind, of creativity and transformation. Our aim had been to try and see if she could become "unstuck" from the prison system, and now we were seeing that this might require detaching a part of herself, peeling off an old persona that was no longer useful. I left her company that day with some optimism that she would be able to reorder her internal landscape and leave behind aspects of an old identity that did not serve her in adult life.

She would soon be eligible to apply for parole again, and the content of our final sessions moved on to what she might say for herself at a hearing and what she wanted others to know about our work together, since I would be called on to provide some feedback to the parole board. She said she thought the best way to put it was that she'd "grown up" in therapy, and I agreed. She wanted to ask for more therapy outside the prison environment, if she was allowed to return to the community, to "help me manage out there." We both smiled at this, recognizing it meant that she had found her relationship with me to be positive. More importantly, it was a sign of her increased sense of security that she did not think it was a weakness to ask for help. I now thought her failure to progress or become "unstuck" might have been because she'd had no haven other than prison. I reflected that as a child, each time she thought she'd found a safe harbor it had turned out to be full of danger, and so she would destroy or disrupt her ability to settle in one place. It occurred to me that her repeated recalls from probation and even the tantrum in her cell soon after our first meeting, which I had thought was all about her being thwarted by authority, could also have been a part of this pattern. She might have panicked that working with me on becoming "unstuck" would set her free, which she found to be a terrifying thought.

Charlotte speculated that she might try to fulfill her ambition of working with disabled people, if possible, or the elderly, venturing that this could be a way to make some reparation "for when I killed Eddie." The fact that she could own the deed in such active language was as encouraging as her metaphor of a "blackened heart." Grasping the idea of making amends and being willing to do so were as important as actually following through, although I hoped she would one day. I wished her all the best as we parted, careful to say, "Goodbye, Charlotte." I still remember her beaming face.

ZAHRA

It was a new year, and I enjoyed the sense of a fresh start as I returned to work with the mental health inreach team at the women's prison after the holidays. Heavy keys jangled on my leather belt as I passed through security and threaded my way through the familiar airlocks and long corridors, stopping to greet colleagues in offices still decorated with bits of tinsel and cards. A check of the calendar showed my first appointment that day was with a woman called Zahra, in the prison health care unit (the HCU) in the central wing.

Approaching the double doors, I was greeted by the sound of raised voices within: loud and furious cursing mixed with a more distant but sustained high-pitched keening, like a widow at a wake. Hasty footsteps and shouts, presumably of staff as they rallied to soothe and restrain people, were underscored by the desperate sound of another person's ragged sobs. I thought of Dante's arrival in hell ("Abandon all hope, ye who enter here" emblazoned over the gates) and the cacophony of "unfamiliar tongues" and "cries of rage" that greeted him. I imagined how a visitor might feel overwhelmed in the face of this; even though I'd been doing this work for many years, I had not become inured to the anguish of both staff and prisoners in such environments, and I hoped I never would. But while Dante covered his ears and wept as he passed into the underworld, I knew that if I dissolved into tears as I entered the unit, it would help no one.

The HCU has a remit to provide basic health interventions to prisoners who are too ill to be in their cells. Some of the patients are physically sick, but due to the prevalence of mental illness in our prisons, the unit has to look after acutely mentally unwell prisoners too, many of whom will wait for weeks or months for transfer to a secure psychiatric hospital. The demands on the HCU are often overwhelming, and the staff can have the harassed look of mothers who are caring for too many children at once. But the officer in charge who greeted me that day was welcoming and efficient. He introduced himself as Terry and led me away from the reception area to a meeting room he had managed to clear for me.

As he moved some papers and boxes aside to allow space for me to set up the room, Terry told me that everyone was just glad I'd been able to come, as they had been concerned about the suicide risk of the patient I was there to see. Like Charlotte, she was "on the book," that system for monitoring prisoners who are seen as a suicide risk and are constantly being watched. He handed me an orange cardboard file with Zahra's name on it. I would write my observations about her in it each time we met, and she would have to carry it around with her when she was back on the wing, in accordance with the prison rules, as a flag to others that she was a risk. "I hope she talks to you—she barely says a word to any of us," said Terry.

The woman who joined me in the meeting room a few minutes later didn't seem obviously distressed. She responded to my hello in a low voice and took my outstretched hand with a grip that was cool and limp. As she took the proffered chair, opposite mine, she glanced at the orange file bearing her name with a flicker of recognition—she clearly knew what it was, but unlike Charlotte, she didn't seem to have a problem with it. She was unremarkable to look at: slim and slight, with her black hair held in a long plait. I noticed she had a fresh cloth bandage on one arm, peeking out from the sleeve of a loose cardigan. She wore a calf-length skirt, ballet slippers, and an air of resignation; her manner suggested that if someone cut in front of her in a queue at the bank, they could be confident she wouldn't object. She made eye contact when we first sat down, but her gaze was dull, with a kind of blankness that troubled me. People who are severely depressed and at high risk of suicide are more likely to describe themselves as feeling numb and emotionally disconnected, as opposed to having feelings of sadness. I thought the staff were right to be vigilant about this woman. I also noticed that although we had had only the briefest of interactions, I had the sense of being judged or silently criticized.

I began as always by explaining, with a friendly smile, about confidentiality and my role in the mental health team. She barely responded. Couldn't she see I was there to help her? It was rare for me to feel a flash of annoyance like that—especially with someone so apparently placid. When I was in training, I had often wrestled with negative feelings like this, and it was only slowly and by making a lot of mistakes and taking them to supervision that I learned to tune in to them and to my patients. This is an acquired skill based on careful listening, much like tuning a musical instrument. "Attunement" develops during the essential therapy we receive in training; it helps us to recognize when our own emotional baggage is intruding into the room and allows us to detach from it. Though she was presenting as blank, there was something in Zahra's demeanor that was generating antipathy in me. Or was I simply mirroring some antagonism she was hiding?

I decided to confront this head-on. "I'm curious, are you feeling a bit annoyed about this meeting?" She said nothing, gazing down, lips pressed together as if to prevent a simple yes or no from escaping. My irritation increased, and I was aware of wanting to raise my voice, to wake her. "Perhaps not annoyed then. What about really, really pissed off?" She shook her head vehemently in response, which was better than nothing; at least she was showing some emotion. I assured her that she didn't have to see me and that nothing terrible would happen if we stopped. I wasn't there to make her do anything. She didn't react; it was as if she hadn't heard me. I reflected that if I were on constant suicide watch like her, it was unlikely it would make me cooperative either. "Zahra?" She glanced up quickly, then down again, and I told her that I understood it wasn't easy, talking to a stranger like this. She mumbled something I couldn't catch. "Sorry, say again?" She raised her voice: "I just want to die."

Zahra had started a fire in her cell a few weeks before the holidays. Thankfully, the smoke set off an alarm and her life was saved.

I was interested to hear from her offender manager that this incident had been a direct mirror of her original offense: two years earlier, in the run-up to the Christmas holidays, she had survived a fire she had caused in her apartment. Each time she had left notes addressed to her mother declaring her suicidal intent, and in both cases she had been fortunate that due to a rapid response, the worst physical consequences for her had been minor burns and some smoke inhalation. But the fire in her apartment had resulted in severe property damage, as well as serious injury to a fireman while he was rescuing her and evacuating the building. The maximum penalty in the UK for deliberate fire-setting (arson) is life in prison, even if nobody is killed as a result, and Zahra was sentenced to fifteen years with a minimum term of ten. She had been well behaved during her time in prison so far, until the recent incident in her cell.

Aside from any material or political motives, arson is not a crime that is well understood, particularly in females, although it is the subject of increasing study.[1] Apparently, Zahra's fire-setting career began when she was seventeen, in her bedroom at home, when she tried to set her bed alight. No great damage was done, but her mother reported her to the police and ejected her from the family. She was taken into care until she reached eighteen, when she was left to fend for herself. According to one social worker's note, she tried to reach out to her parents at that time, but her father had been diagnosed with cancer and her mother did not want her to visit. Her older brothers sent her some money but also kept her at arm's length, prioritizing busy lives and young families. It sounded like she was really on her own, adrift in the world.

She left her native Leicester and went down to London to find work. She began to set small fires, usually in parks or near hospitals or police stations, as if to make it convenient for the public services to deal with the consequences. She did not attempt to conceal her behavior and was repeatedly caught in the act—but starting a fire doesn't equal arson until the police charge it as such. She was eventually charged twice, but her sentences were brief, and she was soon back in the community. Her probation records indicated that she had done well thereafter, finding an apartment she liked and a job in a garden center. She got on well with her boss there, who was kind to her. For nearly two years, it appeared that Zahra did not set any more fires. This kind of pause isn't unheard of with arsonists, and indeed other types of offenders; it is consistent with a pattern we also see in addiction. If people are at an early stage in their offending, and if they are not antisocial, they may go through periods when they feel less distress or find life more manageable for various reasons. They remain abstinent for a while, until one day something prompts them to act out again. My guess was that those two years were important to Zahra, and for me a hopeful indication that she could be pro-social.

Her offender manager had told me that Zahra had a history of self-harming, which had continued in prison, where she would cut her arms and legs. This wasn't unusual; there is a high incidence of self-harm in Britain's prisons, with reports of between a quarter and a third of all women in prison self-harming (five times as many as in the men's system). The figure increases annually, and has tripled over the last decade, according to a recent Ministry of Justice report.[2] Self-harm might explain the bandage on her arm, although it could have been due to burns sustained in her cell. I would not probe her at this early stage, but I thought there could be something in her past that was "unspeakable" for her. Some people who can't manage their feelings will feel bodily pain or become depressed, internalizing their hurt, while those who self-harm or set things alight are externalizing it. Both types of activity can be seen as signal fires, calls for urgent assistance. This can become a habit that is hard to break, and it is a risky one. It is a grave error when people dismiss acts of self-harm as attention-seeking—as if that were a bad thing.[3]

Sitting with her that morning, I was struck by the starkness of Zahra's express wish to die and her toneless voice. Clearly, her suicidality had not abated during her time in the HCU. I would have to be meticulous about alerting staff and colleagues to this, establishing mechanisms to ensure that every safeguarding measure was in place. There would be forms to fill out and notes made in her ACCT file, a paper trail to create. It would protect Zahra, and also serve as proof that she had been heard and had received the appropriate level of care and response, "just in case." This bureaucracy can seem onerous, but it is important; just as I can feel compassion and still remain detached in my role, the people who run prisons must balance concern for the inmates with a duty to maintain order and be prudent in tracking matters of liability and oversight.

I thought if I did not respond immediately to Zahra's stark statement about wanting to die, she might expand on it, but instead she sat quietly, staring down at the floor. I took time to reflect on what I could say to her. It would be a rookie error to express sorrow or worry, making this moment all about me. I thought I'd just leave her space in which to feel her feelings without intrusion. After several minutes, she lifted her head, perhaps a bit thrown by my silence, and I held her gaze. "How long do you think you've felt that way, Zahra?" She didn't waver. "All my life." A bleak, soft admission, like a verbal frost. I was reminded of Keats's line "I have been half in love with easeful Death," even if self-immolation was hardly easeful. How had she accommodated that feeling, how had she lived this long? She shrugged.

I decided it was probably time to change the subject, and remembered my plan to try and talk about her work. I told her I understood that her old boss had been supportive of her, and asked if she could tell me more about him and her work. She responded immediately, in a brief moment of animation. She described the garden center, and how she took pride in setting out displays and helping customers. She missed that, she said. "I was a good worker. Maybe I can get a job there again when I get out." Her reference to a future life and the indication of an appetite to leave prison alive were a relief for me to hear.

It occurred to me that Zahra might be most at risk of acting out her distress if she didn't have work she liked to do. As anyone who has ever enjoyed their work will recognize, once that's taken away, you're left with whatever home or leisure means in your life. If that's a trouble spot or a blank space, then depression can rush in to fill the vacuum. Zahra's recent suicide attempt, and also her index offense, might have been related to that lull in routine and work that holidays can bring. At Christmas, the ubiquitous celebrations of the happy family ideal are intense enough in the world outside prison, as we all know (and they seem to start earlier every year). People inside absorb the same enforced merriment from TV specials, from the radio blaring carols and pop songs ("I wish it could be Christmas every day"), from reading print media and online postings (for those who have internet access) full of imagery of celebration and plenitude. All serve as painful reminders that prison punishment is all about social exclusion. Secure hospitals and prisons are required to develop what are called (with unconscious irony) "festive care plans," procedures tailored to help relieve some of the upset inmates will feel at the memories of Christmases past or the contemplation of what they see as a future without joy. Festivities around the new year or on birthdays and anniversaries can also be tricky, particularly for someone serving a long sentence; they mark another long, monotonous, twelve-month stretch, another chasm of loneliness and boredom to cross. For prisoners with mental health issues, this can go deep, stirring up difficult feelings of dread, paranoia, and anxiety, as well as disturbing dreams and memories of loss or, perhaps, of happier times. As the medieval philosopher Boethius put it so well, "The greatest misery in adverse fortune is once to have been happy."

I wanted to find out more about the specific significance of the season for Zahra and to discover what the question was to which, for her, death by fire seemed the right answer. But our time was running out and I would have to return to that another day. For now, I needed to discuss how we were going to handle her revelation that she was still feeling suicidal. The prison staff were worried, I said, "and we all want to keep you safe while you're here." I deliberately put it in those terms to underline the temporary nature of her stay. One day she would get out; the future was waiting for her. "They already know," she said, her eyes drifting to the orange file. She sounded as if she could hardly be bothered with everyone's concern for her; if she had any worries of her own about dying, it seemed she wasn't conscious of them.

The prison—and, by extension, I—would have to do the emotional work of keeping her alive. If she was going to make it, I thought, she would have to get more invested in her own survival. And if she didn't give up her interest in fire-setting, she could be in prison for a long time, possibly stretching beyond her already lengthy sentence. I asked if she would meet me again the following week. "Is there any point?" she asked. It was a good question, and I had my answer ready. I told her I wanted to stand up for the part of her that had expressed a hope for the future, in the form of a return to her old job, and suggested that she might think of therapy as a kind of work too. I told her I was willing to try that, if she was. To my surprise, she agreed.

I didn't know where I would find Zahra when I came for our next meeting. I thought it was likely she'd still be in the HCU, but I was told on arrival that she had been sent back to the wing, signifying that staff thought her risk of suicide had decreased. I guessed that they would also have been under pressure to free up beds in the unit for some other woman who was more obviously mentally unwell. In a poorly resourced system, this is the juggling act; everyone does their best and we pray that no balls are dropped. I wasn't under any illusion that Zahra had miraculously stopped wanting to die, but perhaps she was willing to gamble on a more positive future.

I took it as another good sign when I found she wasn't in her cell but was at work. She had decided to return to a job she had previously held in the chaplaincy, cleaning the worship room and providing assistance to staff during services. We could have our session there.

Prisons in Britain have a chaplaincy that serves all faiths and none, supportive of all religious practices and beliefs, including paganism, agnosticism, and atheism. Although self-professed atheists are the largest group in our prisons, there is still a sizeable proportion who identify as religious. Visiting priests, rabbis, and imams complement the prison chaplain's pastoral function. This is one way in which these institutions can treat prisoners as individuals and model respect for human dignity, as well as encourage better relationships between staff and prisoners. There is also a recognition that spirituality can play a role in people becoming more pro-social and less likely to reoffend on release.

Work, education, therapy programs, and taking diet and physical health seriously are other examples of dignifying people's experience inside, but there is an inherent tension in the provision of these, beyond the perennial lack of funding. If they are to be seen as fair, prisons must have one rule for everyone, and sometimes options that cater to a specific subgroup are seen as biased; the same is true in secure hospitals. The focus of penal reform, which has existed for as long as modern prisons, has increasingly been on trying to prioritize rehabilitation and, with it, human dignity, but there have been many failures. I'm not naive about this, and I'm also aware that in my role I may be shielded from seeing the worst of the injustices or abuses that do occur.

Each chaplaincy is unique to the institution, but they all seem to have a calm atmosphere and a relative sense of safety. I could hear the quiet rumble of conversation and the sound of bells as I approached the doors—not church bells, but those tinkling ting-sha cymbals used by Buddhist monks to mark the beginning and end of meditation practice. It was quite the opposite of arriving at the HCU. Inside, a prison officer chatted with two women who were waiting to see the chaplain; nature photographs on the walls featured inspirational quotes, including Robert Frost's wonderful "The best way out is always through,"[4] superimposed over an image of a tunnel made of oak trees. It struck me how important this nonjudgmental, hopeful space was for people living with the consequences handed down by courts. Within these walls, sorrow, grief, and forgiveness were well understood.

I spoke briefly with the chaplain, who seemed to like and value Zahra. She told me Zahra was in a stable state of mind and had met with the visiting imam that morning. This was heartening too; it suggested she could be reflective and ask for help. At the same time, I knew there was a risk that as we went on in therapy, some painful feelings would surface that setting fires had probably helped her to avoid. There's a meme that nicely captures the true sense of menace in difficult emotions: a man opens his front door to a crowd of rather cheery monsters, jostling to enter, and responds by saying, "Well, well, if it isn't those feelings I've been trying to avoid . . ." Zahra would have to trust me as we opened that door together, and I knew that wouldn't come easily to her.

She arrived a few moments later, taking the seat facing me and nodding in greeting. She looked more alert and less blank this time but fiddled with the bandage still in place on her left arm, tugging at it and smoothing it as we talked. I told her I was glad to see her and mentioned that the chaplain had spoken warmly of her. I was treated to the briefest of smiles, transforming her face for a moment, but it soon vanished, a light switch flicked on and off. I reminded her that therapy was a kind of work—the work of taking her mind seriously—and that it might mean talking about her past experiences and choices. She frowned, telling me she wasn't sure she could do that. It made her nervous because she didn't want to think about "hard things in the past."

The hard things could wait, I said. We could start with some simple stuff. "Like what?" She might tell me a bit about her family, I suggested. She exhaled, as if I'd given her more than she could handle, but she made an attempt. She was careful not to speak ill of them, I thought later; her true feelings would only emerge over time. She told me her father had died during her first prison sentence, succumbing to cancer. "He was a good and decent man," said Zahra, sounding like she was reading a quote from an elegy or obituary. "And your mother?" I asked. "She's alive." Her voice sounded brisk and impersonal. "She's a busy woman. Seven grandchildren now, you know?" Again, that sounded like a quote, and I found myself thinking she might be parroting her mother. Did she ever visit her daughter in prison? "No, no, it's much too far away." Zahra's tone did not invite another question, and I had a strong sense that this line of inquiry was closed.

There's a cliché, dating back to Freud, that therapists always ask about people's parents and inevitably invite their patients to blame them for their troubles. The work in recent decades on childhood attachments that I've described, which builds on the work of Freud and many who followed, provides empirical evidence that there is a connection between a child's early relationship with their parents and the way in which their mind develops. This in turn influences the function of the adult personality, including the ways in which people talk about themselves and those closest to them. Some research indicates that repeated exposure to abuse or neglect in childhood may affect the development of neural connections between those areas of the brain that manage emotions and support self-reflection. By the time I met Zahra, along with other forensic colleagues I'd published research into how the unresolved distress of childhood attachment insecurity can increase the risk of violence.[5] I had a sense that this work would prove relevant to Zahra, whose self-narrative, such as it was, appeared to be preoccupied with family members who seemed to be absent from her life. I was reminded of the double meaning of "account," as both a story and an honest reckoning.

Good therapists don't probe for evidence of abuse or trauma, but instead listen carefully and attend to what their patients don't say as much as what they do, noticing the all-important spaces between the words. Most of us will also want to draw people out about their positive experiences with parents and caregivers, particularly their memories of being attended to as children, held in mind, and known as an individual. These can have a neutralizing effect on adversity, building resilience and making therapy more likely to succeed. Although I made no early assumptions, I was struck by how Zahra avoided talking about the emotional reality of her relationships with her family; her account was dry, matter-of-fact.

I could see that Zahra was unused to talking about herself and her experience. Reticence early on in therapy isn't unusual, but I thought it went deeper with her. She was educated and articulate, far more so than many people I worked with, yet she struggled to find words for her experience and her feelings. It took several sessions to learn a little more about her life growing up in the Midlands. As I've noted in other cases, hearing someone's history firsthand is always preferable to reports or documentation: their use of language opens a window onto their emotional experience. For example, I knew Zahra had been born to parents who already had two boys in their teens when she came along; she described this as being a "late child." Again, there were two meanings to consider: late can mean either deceased or tardy, and neither word has warm connotations. I had the impression that she may have learned this phrase early on, and that she felt somehow at fault for her birth, as if her life were a mistake.

Each time we met, we would talk about the orange ACCT book she still had to carry around with her, containing notes about her suicide risk. I suggested that together we could think of reflections that we might add to her notes, as if it were a work assignment. As a result, I think she began to see her suicidal feelings as a problem for the non-suicidal part of her mind. This was something that we could consider together, something which she did not have to hide from me. By this method we began to construct a kind of bridge between us. In taking her suicidal feelings seriously through our work together, she began to make a connection between what had happened in her cell and the day when she set fire to her apartment. Little by little, haltingly at first and then flowing more easily, she told me the story of her offense in language that suggested agency and acceptance. I was able to piece together a detailed impression of that fateful day, one that has stayed with me for years, in the same way that a particularly moving or distressing film lodges in the memory, with certain images returning to mind at unexpected moments in my daily life.

Her shopping list that November evening was not long, she began, but she had to go to a few different places. She recalled it was bitterly cold, and I pictured her tugging a scarf higher around her neck to protect her from the chill as she picked her way along the main street toward home. Threading through the crowd of shoppers and commuters, she passed Khan's bakery and nearly walked by, but then turned around and slipped inside. I was familiar with those Asian sweet shops and imagined the brass bell above the door tinkling as she stepped into the damp, cardamom-scented warmth.

She had to queue for ages alongside an almost entirely female crowd, their high-pitched chatter grating on her ears. Through the glass window of the counter display she eyed her favorite sweets, *gulab jamun*: golden spongy balls of pastry dusted with tiny shards of pistachio. The girl at the counter yawned as she took the order. "Cover your mouth or something will fly right in there, stupid girl," she heard in her head, as if her mother were pressed close beside her. But Mum was far away, in Leicester, in the house where

Zahra had been born but was no longer welcome. As she left the bakery to go home, perhaps pinching one of those pastries out of the bag to eat as she juggled the shopping bags holding the other supplies she'd purchased, I'm sure she appeared utterly harmless. Anyone waiting with her for the light to turn green at the intersection would have seen her as one of many: an Indian woman aged anywhere between thirty and forty, well groomed and unflashy, no doubt wearing a sensible winter coat.

When she got home, the first thing Zahra did was text her mum. The non-response came: "Delivered." Again. She'd sent several text messages wishing her happy Diwali, since it was the first night of the festival, and asking her to call sometime. Mum was probably cooking for everyone and would see this message later, Zahra thought. The clay lamp with a spout that she'd pulled out of a dusty box under her bed that morning was sitting on the table, and she took a moment to fill it from the big bottle of oil she'd just purchased. She went to hang up her coat, and then simply dropped it on the floor by her armchair. What was the point? Her phone buzzed—a text! "CLAIM YOUR £10 VOUCHER OR REPLY STOP TO END." Outside, fireworks began. I pictured her standing there listening to the first hiss, whistle . . . pop of the night, peering out through her kitchen window at the display. She heard faint cheers filtering through the glass from the children living next door. Did she think of them, as she made her plan? She didn't want to, she said. She figured they would be fine. The building was mostly brick, wasn't it?

It was day three of Diwali. She said the street outside was teeming with people dancing, laughing, and having fun. The flats were all festooned with decorations, windows full of twinkling fairy lights and candles. I didn't want to interrupt her flow, but I was thinking, "She's from a Muslim family, and Diwali is a Hindu festival, isn't it?" As if she'd read my mind, she commented, "Everyone celebrates Diwali, you know. Any excuse for a party." The five-day festival had fallen a little later than usual that year, butting close to Christmas. "These festivals are not so different, are they?" Zahra mused. I asked her what she meant. She'd grown up celebrating both, she told me, and talked a little about how each of them marked new beginnings and signified a triumph of good over evil, the coming of light into darkness. I listened, thinking about Diwali lights merging into strings of colored Christmas bulbs and the message in John's Gospel of how "the light shines in the darkness, and the darkness cannot overcome it."

The third day of Diwali was when you were supposed to visit a temple, Zahra explained, which she hadn't done. You're also meant to spend time with friends and family—but she hadn't done that either. She had gone to work at the garden center, as usual, arranging all the latest Christmas stock. A few weeks earlier, she had asked her boss if she could make a Diwali display as well, so she checked to make sure all was in order, with tea lights lined up, flower garlands hanging neatly. I smiled at her description of the goddess Lakshmi balanced on her lotus flower, gazing across at Father Christmas and his reindeer in the aisle opposite. She set aside one box of tea lights to buy with her employee discount card on the way out—unlike some of her colleagues, she'd never try to pocket them on the sly.

It was the only job she'd ever had that she liked, she said. Lovely smells of ginger and coffee drifted from the newly installed café at the back. The shoppers, their carts piled with poinsettias and ropes of tinsel, greeted each other with hugs and laughter, huddling together in their cozy groups of family and friends over steaming mugs and mince pies. Seeing them made her feel sad, she told me, but she couldn't explain why. I suggested maybe it was because she wasn't with her family. She shook her head—both of her brothers had invited her to come to their homes for their celebrations that week, like they did every year. But she felt ashamed and angry at them for reasons she couldn't really articulate—and at the time, there was no one else she could talk to about such things. I nodded for her to go on, encouraged that she had come this far.

The truth was, she blurted out, she feared to see her mother at one of those gatherings with her brothers and their families, as much as she longed to hear from her and get some inkling that the woman even knew her daughter was alive. It had been three years since they'd had any communication, and that was just one phone call, curt and abruptly cut off by Mum. And before that, another five since she'd seen her in person. It felt like forever. The bad thoughts had started up again. It had been a long time since she'd felt so low—and even so, she functioned almost as normal during the workday. Nobody knew. When everyone was leaving work that last evening, her manager had wished her a happy holiday, asking, "Will you be seeing the family?" "Off to my mum's!" she'd shot back, demonstrating a big fake smile for me as she recalled how she'd presented this lie. It had cheered her up a little, the idea that he probably believed her.

But when she let herself into her gloomy basement apartment, that bad feeling ambushed her, forcing her to curl up in a ball in the chair by the electric heater. She had to pull herself together. Then she checked her phone again, just in case. Still no reply from Mum. She opened her browser and flicked through her internet searches from the night before, making sure she'd read all the instructions. She was ready. She described how she pulled a stool over to the smoke alarm in the kitchen and, standing on tiptoes, managed, after a bit of a struggle, to disable it.

She told me that she thought about what might happen the next day, imagining a phone call made by a stranger to her mother, thinking about what Mum would do, if she even answered. At that, she stopped short, lapsing into a moody silence. I waited awhile, then prompted her, asking what she had thought her mum's possible reaction would be to such a call. "Maybe . . . I don't know. I figured she'd be gutted—but mainly because people would point to her as a bad mother, blame her or something." There was nothing her mum cared about more than what others thought.

Zahra told me the main thing on her mind was that nobody would care if she died. She had no close friends. Her family might not even hear the news for ages; her brothers didn't answer calls from unknown numbers on principle. When they did find out, they'd probably think they were better off without her, freed from any cloying sense of duty that made them invite her round once a year or send her a photo after the arrival of yet another fat, beautiful baby. "Mummy, please text," she wrote one last time, pressing "send" before she could regret it. After a moment, she saw the word "Delivered." Maybe her mother would read this final message and realize it was urgent. Her voice was flat and her tone pragmatic as she related this, despite the desperation implicit in her words. The dissonance was moving and painful to hear, and staying neutral, holding back tears, took more effort than I thought it would.

After another half hour or so of staring at the phone and willing it to buzz with a message, in a moment of clarity Zahra realized there would be nothing. Time was up. She scribbled a handwritten note to her mother, an apology and a goodbye. She pushed it out under the front door, hopefully out of harm's way. Taking a tray from the kitchen, she lined up four or five rows of the little tea lights she'd brought home and set a box of matches beside them. She didn't usually keep matches around, because her stove was electric, and anyway matches weren't good for her. She knew that. But today she'd bought some specially. Then she opened a bottle of sweet wine—another rare purchase. Drink didn't agree with her as a rule, she explained to me, but that night . . . She trailed off. I nodded. She didn't have to justify it.

She quickly ate the pastries she'd brought home, washing them down with the wine. When she stood up abruptly, she remembered thinking she might vomit. Next, as part of a preplanned ritual, she picked up the clay lamp and, methodically, making sure not to miss a spot, went around the two rooms of her apartment, dashing its contents along the edges of the walls. When it was empty, she went and fetched the bottle of oil and poured out whatever was left for good measure, tracing a shiny wet borderline on the carpet, all around her bed. I imagined her climbing in, sitting there marooned on an island of sorrow, where nobody was going to come to her rescue. Nobody knew.

Picking up the box of matches, she shook it, and she recalled how her heart had started to beat faster the first time she heard that tantalizing sound. There was a power in those little wooden sticks. She lit the tray of lights with care, "like a birthday cake." As the noise increased outside, Bollywood music filtering through the walls, she recalled seeing tea lights on other Diwali nights, long ago, when people would fill her family's home—friends and relatives and relatives of friends. A memory returned as she told me this: she recalled a time when she was ten or eleven years old, her young self peeking out of her room on the landing and watching the line of lights someone had laid out on the stairs. The little flames looked like they were dancing to the music blaring from the sitting room. But she was meant to stay upstairs and study, she said. It was her job to be a good girl and do well in school, so she would grow up to earn money and contribute to the family. Her big brothers were allowed to join the party, though; they were spoiled and adored.

I asked her if she was always a good girl, and she shook her head, telling me that by the time she was in her teens, she had begun to climb out of her bedroom window when she should have been doing homework, drinking and smoking with some local kids who hung out in the park, in defiance of her parents. She risked a beating from her father every time she was caught. She talked of how at sixteen she began to self-harm in secret, cutting into the flesh on her arms and legs. Somehow, it made her feel better, "or at least feel nothing." She covered the angry welts with long sleeves and wore only trousers. Nobody knew.

She returned to the story of the fire, admitting that she couldn't help it—before she struck a match, she had to take one last peek at her phone. There was a message on the screen, but it just warned "low battery." Who cared? Nobody. She picked up the first tea light on the tray and pitched it across the room toward the curtains. Then another, and another, in all directions . . . until the tray was empty. As she watched, her head swimming with wine and her eyes starting to tear up from the smoke, with one great whoosh the flames leapt up, consuming the curtains and licking at the torn wallpaper. Only then did she feel panic. What had she done? That was the last thing she remembered, she told me, until she woke in a hospital bed.

I knew from the trial documents that Zahra and her neighbors had been incredibly lucky: fire alarms outside in the corridor had gone off immediately, and the fire department, already on high alert during Diwali week, was close at hand. The children next door were swiftly evacuated. Zahra suffered smoke inhalation but miraculously escaped with a few minor burns. Unfortunately, the fireman who broke down her door and pulled her out of the smoke was badly hurt. Zahra was arrested in the hospital the next day and sent to the women's prison, where, two years later, we would meet in the HCU.

As she described her memory of that night, I thought again of how difficult holiday times are for the lonely and the unloved, for those who have nowhere to go where they will be welcomed. Some people can manage this by working, as a way to hide from socially enforced delight. It's not only the shops on the main street or Amazon that do the bulk of their business during this season; the Samaritans' hotline receives its highest volume of calls in the last quarter of the year. My mind kept returning to Zahra's fruitless texts to her mother, and the poignancy of this woman's longing for maternal contact, even a few words to give her some shred of evidence that she existed in her mother's mind. If many of us can relate to Zahra's anguish in the holiday context, then perhaps we can also recognize that experience of rejection and fear when someone we love doesn't respond when we call out to them. Why did she think she might get a response, after so much rejection? I found myself considering whether she was in part prompted by the hopeful and maternal symbolism around her: the Virgin Mary tenderly holding her baby son, the holy family surrounded by love and light; little children sitting around a tree with their loving parents. I searched for "Diwali images" after our session and found the goddess of good fortune, Lakshmi, rising from an ocean of milk, full-breasted and broad-hipped.

When Zahra finished her account, she folded her hands and looked up at me, expectant, as if I would have some great insight. I was still absorbing it, like someone who sits transfixed in a cinema after a powerful film, blind to the credits rolling and the audience heading for the exits. I could see Lakshmi and Father Christmas on their facing displays, taste the sticky pleasure of those Indian sweets, hear the fireworks exploding in the street and inside her mind, and feel the sharp pain of the texts that failed to come. I couldn't help but have profound sympathy for her, and for the deep loneliness in her life. But most lonely people don't set life-threatening fires. I didn't share all these thoughts with Zahra, but I did share with her how much sorrow I felt listening to her story, adding that it made me acutely aware of how close she had come to death by fire. "Why do you care?" she asked. It wasn't an aggressive question—she really seemed perplexed. I needed to make a careful response. Again, this wasn't about me; it was about her wish to die. "Well, I am glad that you are here to talk about this with me, and I am conscious that might not have been the case, that you really hoped to die. I'm also aware that you still felt that way not long ago, when you set the fire in your cell." She gave an almost imperceptible nod. "I think in both cases you wanted to hear from your mother. Is that right?"

Zahra didn't respond, and I worried that I had stopped the conversation. Then she spoke, almost in a whisper: "It's all I ever wanted . . . to hear her talk to me as if she cared about me." She said nothing after that, for what felt like a long time. I had to remind myself to exhale as I waited for more. "I think," she began again, with a firmness in her voice that I'd not heard before, "that my mother doesn't really like me. And I don't think she ever has." She admitted that she felt ashamed for saying such a thing. I asked if she could explain why, and she reminded me about the importance in her family and culture of honoring parents. She had always thought it must be her fault that her mother treated her as she did. I recalled the "late child" label she'd spoken of, the expressed idea that she was a mistake, or some kind of a negative addition to the family. In our next session, we picked up that thread again, and she told me about another label she'd been given by her family as a teenager: she was a "bad girl." This led to her telling me about her first suicide attempt by fire, when she was seventeen.

As with the other two incidents, she had been rebuffed by her mum that day. Again, it happened near the year's end, around the holidays; surrounded by festivity, she felt isolated, unable to speak to anyone about the pain she was in. As she sat alone in her bedroom, feeling unbearable and unwanted, the best recourse seemed to be death. I imagined her back then, so young, so vulnerable, scars etching her forearms, rummaging in a school backpack, hand closing around the box of matches. Rattle, rattle. Those little sticks—the outsized power they had for her. Then the smoke filling the room, the mattress smoldering, the panic and the smoke and the coughing and her mother's voice shrieking in her ear, "You stupid, stupid girl! What have you done?"

She was shaken by this memory, as was I. But as this session had to end, I tried to ensure she was settled a little before I returned her to the wing, so as not to send her back in distress. I invited her to sit with me before she left and think about what we should write in her orange book about her thoughts and memories. Together we identified someone on the staff whom I could alert to the fact that she was feeling upset, so that they could help her as needed, and I assured her she was not the first person who had described to me such difficult relations with their mother.

We would talk further about this troubled relationship in the weeks that followed. She had been surprised and relieved to hear that she was not alone and that her experience was not unique to any cultural or ethnic group. I told her that a great many women struggle with mothers, and with mothering, for a variety of reasons, and not all of us are meant to bear children. If someone has difficulty with the role, it may be because they were not cared for as a child or have some unresolved trauma and are transmitting that pain to their own child. As our therapy progressed, I invited Zahra to speculate on what her mother may have experienced as a child and as a young woman. She had come to the UK from India to marry a much older man whom she didn't know, who was violent to her and the children, and who was not a loving partner. That didn't excuse her treatment of her daughter, but it might help explain her deficiencies. Could Zahra forgive her mother for being cruel? Could she forgive herself for wanting to hurt herself? I also wanted to explore whether she could allow herself to receive something from her brothers, if not her mum. There were tears when we got in this deep.

It was also crucial for me to talk with Zahra about how frightening it is for anyone to be neglected or treated with hostility by a parent, even if they never lay a finger on their child. Angry parents generate fear in their children, and over a long period chronic fear can impair a child's self-esteem, their sense of value, and their ability to regulate their moods. Zahra's parents provided her with all the physical and material necessities: shelter, food, clothing.

But what Zahra recalled was constantly feeling rejected, judged, and unloved. Her self-harm was a response to the anguish she felt about an attention that she would never command, and eventually this escalated to arson; as far as she was concerned, her sorry self could disappear in a ball of flames. I thought that it was remark-able—and spoke to her resilience—that Zahra had been able to survive so much rejection and parental dislike. Many people with that kind of history have fared much worse.

I also knew it was important that Zahra realize that as an adult, she had choices and responsibilities. She was speaking again one day about her poor treatment by her family, and I decided it was time to ask if the things she did while living at home may have been damaging to *them* in any way. Zahra was righteous in her anger. She jumped up from her chair, shouting at me that I didn't care about her and I was a fucking bitch who knew nothing, add-ing that she knew I was "just in this for the money." This rage came out of nowhere, and it was so out of character that the heat of it took me aback. I felt like I'd stumbled over a hidden land mine. Then she stormed out of the room, slamming the door so hard it rattled in its frame. After a moment of stunned inaction, I had to hurry after her: she'd forgotten her ACCT book.

Zahra would not look at me when I caught up with her. I apolo-gized for upsetting her, and she watched in stony silence as I made a note about our altercation in the book. I said that we could meet up next week to think more about what had happened, but in truth I wasn't confident she would turn up. Although I'd learned long ago, with patients like Gabriel and Tony, that it was possible for therapy to survive such an "upset," I wanted to look more closely at my part in it.

I took the time to discuss what had happened with a senior col-league, so I could process it. I told them that I felt I had overlooked something and shouldn't have been taken by surprise by this "mouse that roared." As soon as I articulated that thought aloud, I recognized I had been too distracted by Zahra's compliance or "mousy" demeanor; I also admitted that I thought I had some inbuilt belief that she was passive, a "good girl," perhaps in keep-ing with a stereotype I held in mind of the dutiful Asian daughter who shows respect to her elders. I'm not proud of this and I wish I could say it was the last time I took someone at face value, but it's a lesson I have had to keep learning, over and over. There's good reason for that idiom, which derives from the world of finance; as the Israeli economist and psychologist Daniel Kahneman has explored in depth,[6] it's easy for the mind to judge only on superficials, and harder to go into deeper layers of meaning.

My colleague also pointed out that Zahra may well have thought my question about hurting her family was a criticism of her. She had probably experienced me as being like her mother, uninterested in her distress and careless of what she might be feeling. I realized that in the "heat of the moment," all her pent-up fury toward her mother had transferred itself onto me. This kind of "redirection" of feeling by a patient onto their therapist was not a new idea to me; it is a basic part of psychoanalytic theory, and it applies equally to positive and negative emotions, including love, dependence, anger, and distrust.

I knew if I could explain this to Zahra, it might help, and I took it as a good sign that at least she was doing something different with her anger. Instead of externalizing it and taking it out on her body or inanimate objects that might burn, she had protested her pain with a verbal attack on the person who had hurt her, as any one of us might. Although swearing at people and slamming doors is not the best way of communicating, I thought Zahra had done something authentic and healthy by being open and honest in her anger. It was, therefore, crucial that the therapy didn't stop at this point, and thankfully I was able to persuade both staff and Zahra of this.

I could see that she was embarrassed when I came to her cell door to ask her to return to therapy; she didn't want to look at me as I apologized and asked if we could talk about what had happened. Her awkwardness in the face of my genuine regret and my invitation to begin again made it clear that she was unfamiliar with how she might work through a conflict and make a repair. This is such a vital tool to have for building trust in close relationships, and I was grateful when she agreed to another session together.

When we looked at what had happened that day she stormed

out, Zahra was able to acknowledge that there had been a confusion in her mind between the past and the present. The fact that we were working together again demonstrated to her that anger in close relationships is survivable. We were able to circle back to my question about the extent to which she had caused her family alarm and distress, and in time she was able to acknowledge that she had. We also talked about the challenge of how to manage her distress if she didn't use fire or self-harm. Although she didn't look the part, I thought Zahra had a lot in common with Marvel Comics' Hulk, the traumatized child who becomes dangerous when angry. At one point, she even quoted him unconsciously saying, "Don't make me angry, you won't like me if I'm angry." I had to work hard to stifle a smile at the chaos that would ensue if this seemingly meek and mild woman morphed into a muscle-bound monster in the midst of a women's prison.

After nine months with me, Zahra was no longer considered to be a suicide risk, and her ACCT book was closed. She was informed that she was going to be moved to another women's prison to finish her sentence, and before she left we had a final few sessions together. We talked about her future risk to herself and others, and she said she didn't think she would set another fire, but she couldn't promise not to shout and curse or slam doors when people upset her. I made a recommendation to her probation officer that Zahra ought to get further help from the mental health team in her next prison, including some more one-on-one therapeutic work, if possible. She could have benefited from some group anger management therapy too, I knew, but this was rarely offered in the female system, where group programs tended to address trauma and loss. This was almost a decade ago, but the same is still true today. Even if using violence to cope with feelings of anger and despair has led to their imprisonment, that capacity in women continues to be tacitly excluded from therapeutic interventions, which is not an honest communication to the female perpetrator or the public. Whatever therapies she might access, it would be important in Zahra's next case review to highlight the importance of continuing to work on herself, which could eventually lead to her release back into the community.

Some readers of Zahra's story might think she was primarily a victim, hardly comparable to a homicidal or sexually violent prisoner. There is truth in that, but it's worth reiterating that we don't always think that way about men with similar histories and offenses. Their anger and capacity for violence is always taken seriously, but we struggle with seeing women as dangerous to others because it is so rare for them to act those feelings out with violence. Most of the harm they do is to themselves, but Zahra's behavior repeatedly put others in danger as well. Any difference in our sympathy toward her suggests we have a gendered view of evil, whereby men's violence is seen as essentially different to women's, which profits no one. If anything, it bolsters the pernicious concept that it is somehow "normal" for men to be destructive and violent, and that victimhood is part of the essential identity of a woman.

Despite my training and considerable experience in working with female violent offenders, I realized I was just as guilty of this bias when I worked with Zahra. I had not found it easy to stay in an objective state with someone who had nearly killed herself and others more than once. I doubt I would have seen her as "a mouse" if she were a man who had done the same. In the end, what mattered most was not how I or anyone else saw her, but whether she could let go of labels she'd been given, like "late child" or "bad girl." The urgent challenge is to take a hard look at our priorities and prejudices in a justice system and a society where only a few women like Zahra will get the help they need, and only when they literally or metaphorically set themselves on fire.

IAN

"You have reached your destination," the GPS pronounced. I edged my car to the curb on a bland suburban street, peering doubtfully at the faded house numbers. There it was, the two-storeyed brick house at the end. Housing for people on probation has to be discreet, with no signage or other markers. There was some minor security at the door, and I was asked for my ID by a staffer. Much like the neighborhood outside, the man who came down the stairs to meet me was nondescript. Like so many people who've been imprisoned for a long time, there was a certain air of wariness and sadness about him.

Ian had been released from prison a week earlier, after serving a long sentence for the sexual abuse of his two young sons. Middle-aged, with narrow shoulders and a slim frame, he had close-cropped sandy-reddish hair and a sprinkling of freckles across the bridge of a sharp nose, and was wearing jeans and a plain sweatshirt over a collared shirt. Years ago, I recall working in prison with a man convicted of child sex offenses, and a prison officer remarked to me that he "looked like a typical nonce," the term used in British prisons for sex offenders, especially those who molest children. I couldn't make any sense of that assessment; it's important, not least for safety's sake, that everyone accepts that sex offenders don't have distinguishing features, any more than terrorists do. "Neat and boring" was my first impression of Ian, much like other men in his position, who generally don't want to attract attention to themselves, in or out of prison.

He squinted at my proffered ID and mispronounced my surname with a soft "sh," as people do. I accepted his offer of a cup of tea, and he directed me to a room off the hall where we could talk. Mismatched furniture was oriented around a small TV, and I chose an armchair near the door, next to a bookcase holding a range of scruffy paperbacks. Scanning the titles, I couldn't help feeling some amusement that many of them were true crime books or detective novels. "Do you take sugar?" Ian was back, bearing two steaming mugs. The purpose of our meeting was far from the quotidian social exchange, but it was starting like any other English conversation. "If we don't mention the weather soon," I thought, "there'll be a comment about food." Sure enough, Ian added, "Sorry, we're out of biscuits."

At the time, I was still doing some work in prisons, but I had also joined a mental health team that liaised with the probation service to give support to newly released prisoners like Ian. There was increasing concern about the risk of suicide in men on probation, and the request for me to see Ian had come about partly for that reason. He'd been treated for depression while in prison and was transitioning back into the community after a decade inside, which is never easy. I had been told he'd accepted my offer of this meeting without question, which could indicate receptivity, but I thought it might also mean he was institutionalized, used to doing as he was asked.

We sat facing each other across a wooden coffee table, which was scarred with cigarette burns and scald circles. The house was quiet. It was probably filled to capacity, given that hostel beds are in short supply and always in demand, but residents are expected to be out during the day, looking for work or meeting with the probation or housing services. I began with a few general questions, nothing too intrusive. Did he like the house? (Yes, it was fine.) Was he getting out much? (Yes, there was a bus at the end of the road into town.) What sort of work would he be looking for? (Maybe construction, but it's winter, so . . .) His voice trailed off, and he sat gazing into his mug, as if the tea leaves might reveal something about his prospects. These banalities could easily fill the whole appointment time, and I knew that I was going to have to go deeper, even though I was aware that both of us might be reluctant to do so. I had a sense of

Ian standing on a ledge, waiting for me to say something that would tip him over into feelings of hurt and shame.

I went forward gently, asking whether things had changed much since he last lived in this area. On release, most offenders are rehabilitated in their home district, unless there is some objection or restriction. Ian had been placed only a couple of miles from his old neighborhood, but there was no need for an "exclusion zone" because his family had long since moved away. A red flush crept up his neck to color his sallow cheeks, and his hand gripped the arm of the sofa. "The neighborhood's not changed much," he said and shrugged. "I don't know anyone round here anymore, and the family are long gone . . . I mean . . . I don't know where." He swallowed hard and added, "There was no return address on that . . . you know, the letter."

This letter was another reason why I'd been asked to see Ian. One of his sons, who was now nineteen years old, had recently contacted the probation service to ask if he could meet with his father, in a letter that was brief and polite, revealing nothing of his feelings or intentions. In cases like this, it's unusual for family members to reach out, and the request was causing the probation team some anxiety. The young man was of age, and a private citizen. Nobody had the right to question or control his actions, nor was there a duty to protect him—but they did have a responsibility to support Ian, who was already exposed and fragile. The team had debated holding off telling him about his son's wish, perhaps just for a few months until he got settled, but decided that such dishonesty would undermine their work with him. When Ian had come in for his weekly meeting with his probation officer a few days earlier, he had been shown the letter. I was told he responded with a mixture of shock and alarm, and I tried to reassure him I wasn't there to make matters worse. "We don't have to talk about the letter today, if you don't want to."

"I suppose I do," Ian said wearily. "I mean, nobody likes it." "Who doesn't like what?" I asked. "You know, the whole idea." I asked him why he thought people wouldn't want him to meet . . . I reached for his son's name, even as I wondered if it was a good idea to summon him into the room in this way. ". . . Is it Hamish?"

Ian flinched a little, an involuntary response alerting both of us to the fact that the past was live and painful. By this time, I knew how important it was to read a sign like this, and to wait until we had built some rapport before trying to go deeper. I realized it would be difficult.

I let Ian know that I would need to take a history as part of my assessment, but we didn't have to go there today. He seemed much relieved. Could he tell me how he felt about his son's letter? Ian sat forward, becoming a little more animated. "They don't want me to reply, I know. How would it look, if it got out in the local press?" An interesting response, because this wasn't addressing how *he* felt; he was thinking about the minds of the probation team. That was hopeful—it might mean he could mentalize his victims' emotions too. But it could also imply a self-centered motive, dressed up as concern for others: a worry about how public exposure might affect *him*. Ian's voice turned bitter, almost a snarl. " 'Local pedo visits son,' right? That's what they'd say, I bet you."

I had already been given some background by his probation team. Ian had been released on probation by the parole board, after serving ten years of a twenty-year sentence. Although it does mean freedom from incarceration, release on probation is not equivalent to liberty. It is an extension of prison, with strict regulation and communication systems put in place meant to scrutinize the offender and prevent recidivism through a recall to prison, if the risk justifies this. Ian's crime was abusing his two sons: Hamish, then nine years old, and his brother Andrew, aged eleven. His wife Sheila had reported him to the police. While on remand, he had denied the charges, but ultimately he pleaded guilty. As far as I knew, Ian had not had any contact with his family since the night of his arrest, and Sheila had divorced him while he was inside.

He was right that local journalists would probably pounce on a piece about a close-to-home crime like this, to serve up on the front page with a mug shot. A pedophile is sure to grab the readers' attention, as someone we're all allowed to hate. I've noticed how the most famous contemporary fictional account, in Nabokov's *Lolita*, will routinely come up in media coverage, especially if there's a young girl involved; Mr. Humbert is the iconic "pedo."

But for me, the narrative of a man like Ian has much more in common with the inexorable path Dostoevsky charts in *Crime and Punishment*: the gradual conception of a foul thing, its emergence into being and action, and the slow unwinding of consequences, the tortured aftermath.

If we surveyed a representative cross-section of people today, asking them to rank the worst examples of human evil, there's a good chance that "pedos"—or, to use the professional term, child sex offenders (CSOs)—would come first. I am skeptical about the notion of any kind of hierarchy of evil, but I know the public fascination with CSOs verges on obsession in its intensity. I don't recall this being true in the early part of my career, nor do I think it can be explained by an increased number of convictions for child sex abuse in recent years. Those figures have remained steady for three decades. Even allowing for underreporting, sexual abuse of children is less common than other types of child maltreatment.

One explanation for this contemporary focus on CSOs must be the internet and social media, which increase awareness of every kind of activity, near and far, and the surge in the production and use of child pornography, which is obviously a form of sexual abuse of children. We also know that violent victimization, in all its forms, has increased lately, for the first time in half a century. Intriguing research by American colleagues, including Professor Jim Gilligan and others,[1] finds a correlation, particularly among men, between shame and higher rates of violence in times of increased social instability and wealth inequality.

Different countries and societies mount different social and legal responses to the demon "pedo." In the UK, as in much of the US, it is a requirement for communities to be informed when a convicted CSO moves into the area; this has given rise to some press and community reactions that look a lot like vigilantism. In some jurisdictions, people are kept on registers (signing up with local authorities, restricted from working with young people, etc.) long after they have served their prison sentence and done their probation. Sometimes this will be for life, which is not the case for a range of other serious or even fatal crimes; this is another way society reinforces the notion that child sex offenses are the "worst" evil. It has occurred to me that this extreme level of commingled interest and disgust about the sexual abuse of children might have a quality that is hard to articulate. C. S. Lewis spoke of a "felt evil" for things that have an exciting "tang" about them, precisely because they are forbidden.

All the activism in relation to, and condemnation of, CSOs suggests we know our enemy, but it is not as straightforward as it might seem. For starters, the Greek word *paedophile* (denoting someone with a love for children) is wrongly used as interchangeable with someone who causes sexual harm to children. Instead, it denotes a primary sexual attraction for children, and not all those who have this desire act on it; in fact, many define themselves as actively "anti-contact."[2] To complicate matters further, the majority of people who are convicted as CSOs are not simply pedophiles; many are married or partnered and have an ordinary sexual interest in adults, even as they abuse their sons or daughters. Although it has been with us since ancient times, up until the last century sexual offending against children was barely recognized or spoken of, and until the civil rights activism and social revolution of the 1960s, there were minimal protections for CSOs' victims under the law, in any jurisdiction. Today, protective laws in most countries define victims of child sexual abuse as anyone under eighteen.

But this protective stance doesn't allow for another societal development on a worldwide scale, which is that so many "children" under the age of eighteen are engaged in sexual relationships, with diminished legal protections where the age of consent (sixteen in the UK and much of the US) is lower than eighteen. And where there is sex, there may be cases of sexual assault; we know that the overwhelming majority of all sexual assaults occur within the context of relationships. Although identifying accurate data is difficult, mainly due to underreporting by victims who may be afraid or unwilling, there are some statistics that stand out. Research into the scale and nature of child sexual abuse in London in 2017 and 2018 noted that girls between the ages of fifteen and seventeen reported the highest incidence of sexual assault.[3] According to a survey in 2015 by the Scottish charity Break the Silence, one in three teenage girls in a relationship suffer an unwanted sexual act.[4]

A recent study by a leading American researcher in this field, the sociologist David Finkelhor, showed that in the fourteen- to seventeen-year-old age bracket, "most offences are at the hands of other juveniles (76.7 per cent for males and 70.1 per cent for females), primarily acquaintances," and of that number, girls are four times more likely to be the victim than boys.[5] It appears that while media and public interest is intently focused on the idea of the "typical" CSO as a creepy adult stranger targeting a pre-pubertal victim,[6] the most common victim of child sexual assault is a teenage girl, her assailant a teenage boy.

There is also the question of what desire entails. Traditional bio-scientific accounts of sexual desire tend to emphasize the importance of looking and seeing, as a basis of lust, and wanting it more if you can't have it. But my experience of assessing sex offenders suggests this is simplistic. Not all of them describe a visual focus for their sexual desire, and other motives, such as anger or jealousy, may drive a heterosexual married man to abuse his sons. I have found it helpful to break down the concept of desire into three different domains: the carnal, the sensual, and the erotic. All three may coexist in one person at different points, but they communicate different things.

The erotic is easy: it is the use of sex to express intimacy and attachment, and primarily it is playful and profound, messaging, "I want you as you, and you and me as we." The sensual is shallower and may involve little mutuality or connection, but it can be comforting, if only because touch expresses a message of "I'm with you." Many heterosexual prisoners will talk about this when describing their same-sex relationships in prison. Carnal desire is not playful, and it is uninterested in cooperation or exchange; it is about appetite. The object of desire is something to be had, and the message might simply be "Fuck you" or "I own you." Child sex offending (like all other sexual offending) is violence, and it is carnal. Victims of CSOs do not have an erotic or sensual experience, and most describe feeling used, controlled, and consumed. I doubted whether Ian would have been able to explain any of this to himself, let alone to his son, if they were to meet again.[7]

Some years into his prison sentence, Ian had agreed to join

a sexual offenders treatment program (SOTP). These have been developed in the UK over the last two decades to help sex offenders reduce their risk by attending to the harm done and building self-awareness. In the US, the Federal Bureau of Prisons provides similar programs for convicted sex offenders, although they are not widespread and vary state by state; as in the UK, the primary focus there is on risk management rather than rehabilitation and therapy. In contrast, the European Parliament passed a directive in 2011 addressing the reduction of child sex abuse which emphasized the value of prevention and intervention programs for CSOs. Colleagues in Scandinavia and Germany have been active in trying to reach out to help potential CSOs *before* they offend. Their attention is focused on adolescents, trying to halt a pattern of offending before it can become compulsive, especially if the person has other risk factors for crime, like substance abuse and social isolation.

SOTPs in British prisons may involve adult sexual abuse survivors who are prepared to come and speak about their past experiences. Such talks can help offenders to take seriously the harm they have done. I gathered that Ian had been deeply moved after hearing a young man talk about being abused by a relative. He told his offender manager in prison that he had gained a new understanding of what his sons had been through and fully accepted responsibility for his assaults. He subsequently fell into a prolonged depression and had been suicidal at times, which can happen when people wake up to the reality of what they have done. Ian told me at our first meeting that he was happy to continue taking the antidepressants that had been prescribed to him at that time, because he knew they helped him, and I took that as a good sign. Investment in self-care can be the first step to caring for others.

I would see him for six sessions, with the specific and limited task of advising on risk and helping probation think through the pressing issue of possible contact with his son. Quite apart from the question of how it might look if reported in the press, enabling such a meeting had ethical and practical considerations, which we discussed in the team meeting. What if Hamish wanted to exact vengeance, someone asked, or what if Ian tried to "groom" his son again? I dislike that word, because it is often overused and ignores the complexity of the ways in which offenders get their victims to comply. The idea of grooming also fails to convey the victim's dilemma about their relationship with their abuser, and how hard it can be to refuse someone you trust and love. I suggested that I thought it unlikely Ian would attempt anything of the sort with his adult son and was doubtful at this point that he would even agree to see him. Ian's senior probation officer, Peter, proposed to have a preliminary meeting with Hamish as a next step and suggested that I might come along and observe. I wouldn't talk about Ian specifically, and I wouldn't be acting as any kind of therapist to Hamish, but I could be on hand to answer some general questions about CSOs and their treatment. It is not the norm for me to meet the victims of my patients, but it is not unheard of in my community work, and I was willing to do so if it was helpful to everyone involved. In the interests of transparency, I would let Ian know beforehand.

At our next session, I broached this with him, and he bristled at the idea. Was I going along to warn Hamish about him or something? "Tell him stuff I've said to you?" I assured him I would not be sharing anything he told me with his son. His tone changed, softening. "And are you there to see if he's . . . like . . . strong enough?" No, I said, I was not there to be Hamish's therapist. My priority was Ian. I added that it sounded to me like he might have some curiosity about his son and what he was like now, as a young adult. Was that so? Ian dropped his head into his hands, his response muffled. "I don't know . . . I don't know anything." I sensed his despair and feelings of loss, and his sadness seemed to fill the space between us.

I am aware as I write this that the reader might be experiencing powerful negative feelings imagining this encounter. It is understandable and human that a kind of righteous anger arises when faced with a person who has hurt a child, who has exploited an innocent's trust. How dare a pedophile present himself as sad or vulnerable? How could I possibly have compassion for such a man and offer to listen to and understand him, especially when victims of sexual abuse so often fail to get such support? And what good will it do anyway? I am asked such questions regularly, and part of my response is that depriving people like Ian will not improve services for victims. In fact, it might make things worse for future victims if offenders are not supported in their efforts to rehabilitate or offered a chance to make good. And as a doctor, I know what I'm getting into when I sit down to work with CSOs, just as surely as a lung specialist walking into a respiratory unit knows his patients will cough.

People also ask me how I, "as a mother," could ever get involved in this work. I explain that my initial experience with CSOs was in the mid-1990s, before I was married or had children. At that time, I was a senior trainee and trying to gain experience as a psychotherapist. Therapy groups for sex offenders were being tested by the probation service, and an opportunity arose for me to take part in a group treating male CSOs. For some participants, it was a condition of staying out of prison, while for others it was a condition of their probation on release, having already served a sentence. Group work was becoming more prevalent in the forensic field and was indicated for offenders because it promoted prosocial behavior by requiring them to work with others, listen with respect, and speak in turn. It was also effective because many people with a history of offending were averse to being alone with an authority figure or a person in a caregiver role and needed to be in a group to feel safe. For CSOs, there was a specific value because they had to manage feelings of shame and guilt, emotions of self-assessment that imagine an audience's response.

In this group we saw a recurring script emerge, a "neutralization discourse," as it is called by criminologists. This entails using language that reduces agency, as all of us do when we feel defensive, from an early age—phrases like "It wasn't my fault" or "They started it" are familiar examples. The careful constructs I heard in the group also framed the abuse as somehow consensual, with lines like "She flirted with me," or "She never said no," or even "I loved her . . . This was how we showed our love for each other." There were also overlapping descriptions of how the CSO leveraged affectional bonds ("Don't you love your daddy?") or offered veiled threats ("Mummy will be angry with us").

In almost every case, their victims were children they knew

and cared for as a father, grandfather, stepfather, cousin, teacher, or family friend. Data prove beyond a doubt that this is typical of the overwhelming majority of CSOs, whose crime happens in the context of an existing relationship.[8] As we've seen with other forms of violent offending, the media focuses on the exceptions to the rule. The forcible abduction of young people by strangers is newsworthy, of course, but the way it is handled can be misleading, as if shocking cases like the kidnap and abuse of Jaycee Dugard in the US or Natascha Kampusch in Austria were some kind of awful norm. Tragically, that kind of stranger abuse does happen, but it is the offending equivalent of a plane crash. It wrongly persuades us to think of some omnipresent threat that is "out there," as if danger comes from some evil and unknown bogeyman. This idea probably persists because it is too terrible to contemplate such a threat being close to home.

Contrary to the grotesques of tabloid fantasy, the men in the CSO group were not generally cold or psychopathic, and in many cases, they seemed quite empathic. Each of them was asked to write an account of their offense, before taking the "hot seat" and reading it out to the others, which was not easy. The men would point out one another's distortions of reality, which they recognized easily because "it takes one to know one." If this process is managed properly, it is truly remarkable. I learned so much at that time, especially about the need for delicacy and precision when leading a group. With qualified and sensitive facilitation, CSOs in group therapy can be helped to walk a tightrope of honest self-revelation without dying of shame.

After I started at Broadmoor, I had few opportunities to work with CSOs because there were only a small number of them held there, and unlike the men in the probation group, they had nearly all killed their victims—which is statistically exceptional. I came to work with CSOs again within the probation service decades later, and by then I was a much more experienced psychotherapist. I'd had a chance to study with some remarkable colleagues in the meantime, including Professor Derek Perkins, who had done groundbreaking work on the treatment of sex offenders, and Dr. Estela Welldon, a pioneer in running therapy groups that put perpetrators and victims together, enabling them to learn something from and about each other on their path to recovery.[9]

By this time, I did have growing children of my own, and I found it made the work both harder and easier for me. I could better appreciate how it was possible to see your offspring as an extension of yourself, almost as an object you control, which were themes I'd heard often in the "scripts" of the therapy group. It was as hard as ever to imagine a child in distress, but I don't think this was more acute for me now than it had been before I had children, or indeed when I think about any victim of violence. I may have had increased empathy for the wives of CSOs who abused their children, thinking of their shock and fear when they found out what was happening, and the shame and sense of failure they may have experienced because of the cultural expectation that mothers will protect their young.

Soon after my initial sessions with Ian, I sat in a meeting room in a typically drab public office building in town, waiting for Hamish with Peter, an old-style probation officer who could remember when making a positive and therapeutic alliance was the mainstay of the job, as opposed to the basic risk management which was now offered. He was a big man with a soft West Country accent and a gentle manner. I found his air of calm reassuring, and I imagined his clients would too. Offenders tell me that they often find it easier to work with older probation officers than younger ones, who can sometimes present as more rigid and controlling. I sympathize with that when I remember my younger self sometimes covering up a lack of confidence with a bossy attitude. In hindsight, I can see that a lack of experience in caring roles, such as looking after a parent or children or even a pet, is a real disadvantage when dealing with people who are dependent and sometimes demanding. Handling power differentials is an acquired skill which takes years of practice.

I had taken a seat at the end of a rectangular table, where I would be able to see both men without swiveling my head from side to side, tennis-match style. I was conscious of feeling nervous, even if I couldn't say why. I reminded myself I was just there to observe. Hamish was ushered in, looking younger than his nineteen years, with a clean-shaven round face, fair hair, and a slim build. He apologized for being late, when he really wasn't, and made good eye contact with me, shaking my hand firmly, just as his father had when we'd met. After brief introductions, Peter thanked him for coming and kicked off by saying that we'd like to understand a bit more about what Hamish's request to see his father was about. The young man sighed. "Nobody wants this." Another unconscious echo of his father, I thought.

"I just feel I need answers," Hamish was saying. "My mum and my brother . . . they don't think I should see him. Mum says it's best to put the past behind us, and after all, we've been fine without him for so long . . . And it's true—we have." He looked from me to Peter, his gaze level. "Anyway, Andy had it worse than me. And we had therapy about this, right after . . . I mean, not for long, Mum couldn't afford it. But I remember the therapist said that I might want to get closure, later on, about what happened." "Closure?" Peter raised an eyebrow. "Thing is, I have memories of him from before, some good ones too, you know—football, holidays, stuff like that. I mean, he was just my dad, and then it all happened and, whoosh, he was gone overnight and . . . I know that he's not . . . like, he's not Dad anymore, but who is he now? And what's meant to happen now that I know that he's out? I could bump into him in the street or something."

I couldn't stop myself. "Are you frightened of your father?" Peter shot me a look, and Hamish frowned as if the question was absurd. "Not at all . . . I'm not sure I have any feelings about him. I just want to see . . . I don't know, this bogeyman we haven't been allowed to talk about for ten years. I'm still related to him, aren't I?" I sensed some anger simmering not far below the surface. As if he could read my mind, Hamish quickly assured us that he had no wish for revenge, and I began to feel a reluctant admiration for a young man who was taking his courage in both hands to do something so difficult. Neither Peter nor I were responding immediately with a plan for contact, and Hamish's tone turned appealing, almost desperate. "Isn't there a kind of process that I could get here? I've read about this, where a victim and the person who hurt them get in a room together . . . That's all I want, just one meeting where I could just ask . . ."

He was talking about restorative justice, a reconciliation practice that first originated in Canada in the 1970s, in experimental programs involving the making of verbal amends by offenders to the victims of their petty theft or vandalism. Ultimately, the programs contributed to the development in the 1990s of formal victim-offender mediation, and its adoption and promotion by the UN, the Council of Europe, and other organizations, including the American Bar Association. By the time I was working with Ian and the probation service, the practice was increasingly making its way into the public consciousness in the UK. But I knew that no victim was entitled to this kind of relief, despite what they had suffered; the perpetrator always had the right to decline, for whatever reason.

"If you had that meeting, what would your first question be, do you think?" Peter's voice was low and kind. Hamish flushed, and for a moment I saw his father's face as it had been when I first sat down with him at the hostel. "I don't know, just whether he's sorry now? And . . . why did he do it? *Why?*" The three-letter word was heavy with years of pain. Peter nodded. "Okay. We'll have to discuss this further. But we'll think about it, I promise." Hamish's face fell, as if he had expected this meeting to be more conclusive. My impression was that this young man was unlikely to harm his father. But he was still not entirely adult and hadn't fully thought through what the impact of seeing his father after so long could be—not only for him but also for his mother and brother. Such an encounter could disturb the family dynamic in unpredictable ways. I was also concerned about the impact on Ian, especially with his risk of clinical depression. In my mind's eye, I saw him hunched on that lumpy sofa with his head in his hands, and I thought that if I were him, meeting with Hamish could be heartbreaking.

We couldn't resolve this overnight. There would be the usual official process of information-sharing in the team, and I'd be asked for my considered view after I'd finished my allotted sessions with Ian. After Hamish was gone, I asked Peter about the restorative justice idea. "Is it remotely possible?" He looked dubious. "In theory, yes, but I don't know that anyone's done it in a case like this. It's more muggers or burglars meeting up with people who've not been badly hurt. I can't think of anyone who could facilitate this." It certainly wasn't something I was trained for—and yet, when I looked back at this moment later, I would think, "Could I have done something more?" But even if we had found a skilled mediator to help, what answer would Ian have given to Hamish's great big "why"?

The next time I met with Ian at the house, I thought he looked more alive, less haggard. He didn't seem depressed and he told me he was eating and sleeping well. I commented that he appeared to be allowing himself to enjoy being out of prison now, and he agreed. As soon as we took our seats in the TV room, he wanted to hear how my meeting with his son had gone, and I filled him in. "He wants to ask me things? What things?" I turned that around. "If you were Hamish, what would you want to ask?" But Ian shook his head rapidly; he couldn't or wouldn't answer. He turned away from me to face the window, pressing the heels of his hands to his eyes as if to hold tears in. After a bit, I spoke again, hoping to keep him engaged. "I can't know this for sure, but I wonder if he wants to put a name and face to you, as you are now, so you're less frightening to him?"

"He's frightened of me?" I had to think how best to answer, and I put it to him that it might be that he was linked in his son's mind with a time in his life he didn't comprehend, a time when he felt fear. "Oh." Ian still sounded surprised, so I asked him if that came as a shock, or if he couldn't understand why his son wanted to see him at all. "After what I did? Too bloody right."

"Ian," I said quietly, holding eye contact, "could you try to talk to me about that, as you see it now, with the benefit of hindsight?" Telling me about his offense was not going to be easy, but I knew he would have had to go through it before with police, lawyers, therapists, and others. As part of my assessment, I needed to know how he thought about it now. When he went through the history, I would be alert to any small linguistic "spikes" that could indicate ongoing grandiosity or entitlement, a sense of injustice or a defiance of rules—all things which can indicate a present risk.

He chose to begin back in his childhood, perhaps because it was at a distance from the offense. He started by telling me that he had always had a problematic relationship with his parents. His mother was an alcoholic, in and out of rehab and hospitals for much of his young life. When his parents divorced, she left him with his father. Ian was just thirteen, his younger brother twelve. Ian described his father as a remote and hostile parent, a man who was "cold as a block of ice," adding that he was "shit scared of him." I didn't comment on that, but Ian may have sensed my interest and was quick to assure me his father had never physically or sexually abused him. I had no reason to disbelieve him. While it is true that some CSOs will perpetuate the abuse they experienced as children, it is just one risk factor. A history of sexual abuse as a child is neither essential nor sufficient on its own to cause someone to shift from victim to perpetrator.[10]

Ian left school and home as soon as he could, apprenticing himself at seventeen to a builder in another city. I knew from reviewing the police record that he had had only one previous contact with the police, a caution for indecent exposure when he was nineteen. He didn't mention that and looked embarrassed when I interjected to ask him about it, saying it was nothing, that he'd been drunk and was caught pissing in a public park at night. He said that he'd talked about it when he was in the SOTP group in prison, and loads of people had similar stories—it didn't mean anything. I wasn't sure that was true; many people with convictions for indecent exposure do go on to commit some other sexual offense, but the converse is also true, that many indecent exposers pose no risk to anyone. We didn't have the time to get into it, but I did note the use of alcohol, a disinhibitor. So far, this was one of the few bicycle-lock "numbers" I could discern in Ian; but useful as that model for assessing risk was, I was learning all the time that the overt absence of known factors for violence (which were so evident in lives as full of adversity as Gabriel's or Charlotte's, for example) could be just as telling. I had only to think of Zahra to be reminded of that. Ian and I took a break there, agreeing to pick up where we had left off in our next session.

I returned the following week knowing what lay in store, like

an ER doctor reporting for a Saturday-night shift. He resumed at
the point in his mid-twenties when he met his wife, Sheila, then
a secondary-school teacher. Their courtship and marriage were
"normal," he said, without elaborating much. "Tell me about her,"
I suggested, but he blocked that avenue, his body language almost
a cliché as he crossed his arms over his chest and stuck out his chin
like a stubborn child. "There's nothing to say." "Nothing at all?" I
asked gently. He shook his head, adamant. He wasn't going to let
me see into his marriage, it seemed. Then, after a moment, he said
quietly, "I let her down." He hurried ahead in the story, talking
in generalities about those early years together, when they were
doing up their first home and planning a family.

He was not glib, nor did his account lapse into self-righteousness
or self-pity; it was more that he seemed detached from it, as if he
were describing another man's life. He told me that when his father
died, he and Sheila had come into a little money. She received a
promotion at school, and they agreed he would stay at home and
be a house husband for a while. Her new role meant Sheila had
to work late a couple of nights a week, and I asked if it bothered
him, being apart from her that much. He looked taken aback, as if
the thought hadn't occurred to him. It was fine, he'd encouraged
her, because it was a good job, good money. He was proud of her.
But he admitted that, over time, he did begin to feel irritated at
having to take on more of the caring role for the boys. It was all
right playing football with them or making supper together, but
he'd get anxious about things like helping them with their homework, not having been much of a student himself. They would
argue about TV and computer time, and he'd give in rather than
enforce his wife's strict rules. He hated being "the bad cop" and
"doing everything." He started to feel like a single parent. I nodded to show that I understood this was not an easy role.

"That's when it started, I guess." He lapsed into one of his long
pauses, and I sat patiently, listening to the clock ticking and the
shush of the occasional car in the rainy street outside. When he
began to speak again, after taking a deep breath, I had the mental
sensation of linking arms with him as we both moved toward a
precipice together, keeping him company as he faced the abyss. I

wouldn't interrupt him from then on, other than encouraging him if he faltered.

It had begun with Andy, his eldest, then eleven years old. Ian couldn't say when the first feeling of wanting to touch him had started, only that an image came into his head one day, just a flash of seeing his hand on Andy's penis—not that he'd ever done it. It gave him a little "blip" of warm excitement, as if imagining a distant thing could bring it nearer, make it possible. It sounded like sexual radar, homing in on a distant but definite sense of excitement, bringing to my mind what Evelyn Waugh called "a thin bat's squeak of sexuality, inaudible to any but me."[11]

He pushed the thought away at first, but it kept returning, getting louder. One night, after the boys were in bed and he was alone in his room, with Sheila out late again, he masturbated to the image in his mind and imagined that Andy had smiled at him, a lovely welcoming smile. Then he imagined Hamish, aged nine, into this fantasy, thinking how they all might touch each other, which was arousing for him. The thought that he could actually do it began to take hold, starting with the notion that maybe Andy would think it was an accidental touch. He hadn't supervised the boys at bath time in years, but now he began to go into the bathroom when they were getting ready for bed. He started a water fight, which they loved—Mum would never allow it. Then he suggested they play a game of "submarines and sharks" together, the boys in the water and him sitting on the edge of the bath. He told me the boys loved all this, and it became routine whenever Mum was out, the three of them making a real mess in the bathroom, water and bubbles all over, shrieks of laughter, no washing of hair or teethbrushing required. At this point, I was able to fill in some blanks (for myself, not aloud). I'd seen enough in the court documents, but I'd also heard so many versions of this before, in other cases. The script moves inexorably toward its brutal conclusion.

When Andy first felt his father's hand touch his penis in the bathtub, he told a specialist police officer, trained in working with children, he thought it was an accident. He tried not to think about it, but then it started to happen again and again. He began to feel "funny" about it, "weird" and embarrassed. What was Dad doing? He'd heard about sex and stuff at school and from his friends, even seen a few things online at his best friend's house, and he began to worry that his dad was gay. Or maybe he was. But it was his father, so that was impossible. Then he saw Dad doing it to his little brother Hamish too. The brothers talked about it a bit, lying in their bunk beds late at night. I pictured these children staring upward, whispering into the darkness, rather than facing each other as they struggled with such difficult words and thoughts. They didn't know what to do. They knew how cross Mum would be—and Dad too. It was their secret with him. They said nothing.

Ian had promised them a treat: they would all go to the new superhero release at the cinema next time Mum was out. Sitting between his sons, Ian put his hands down both the boys' trousers while they were watching the movie. The boys said that they were stunned—and terrified in case anyone around them saw. Ian told me that his memory of this incident was that his sons consented; after all, they didn't move and they didn't rebuff him, they just watched the film. At home, as he was putting them to bed, he got them both to touch his erect penis, like in his fantasy. They did it, without argument. Hamish and Andy recalled that after that night, he gave them extra pocket money and other treats, telling them they were "good boys." It was another familiar line to my ear—as was their mother's testimony.

Sheila had been preoccupied with her challenging new job and considered herself lucky that her husband was so good with the kids. In hindsight, she realized the boys had become quieter and more irritable during that time. Then one night, Andy had a blazing row with her "over nothing," and for some reason smashed a new toy, a gift from his dad, into little pieces. It was particularly shocking because he was always the better behaved of the two boys, the responsible big brother. Ian was a real help that night, Sheila recalled to the police later. He calmed everyone down and cleaned up the mess, assuring her that it was probably "just hormones"— "You know, boys will be boys." He'd been a tricky teen himself. But Andy wasn't a teenager—he was eleven. After that incident, she had tried to cut back at work, but it was hard: there was an Ofsted (the UK's Office for Standards in Education, Children's Services and Skills) inspection coming, and everyone had to do extra hours.

Then the night came when Sheila was out of town at a conference, and Ian tried to have anal sex with Andy, in front of Hamish. Ian rushed through this part of the story, and I didn't press him. I had read the witness statements from the boys, which gave me the gist, their words eloquent in their terseness. After the assault, Andy barricaded himself and his brother in their bedroom. Ian told me he knew he'd gone too far and was panic-stricken. What would happen? He lay awake all night. But the boys got up the next morning and left the house for school. Nothing was said. A few days later, Sheila received an emergency summons from the boys' school. Andy had disclosed to a trusted teacher what had happened at home. Hamish was brought in, and he confirmed it.

Ian talked about that last day in his former home, how it stretched into a long, terrible evening. Sheila was working late again. The boys didn't come home after school, but at first he thought they might be at a friend's. His mind was confused and his heart started racing as the hours went by and they still hadn't returned. He called Sheila to check with her what was happening, but she didn't answer her phone. He tried her several times again, without success. Then he tidied up the house and started to get dinner ready, hoping that at any minute the front door was going to bang open, the boys chattering and their schoolbags thumping onto the bench in the front hall. As the minutes passed, he realized that wasn't going to happen. He understood, he said, that it was over. "What was over?" I asked quietly. It was my first question since he'd begun this painful chapter. "Life," he said. That was when he first thought of killing himself, initially contemplating a desperate night drive down to Beachy Head, Britain's infamous suicide spot on the Sussex coast. But it would be far simpler to take an overdose of paracetamol, washed down with whisky. He scrambled in the medicine cabinet, shaking out the pills into his hand, pouring single malt into a coffee mug and chugging it all down. Then the doorbell went. It was the police. When Ian opened the door, he was obviously drunk. He told them he'd taken an overdose, adding, "I'll be dead soon, don't worry." That struck me as odd. Don't worry about what? That he'd do more harm to his children? That he'd put up resistance? They bundled him into the car immediately and took him to the hospital.

I understood from Ian's probation record, which included some of the police reports and trial transcripts, that Sheila didn't hesitate or question what the boys had said; she called the police and took the children to her parents. She did not go home or contact Ian—they never spoke again. Like so many mothers before her, she was full of self-recrimination, telling the police, "I'll never forgive myself." I noted that after Ian's arrest, as a matter of course, social services had thoroughly investigated the poor woman for failure to protect her children. This may sound heartless, but both in the group I worked with back in the 1990s and subsequently, I have seen many married CSOs who abuse not only their children but their grandchildren, sometimes with their wives' assent and cooperation. These couples would not only reject the idea that the man was a pedophile, they would also not classify his behavior as a sexual offense. Both husband and wife would think that the man of the house could do what he liked with his partner and children. On the other hand, I have assessed numerous parents who download child pornography and who would deny they are deviant and be genuinely baffled by the idea that their own children could be at risk from them. They don't see their children as sexual objects precisely because they have a parental relationship with them.

When Ian and I met for our final session, we returned to the subject of responding to Hamish's request to meet. Ian was ambivalent at first; he talked about wanting his son's forgiveness if he could get it, but commented that even then it would not be over for him. How could he forgive himself, even if Hamish could? What purpose would it serve for the two of them to meet? He had wiped out their future when he made Hamish complicit in his abuse. He felt that he understood Andy's rejection more; he knew what it was like to be Andy and break off all relations with one's father. After some discussion, he announced that seeing Hamish would be too much for him. He could not give his son what he wanted, not now. I relayed this decision to Peter, who was much relieved and told me the whole team of professionals involved with

Ian's case had felt this would be the best outcome. Hamish would be disappointed (but he had got over worse, was the unspoken comment). Maybe someday things would change, I offered, when Ian had made a new life. One day he might be able to contemplate a meeting. Peter looked at me, his humanity tempered with a realism born from long experience. "Maybe."

Later, the image of Ian came back to me, sitting on that old sofa by the window, head bowed and spirit crushed, wrestling with his shame. I reflected on how complicated forgiveness is and how little space there is for it in our justice system, thinking again about restorative justice and whether it could have worked for Ian and Hamish. Keeping Ian in prison had done what, exactly? Our society had shown him and the world how much we hate the crime of sexual assault on children. But ten years of imprisonment had cost us the best part of £500,000 (almost $700,000). Could we have achieved the same result or better by keeping Ian in a community house for offenders, wearing an electronic tag? Resources might have been allocated to giving both him and his whole family, separately or together, a lot of therapeutic time to work through this grievous assault on their security and love. Such therapy would not assume reunification or even forgiveness. However, it would have ensured both father and sons got the help they needed, and the terms of the sentence would still have controlled Ian and conveyed societal condemnation of his actions. I have to think that spending a decade in prison was a contributing factor to his story's conclusion.

"I'll be dead soon, don't worry," he had told the police a decade earlier, on the night of his arrest. He made good on that promise six months after our last session. He had found a room to rent and taken on some night-shift work. This was perceived as a good outcome; I have seen people in his circumstances who move on, who seem to let go of the past and make a new life. But even if he appeared fine on the outside, Ian was living in what Thoreau called a "quiet desperation." One morning, he clocked off at dawn, made his way to the station, and threw himself in front of an oncoming train. Peter contacted me as soon as he got the news. He would have to break it to Hamish, and I knew he would bring to bear his compassion and long experience on any concerns the young man might have about whether his request for a meeting had contributed to Ian's suicide, the act that stops all conversation. I was sorry for Hamish's loss of his father and for the fact that this earnest, anxious young man would never have the "closure" he had sought.

In my work there is always a danger of being blinded by a fantasy that you know what is in a patient's mind. The probation and mental health services would come under scrutiny in the wake of the tragedy, in case we'd missed something. But the fact is, even if we'd had an inkling of Ian's planned suicide, we didn't have many options to support or deter him, such as "sectioning him" (a British colloquialism for involuntary commitment to a psychiatric unit) for his own protection. Even if we had, and if by some miracle a bed had been readily available, I suspect the local mental health services unit would have refused to allow him on their ward, arguing that he didn't have the kind of disorder that made him detainable under the Mental Health Act.

We had done our best to help Ian survive from a practical perspective the challenge of coming out of prison: he had a home, he'd found work, and he'd been given some support from the probation team and me. In a psychological sense, we couldn't offer more. Ian had been unable to come to terms with himself, and in his mind, death became his best or only option. With or without Hamish's letter, Ian had his shame, and as I've said, shame is a powerful motivator of violence, including violence directed at the self. Long ago, I read a book about the effects of incest and child abuse, memorably entitled *Soul Murder*.[12] I have since heard many survivors of sexual abuse talking about that feeling, the notion that some part of them has died. It may seem alien to think about this in terms of how it also applies to perpetrators, but based on my long observation and work with CSOs like Ian, I believe that many of them experience this feeling too. They are doing something suicidal as soon as they abuse a child. Shame is such a soul-eating emotion.[13]

LYDIA

I wonder if someone passing the prison visiting room that day, glancing through the glass walls on their way to their own meeting, would have known for certain which of us was the professional and which the soon-to-be ex-prisoner: two women, both fair, both in middle age, in the act of shaking hands and settling into bum-numbing metal chairs that were screwed to the tiled floor on either side of a small table. Subtle waves of normality must have emanated from both of us, with our similarly simple earrings, slim watches, and unremarkable clothing. The one with short hair, cut in a neat bob and silvering around the hairline, wore black—a sweater and slim trousers. The one with longer hair, piled high in a messy bun, was me, as usual dressed for comfort and reassurance. The only giveaway would have been the heavy gray overcoat hanging on the back of my chair, but at a glance, that would have been easy to miss. I'd come in from the February cold for this visit, while the other woman, Lydia, would soon be escorted back to her cell.

That hypothetical passer-by is an apt metaphor for me, in cases like Lydia's, where I failed to see something significant because I had focused on the surface. This had happened with Zahra, but as I've said, learning not to take others at face value is a long process; at least, it has been for me. I have described how I like to think of the mind as a coral reef, mysterious and complex, ever metabolizing, teeming with things of beauty and danger. The father of American psychology, William James, also chose a watery metaphor when he coined his famous idea of the "stream of conscious-

191

ness,"[1] and this is a particularly useful image in any discussion of human obsession. Picture the flowing water, full of the flotsam and jetsam of thoughts. There can be eddies in the flow here and there, a brief divergence caused by a fallen tree or some carelessly discarded rubbish; these are the mental ripples that develop around certain thoughts. We've all been there: think of one of those musical earworms—a pop song or a jingle for a commercial that goes round and round in your head. This is uncomfortable but temporary and does no harm; soon dislodged, it will be swept on its way downstream.

The problem comes when a great big boulder of preoccupation gets stuck in the flow. The little eddy becomes a whirlpool, pulling in other thoughts and feelings that swirl in the mind until a delusion is created. This is gradual, not unlike the development of an addiction, which may start small, with the first inhalation of a joint or a teen outing to the pub, before it progressively takes control of the self. The first casualty of obsession or addiction is truth, when people succumb to the dangerous fantasy that they can walk away anytime.

Such fixated thoughts or neuroses are the basis of the pattern of behavior known as "stalking," which has been variously defined as "obsessional following," "unwanted surveillance and pursuit," or, by the US Department of Justice, as "a crime of terror, one part threat and one part anticipation of a threat being carried out." A 2019 British crime survey[2] indicated that 10 to 20 percent of the population have engaged in stalking behavior, not including the millions who regularly indulge in some of that familiar post-romantic-breakup or pre-job-interview activity widely known as "Facebook stalking." On average, actual obsessional stalking may last for a year to eighteen months, but around a tenth of stalkers pursue it for more than five years, and in a small subset of cases it can go on for decades. The survey indicated that stalkers in the UK are more likely to be male with female victims than the other way around, but one in ten men reported having a female stalker. As part of my ongoing work with the probation service, I was going to assess a woman who was among their number, and who was soon to be released from prison.

That first visit with Lydia was a "hello"—a courtesy call, not an assessment session. She had just been granted parole and would shortly be released from prison into the community. I had stopped by to introduce myself because we would be meeting together outside the prison for a series of five or six sessions, at the request of her probation team. When I wrote to her about the referral, I had explained my role. I would be evaluating her risk and supporting her in staying safe by exploring the roots of her offense with her: her life experience, personality, how she coped with stress. I had the impression that no one on her team was too concerned about the risk to the general public. After all, there was only one person in Lydia's sights.

Two years earlier, after previously living a blameless and crime-free life, Lydia had begun a campaign of harassment against her therapist, a Dr. W, making threats to him, his family, and his property. The police intervened to caution her, and Dr. W took out one restraining order after another. These are protective orders issued by the court that are intended to prevent a violence perpetrator from gaining physical access to a victim, and they are mostly used in domestic violence cases. They can attract fines or other charges, depending on the circumstances and the jurisdiction; if the behavior continues, it can result in a criminal charge and a prison sentence.

Like many stalkers, Lydia had ignored the court orders and carried on, until finally she was arrested, pleading guilty to harassment. Sentences for stalking in the UK have become tougher over the last decade, but at the time (about ten years ago), Lydia got three years and served two, at which point it was determined she could serve the remainder of her term on probation in the community. Her referral to me was meant to offer her an extra layer of support. I would help her to help herself as she reassimilated. She wasn't obliged to accept the sessions, but I had been told that she agreed immediately when the suggestion was put to her. I hoped that meant she was welcoming of support and able to trust. The brief referral letter I'd had indicated that Lydia had completed a few courses or group treatment programs while in prison, similar to the SOTP groups that Ian had attended for sex offenders, which tend to focus on promoting an understanding of victims' experiences. Mine would not be the first intervention she had received following her conviction, but as far as I knew, this would be the first time she had talked one-on-one like this since then—or since she had last had therapy with the man who became her victim.

Keeping an open mind about anyone referred to forensic services means being attentive to even the most subtle of first impressions, whether positive or negative. At our initial meeting Lydia really seemed a picture of serenity and calm, and it was difficult for me to imagine this woman making someone so fearful they would ask the authorities to restrain her. There was certainly nothing about her that made me think I should be wary; even though she had become obsessed with her therapist, he was male, and it was a romantic attachment for her. She wouldn't have a generic interest in all therapists, any more than Ian was sexually interested in all children; as with the majority of violent offenses, there was a clear relational foundation.

Later, I would try to recall if some of her lines had a rehearsed quality, but at the time I was probably just glad to find her so willing to talk. I began our chat by running through a few general questions about her offense and imminent release. Yes, she had pleaded guilty at trial, that's right. Now, she said, she could see that the way she had gone about things in the past had been "a dreadful mistake." It was as if we were talking about a social faux pas or an ill-judged bit of parking. I thought I'd bring in her victim's name, in case that altered her tone. Had she given some thought to Dr. W and whether she might be tempted to renew contact with him once she was released? Before I could say any more, she put up her hand, palm out, as if to stop me from even considering such an idea, her voice turning rueful and serious. "Oh, him—I have no plans to make contact. Of course not. I know that's not allowed. And I so appreciate your help, Doctor. Frankly, I don't want to end up in here again, not in a million years."

I asked what her plans were. She had a place in a temporary hostel on release, didn't she? She told me that she actually owned an apartment, which had been taken care of by a friend while she was inside, and she would move in there as soon as the tenants had left. She was fortunate, I reflected; as many as half of all women leaving prison have nowhere to go and can expect to be homeless, and many dread coming out for that reason. One female prisoner I spoke with, who had yo-yoed in and out of prison for years for a range of minor offenses, told me, "This is the best place I've ever lived." But Lydia talked about how much she was looking forward to going home, adding that once she had settled, she thought she might get a cat. "I just adore animals," she said, and she had missed having them around. Although she'd been a lawyer "before all this," someone had suggested she might initially get some work dog-walking, just to ease back into things, no pressure. "Lovely to think of walking in the park every day. I can't wait." I nodded. It all sounded very sensible.

There was just one moment of tension at the end, when I asked her if she had ever met with a psychiatrist like me in the past. I thought I knew the answer, based on the brief conversation I'd had with her probation officer, Jane, when I called to prepare for this meeting. I had caught her at a busy moment, she had said, and we shared a laugh at that, because every moment was busy in her work. Then, when she'd tried to log in to access the file on Lydia, she discovered the system was down and suggested I try the offender-management unit at the prison. I was well accustomed to this procedural rigmarole, as I've described in other cases; despite all the technological advances since I started out in that long-ago era of box files and handwritten notes, the lack of centralized systems for the use of forensic mental health professionals and law enforcement has continued to be a problem.

Jane did recall that there had been some psychiatric reports submitted by the prosecution during Lydia's trial which described her as hostile and fixated on her victim, with one expert suggesting she might be paranoid. Or perhaps that was wrong, or I'd misunderstood, because Lydia was firm in her response: she'd never seen a psychiatrist in her life. "No need!" She could have been lying to me, or believed it was true somehow, or known she had seen someone at the time of the trial but discounted them as irrelevant. There was a challenge in her level gaze now, and I thought I detected a stiffening in her posture. It was not my job to argue with her. Instead, I asked her what it meant to meet with me, whether it was problematic for her.

"Not at all, Dr. Adshead! Quite the contrary. This is for my own good, isn't it? And my probation officer, Jane, she recommended I do this. I must say, it has been rather stressful in here, and I'm sure they've told you I even had some suicidal thoughts at the beginning. But now, thank heavens, I can go home! Get up and running again—make a fresh start. Best foot forward, as they say." A positive, word-perfect response. I was conscious of feeling bewildered; the flash of negative emotion I'd registered moments earlier had vanished. I decided I could return to my question about psychiatrists later. I had only wanted to build enough rapport so that we could feel a sense of psychological recognition when we next met. We parted, the officer coming to usher her back to the wing, while I shrugged on my heavy coat. As Lydia left the room, she fluttered her fingers in a little wave, with a friendly, lilting "Bye for now!" I was conscious of a sense of relief that she'd gone and aware too that I'd been holding myself in tension for several minutes. What was that about?

So far, this woman might not fit anyone's notion of a "typical stalker," but as we've seen, there really is no one typology for any category of violent offender. Stalking, a term once associated with animal hunting and poaching, is a relatively recent category of offense. The word was first appropriated in the 1980s by the media, in relation to some high-profile and particularly lurid murders involving fans who had become obsessed with Hollywood stars. As a result, California was the first state to pass specific anti-stalking laws; most other states followed suit within the next five years. Prior to this, unwanted surveillance and stalking-type behaviors had been prosecuted in the US as criminal harassment or elided with attempted or premeditated homicide, most famously in the cases of Ronald Reagan and John Lennon. After the legislative changes in California, the press tended to align the word with female celebrities, with breathless headlines like "Look Who's Stalking" accompanied by images of beautiful women looking haunted or hunted. Such narratives of women as prey have excited a certain kind of male imagination for centuries; reports of "celebrity stalkers" seemed to trivialize the experience of the victim, as if obsessive pursuit were the price of fame or even a weird sort of accolade.

Relative to the US, the UK took its time, and would only make stalking a specific criminal offense in 2012; prior to that, offenders (including Lydia) were charged with "criminal harassment," under legislation dating back to the mid-1990s. Our justice system has traditionally limited its involvement in the complexities of private personal relationships. The law prefers binary arguments, and criminal statutes tend to be drafted so that actions are right or wrong, which can work well enough with something like homicide. But no matter where they occur in the world, crimes relating to stalking tend to raise trickier questions of perception and degree, depending on local gender roles and cultural attitudes and norms, which may vary widely. The advocates for legal change in regard to stalking in Britain, such as the Suzy Lamplugh Trust,[3] were ultimately successful when they framed stalking behavior as more than "harassment," arguing that not to do so was dangerous and simplistic because it did not address the chronic fixation at the heart of the action or the heavy psychological toll on the victim over time.

Most European countries and some others farther afield have adopted similarly specific legislation over recent years, but much like other violent crimes, it is difficult to measure the incidence of stalking on a global level. This behavior may well exist everywhere, but it might not be reported, particularly if some cultures still don't see it as problematic, due to different attitudes to gender and civil rights. Stalking seems to be less common in cultures where relationships between women and men are subject to greater social scrutiny, or where men are reluctant to report harassment by women.

Lydia's victim, Dr. W, was a therapist in private practice whom she had seen for grief counselling after her father's death. Lydia had contacted him at her GP's suggestion, after complaining that she couldn't sleep. They had several sessions, which seemed to help her, and her therapy ended after an agreed period. Some six months later, Dr. W was alarmed to get a Valentine's card from

Lydia expressing her love for him and written in familiar terms. "I can't wait to see you," she wrote, as if they had been having a relationship. He responded carefully, saying that their work had come to an end and he was unable to meet her again, but she could seek therapy from other sources. When she wrote back asking for "just one last session," he responded courteously that he did not feel a meeting would be helpful. I expect he hoped that would be the end of it.

To Lydia, this refusal was unacceptable, and she began a campaign designed to make him agree to see her, bombarding him with hundreds of emails and texts. When he did not reply, she reported him to his regulatory body, claiming that he had initiated a sexual relationship with her when she was his patient. This caused Dr. W professional embarrassment and anxiety; he was the subject of a disciplinary inquiry and had to cease working while it was ongoing. Things escalated when he encountered Lydia outside his home and had to insist she leave. He had never experienced such a thing before, he later told the court, and he began to feel afraid.

A century ago, her behavior would have been seen as evidence of "erotomania," or de Clérambault's syndrome, named for the nineteenth-century psychiatrist who first described patients with delusional beliefs about a love relationship with another person. They usually think these feelings are reciprocated, even if they have never met the object of their love; in some cases that person is imaginary. The early psychiatric textbooks indicated that a "typical" case of erotomania involved a mature woman whose amorous fantasies were a nuisance but not considered risky. This account of erotomania as a mental illness in women that gives rise to low-risk behavior stands in stark contrast to the familiar male obsession with female ex-partners that we are more likely to associate with stalking today, and which sometimes leads to high-risk behavior or, in rare cases, to fatal violence. The latter are the ones we come to hear about, of course, along with accounts of the occasional celebrity stalker.

Over the last few decades, researchers have shown that there are many different kinds of stalking activities. Some stalkers will stay within the law, using tactics like launching court proceedings over questions of child custody to pressure and intimidate their ex-partner. Others have never met the object of their obsession and tend to pursue them virtually, including approaching their family members or friends, which also exacts a high toll. One victim described how the stalking she had experienced from a stranger was "like a virus infecting her life." The myriad options available to people caught up in a fixation like this and the possible migration of many stalkers into cyberspace makes it difficult to gauge whether or not this crime is on the increase in our society. I wonder if, like testing for a virus, the more it is explored and discussed, the more cases will be uncovered.

Recently, a man who was convicted of stalking commented to me during an assessment, "I think when you love somebody, you don't try to kill them." This apparent truism hides the deeper complexity in human relationships, where love and hate can be finely balanced, and ambivalence and ambiguity coexist with intimacy. I think it is erroneous to believe that stalking and harassment are always about love, which may be a hangover from those early ideas about genteel ladies and their harmless fixations on imaginary suitors. Many stalkers do not purport to love their victims; some want revenge, some want to communicate, some want to ensure the victim does not forget who they are. I think that even those who do insist that they love their victim want only to control them. There is an absence of the kind of care and concern that we associate with love; if love means "to be known," as Paul writes to the Corinthians, then stalking demonstrates a most profound lack of knowledge and an utter lack of interest in another person's feelings and perspective.

According to the textbook definition of risk, Lydia did not pose a high risk of harm to Dr. W, but that was not what he felt or experienced. Her persecution of him was invasive and prolonged, lasting well over a year, potentially impacting his livelihood. Despite the fact that she had repeatedly expressed her love for him, this quickly turned to a sense of grievance that he would not do as she asked, leading to her complaints about his professional conduct. Her overriding goal was to be with him in person, even if that meant seeing him in a regulatory hearing; for someone trapped in a delusion, negative contact is better than no contact at all. When that didn't come to pass, she went to the police with her claim that Dr. W had sexually assaulted her while she was his patient, which meant another investigation was launched. This piled further distress on Dr. W, who had to hire a lawyer and suspend his work again.

When it became clear that there was no case for her therapist to answer to, the police cautioned her. This can be enough of a deterrent, especially when someone is otherwise as pro-social as Lydia still appeared to be. But it only fueled her sense of grievance. She staked out Dr. W's home, and when he parked his car and went inside, she attacked the vehicle, scraping the paint with a key and breaking the windows. Then she put a card through the letter box addressed to his wife, with graphic descriptions of the rape she had accused Dr. W of committing.

He was advised to take out a restraining order at that point, but Lydia ignored it and appeared at his home once again, this time throwing rotten meat over the fence, intending that the family's dog would eat it and die. Such cruelty to a victim's pets (reminiscent of the "bunny boiler" in the 1980s film *Fatal Attraction*) is not unusual, and it is an alarming escalation because it targets a living thing the victim values; they or their human loved ones may be next. Lydia's behavior was now seen as high risk, and when she continued to be found near Dr. W's property, she was eventually arrested. During her police interview, she told them that it was all a misunderstanding. She just wanted to meet Dr. W face-to-face so he could apologize to her for all the harm he had done to her; she was the victim, not him. She was convicted and sent to prison.

When I read through the history of her case, I couldn't help feeling, for the nth time, that I was lucky to have spent most of my working life as a therapist inside high-security institutions, where it would be impossible for my patients to act out as Lydia had. As a forensic psychiatrist working with high-risk offenders, I do have an extra level of wariness about potential stalking by patients, but in fact, my only experience of anything like it arose in a community setting, and did not involve a patient. Someone whom I'd never met took exception to an article I wrote for an academic journal and complained about it and me to my employers, and eventually to the medical regulatory body, the General Medical Council (GMC). I tend to think complaints about one's work can be as illuminating as they may be chastening, but in this case, when the person's letters persisted across several months, their campaign began to feel more like harassment than critique—especially when one of the letters arrived at my home address. I later learned that the author made a habit of complaining about psychiatrists, and it was somewhat reassuring to be one of many, even though at the time it did feel personal. When the letters eventually stopped, I presumed the focus on me and my work had been swept away by newer objects tumbling through the person's mental stream.

Assessing Lydia's risk in our forthcoming sessions was going to mean paying close attention to her description of what had occurred and the meaning of it for her. I was particularly curious to learn why she couldn't let Dr. W say no to her, or couldn't hear it. Our first encounter had been reassuring, and I knew that her probation officer, Jane, felt she'd come a long way. Lydia had done well in prison, I was told, and quickly got "enhanced" status through good behavior, meaning she was trusted with a variety of jobs, including working with older people and helping others to read. She had also attended a mandated course in prison aimed at increasing empathy for victims, and had expressed remorse and regret for her offense. That all seemed positive, but one of the reasons mental health care teams work with the probation service is that there is a known increase in the risk of reoffending immediately after release. Transition back into the community brings many stressors, and support is important in promoting desistance.

Our first proper session together came a few weeks after Lydia's release. I suggested that she come to see me at the local secure unit where I was doing some work; there are some rooms outside the locked environment that are made available for professional visits. I booked a small but bright space, with two chairs facing each other in front of French doors that led to a garden area, where spring was just beginning to make a tentative appearance. I reflexively pulled one chair back a bit and settled down to meet the "free" Lydia, mind open to whatever changes I might notice.

At first, there seemed little difference. She was as pleasant as in our initial encounter, and much the same in appearance too, wearing black again, this time with a plain white blouse. She related with me as an equal, chatting about her plans to move from the hostel for prisoners on parole back into her own apartment soon, and the small frustrations involved in restoring things like broadband and registering for council tax (the UK equivalent of property tax). She dug into her handbag and showed me a flier she'd made to advertise herself as a dog-walker, with a charming cartoon in black ink of a slight figure who was smiling as she strained to hold on to the leashes of half a dozen large dogs as they pulled her along a path. Even as I complimented her on the drawing, I struggled to reconcile it with what I had learned about her offense, including her attempt to harm Dr. W's family pet.

I wanted to know more about her past, to get her account of herself in her own words, in order to make an accurate assessment of her risk going forward. But for this first session I let her lead me, and she meandered along, describing some renovations she wanted to do in her kitchen and commenting about the weather. "I actually saw daffodils on my walk this morning." We both smiled at this British code for the fragile relief we feel when winter might just be on the wane. "Are you a gardener?" I asked. "Oh no," she said quickly, "that was my father's domain, not mine." I knew our remaining time was short, but I wanted to pursue that. "Do you take after him at all?" Maybe this was too much, too soon, and she prickled a little. "I wouldn't say so, no." At the end of the session, I felt we'd connected pleasantly enough, but I didn't know her any better than I had at the start.

We made an arrangement to meet again, and I held the door for her. She started to walk away, then paused and turned. "Oh, I meant to say, I googled you." I nodded, unsurprised. Most people meeting a professional will google them first, and it doesn't mean anything sinister. I'm thoughtful about cybersecurity, as most people are, and I try and keep my cyber footprint minimal and banal. Given Lydia's history, I'd maintain a level of wariness, but I didn't feel in any danger from her because there was no attachment to me. She saw me as a task to be got through, or so I thought. "Bye for now," she called, as she walked off down the corridor, her back straight and head held high. The word "control" came to mind. She had led the conversation entirely — the dog-walker with a tight leash.

I thought how important it was that I hear from her about her childhood, especially since her attachment to Dr. W had arisen after the loss of her father. I've described my deep study of the importance of childhood attachments for later adult relationships, and it was, therefore, unsurprising to discover that several prominent researchers into stalking understood the behavior as a manifestation of a toxic early attachment. One of these, J. Reid Meloy, an American forensic psychiatrist who has worked closely with the FBI, published some work on attachments in stalkers back in the 1990s,[4] and there have been several studies since then which have shown that nearly all stalkers have a history of insecure childhood attachment to their parents, more so than might be expected in the general population or even among other types of violent offenders.

I imagined that when Lydia went to Dr. W with unresolved distress about the loss of her father, it may have triggered memories of other unresolved losses. I suspected that she wanted Dr. W to act as an emotional regulator and control her distress for her. It was similar to the scenario where someone makes a disorganized and preoccupied attachment in a romantic partnership; it is unreasonable to expect that a partner (someone who is not your parent) can make you feel safe, secure, and happy at all times. When they fail to do so, as they inevitably will, the disorganized individual feels hurt and frightened, which can lead to controlling behaviors and even hostility. That's when the partner often decides to leave, which is then interpreted as abandonment and rejection, generating anger, hostility, and sometimes violence. The data show us that when people try and leave their controlling partners, they tend to be at most risk at the point of their departure, and if I was right about what had happened, I thought that this might explain why Lydia had started to stalk Dr. W after he insisted that their work together had ended.

This kind of attachment has also been found in some battering men and their victims,[5] although the perpetrators' behavior is also influenced by cultural narratives about women and children as possessions of the male in the family. Such attitudes are central to the concept of "toxic masculinity" and include the belief that, as a man, "nobody gets to say no to me." A harrowing recent example is that of Australian professional rugby player Rowan Baxter, who threatened and then stalked his estranged wife and their children. When he found them, he poured petrol on their car with them inside and set it alight. He then fought off people who rushed to try and put out the flames and, while his family suffered their awful fate, took out a knife and stabbed himself to death. It seems incredible, but I am sure his actions had a perfect symmetry in his mind: his wife and children were "his," and if he could not live without them, then they should not live without him. There are toxic femininities as well as toxic masculinities, but in the context of violence, this concept of entitled possession is particularly risky.

Psychological explanations of the chaotic results of insecure attachment are not intended to provide any excuse for violence in either gender, but they are essential if we are to understand the meaning for a perpetrator and develop strategies for risk management and intervention. As I've indicated, I have increasingly found that the meaning of offending behavior comes more easily into focus when I see it through the lens of early childhood attachments, and this is especially true in cases that involve offenses of lust and love; there's been quite a bit of study of this connection in recent years as it relates to female stalkers.[6]

Lydia had clearly invented a narrative of being abused by Dr. W to justify her feelings of grievance and hurt: "If I feel this bad, he must have abused me, and he should be punished." In preparation for my next session with her, I read the psychiatric reports from the trial, which had drawn on Dr. W's notes. It transpired that after her father's death, Lydia had been disturbed by memories from her teenage years, and she had revealed to Dr. W that her father had sexually abused her. She had never told anyone about this before, and it was only the recurring nightmares that made her disclose her secret to Dr. W. It was possible that the painful retelling of this abusive relationship with a much-loved father had triggered some deep emotional confusion in Lydia's mind between her father and her therapist.

When she came to our next session, I would talk with her about her memories of her family relationships. I like to use some standard questions about childhood, but when I began to do this with Lydia, she frowned. "Why is that relevant?" I explained, as I often have to with patients, that early experiences in life have an influence on adult relationships and behavior, and it was important to gain an understanding of the past to help people in the present. Lydia nodded assent, but she seemed a little preoccupied. I had noticed when she arrived that she was carrying a large leather briefcase this time, instead of her usual neat handbag. She had tucked it beside her chair without comment, and I resolved not to inquire about it but to get on with the job at hand.

I began with a few general questions about Lydia's childhood situation: where she was born, what her family was like, where they lived. Her answers were brief, almost terse. She was the only child of older parents, looked after by a stay-at-home mother and a father who was a lawyer. She had grown up in an English provincial town, done well at school, and followed her father into his profession, specializing in property and contract law. I asked her for five words to describe her relationship with her father, with a memory provided for each word. So, for example, I might talk of my relationship with my father as "loving," and recount memories of him coming to meet me after piano lessons so I wouldn't have to walk home in the dark, and how I would see him arrive and run toward his open arms.

Lydia seemed stumped by the question, and we sat in silence for a few minutes. This was not unusual. It was a new task, which can take some thought. She had been so articulate up to this point that I doubted she'd struggle for long. But the silence deepened and grew. I gazed out of the window behind her and watched the sky turn dark, and I waited. Eventually I started to say, "I know this can be a bit difficult—" but she stopped me with a raised hand. "Don't. I'm thinking." I waited some more. Then she exhaled deeply and said,

"Sorry, no. I can't think of any words. I mean, he was an excellent father in every way. Provided for our family. A really excellent man." "Is there any memory you have to go with that word 'excellent'?" Lydia furrowed her brow and gave no reply.

As the silence extended again, I began to feel uncomfortable. In attachment terminology, Lydia's responses were "dismissing" and detached, "avoidant" of emotion and implying that my questions were pointless. I had a sense the atmosphere between us had cooled somehow, and the interview no longer felt relaxed. I also began to feel on my guard, and no forensic psychiatrist ever ignores these sensations. We are trained to recognize that every emotion we feel in the room is clinically relevant, whether it is irritation, as I'd experienced many times with patients like Marcus, or sympathy, as I've described in Zahra's case. What I was feeling now was a nagging fear. I glanced at the panel in the door to see if anyone was out in the corridor, newly aware of the alarm I always wore attached to my belt, even when I was not in the closed areas of the hospital. I wondered what I'd said to her to effect this change, or whether I was imagining it.

My train of thought was abruptly halted by a jarring sound, a thudding click-thunk-click-thunk. Lydia had twisted in her chair and was bent over her briefcase, releasing its metal fasteners. What was in there? A weapon? As my anxiety level began to rise, she made a little grunt of effort and hauled out a fat lever-arch file from the case (similar to a three-ring binder), stuffed to bursting with papers. She pulled it onto her lap and flipped it open. I relaxed a little, until I noticed that the papers she revealed were densely handwritten, not typed. Even upside down, I could see the text was full of underscorings, multiple exclamation marks, and emphatic capital letters, with a manic quality that made me think something was very wrong.

When she began to speak again, it seemed to me Lydia's voice had changed. It was colder, crisper, with the tone of a sergeant speaking to a subordinate. "What I need to explain, and what you need to get, Dr. Adshead, is that this has nothing to do with my father. I don't like your questions, and frankly I find them inappropriate and unprofessional. What I want to talk about today, and what you must comprehend, is that I have been the victim of a serious miscarriage of justice." My mouth felt dry, but I encouraged her to explain herself further. "I can show you exactly where the prosecution lied and conspired with my alleged 'victim' " — she almost spat the word — "to have me falsely convicted of a spurious offense."

Her vocabulary had gone from genteel patter to curt legalese in an instant, a change as concerning to me as those hectic scribbled notes, which she was now riffling through with high energy, looking for a particular page. Clack — she released the binder clip and pulled out a hand-drawn flowchart, a complex mesh of lines and arrows between various boxes containing different initials and color-coded markings. Holding it up for me to see, she traced her "logic" by moving her finger from box to box as she spoke, as if presenting forensic evidence to a jury. This was verging on comical, I thought; the conveyancing lawyer turned dog-walker was acting the role of counsel for the prosecution. But she was deadly serious.

"I will set out the evidence to you that Dr. W is a serial sex offender who has preyed on myself and another four unsuspecting female patients, to my certain knowledge. I propose to appeal against my conviction and will see to it that Dr. W is charged with aggravated sexual assault. I will show . . ." — she peered at the chart for a moment as she deciphered her own handwriting, then finished firmly — ". . . I will prove beyond all reasonable doubt that the prosecution deliberately withheld evidence that would have supported my case." Thwack — she brought her palm down hard on the thick file to emphasize her point. I tried not to react, but I felt myself flinch.

I needed to take a few breaths. She seemed to be untethered from reality, and I knew she was not in a state of mind to welcome my reflections about what she had just said. I decided it would be best to stick to what was in my own mind. I was confused, I told her. "When we first met, in the prison, you said you knew what you'd done was wrong, didn't you? And you realized you had to move on from the past and wanted our support. Did I misunderstand anything?" She looked askance at me, forehead furrowed, as if I were the one behaving strangely here. "Of course I want support. I need your help in my appeal against my conviction, so I can return to my work as a solicitor. I mean, I'm the victim here, the victim of assault and baseless lies, the one who has been forced to serve time in prison, can't you see? It's absurd! Dr. W is a *rapist*, a man who preys on vulnerable women needing therapy. Doesn't this disgust you? He was *cruel* and *abusive* and *unkind* to me, and I did nothing but bring his crimes to the attention of the police and the world." I began to wonder if my questions had tripped a mental switch. Those adjectives she was listing might sum up her father. Lydia had paused. "Are you listening to me?" She didn't wait for an answer. "Don't you see, Doctor, I'm the one who's suffered. You and I—we need to stand together." This seemed to be a reference to us not only as fellow professionals who might take up arms against a corrupt system, but also as the sisterhood; it was up to us to stand against the patriarchy together.

I had to think carefully and quickly. If she did not see herself as an offender or have real insight into how others saw her, then perhaps her mental state was much less settled than her probation team had thought. In fairness, she had been described as doing well in prison, and no signs of mental illness had been present. I thought back to an early call I'd had with Jane, her probation officer, who had mentioned that she thought stalking was an odd crime for a "woman like Lydia." That was a kind of red flag I'd missed with Zahra too; it's always worth exploring such assumptions of normalcy, which can serve to hide another reality. I also remembered that when we first met at the prison, Lydia had touched lightly on some past suicidal feelings, as if they were of no interest, like passing clouds in a blue sky. It occurred to me that perhaps, just like Dr. W, all of us professionals who were keen to help Lydia had missed the signs of chaos and danger in her mind that could manifest when she felt exposed or needy. Her good behavior was a mask, a persona she could put on or take off at will.

I went over her list of assertions about Dr. W with her, one by one, as she snapped "Correct" to each point. In a kind of mirror of her criminal lawyer performance, I seemed to be acting as prosecuting counsel and she was in the dock. "To be clear, Lydia, you don't accept the evidence presented to the court that you rang

Dr. W daily and sent him hundreds of texts begging to see him and saying you loved him?" Lydia looked at me with contempt. "Lies. All a fabrication to try and silence me, to punish me for speaking my truth. Can't you see that?" I tried to make my tone more conversational, but it was difficult when I'd read all the transcripts, knew the details. "So did you not damage his car or leave rotten meat for his dog? Did I get that wrong? Were you not convicted of criminal damage?"

"Oh, Doctor. Look. Don't you see? I had to do those things because the police were simply not taking any action. It wasn't 'criminal damage,' it was the tiniest scratch with a key on the door of his car, for heaven's sake. A bit silly, but certainly not worth arresting me for, or sending me to prison. Nobody was hurt, were they?" I tried to nod, hoping I looked thoughtful and open-minded. "And it worked! The police finally took notice, and then I was able to explain everything to them in detail, at last: how he'd lured me in, gained my trust in my time of need, only to take advantage of me, as he had all the others." I mustered an unconvincing "Right . . . ," and she cut across me. "There you have it. I was the victim. And they did nothing. Nothing to him, anyway."

I knew I shouldn't reason with an unreasonable person, but I had to state the obvious. "Dr. W was investigated by the police, I believe? And no evidence was found against him." Lydia waved her hand, dismissive. "A cover-up. A classic perversion of justice. And now look, he's still out there, a menace to any unsuspecting woman who walks into his office. Back in his practice as if nothing ever happened, offering his so-called 'Grief and Loss Counselling for Families and Individuals.'" She must have googled him as soon as she emerged from prison, just as she had done with me. But before I could ask her, she went on, sotto voce, as if instructing me for an important secret mission: "They were all in on it, Doctor, don't you see now? The police, the lawyers, the judge— everyone. Even my probation officer, I'm sure. They're all against me. I know it. He must admit to what he did, to my face, and be punished. I just wanted—" Her voice fractured, as if she might break into tears, but she wasn't crying, she was furious. "I just want someone to make him apologize to me for taking advantage when I was so low. No one is helping me! No one ever has." Her tone didn't match the plaintive words, I noticed; there was no emotional activity or warmth of feeling in those vulnerable statements, and the atmosphere in the room was still hard and strange, and confusing to me. I tried to steer my way back to her appeal for my assistance. Gently, I pointed out that I had no legal authority; I was a doctor. "What could I do that would be helpful to you?" She leaned back in her chair and crossed her arms, gazing at me as if assessing my potential, or lack of it. "I read all about you online." I had no idea where she was going with this. "I know you work with sexual predators. You're an expert. You've written about them, done lectures. You've seen it all. I want you to testify at my appeal that Dr. W is one of them, that he assaulted me and that you believe me, that you're on my side."

Finally, it was clear. I was being cast in a supporting role, or at least in a bit part in Lydia's drama. I realized that rational discussion was now impossible, and if I said anything else, she could lose control altogether. I slid another glance at her open briefcase, again wondering if it held a weapon, and I had a whiff of the real fear that Dr. W must have felt. My own thinking was becoming disorganized by anxiety, and I might also have been reflecting her paranoia with my own. I needed to close this down and get on the phone.

"Lydia, can we leave it here for today? I need to think carefully about what you've told me. And will you talk it through with Jane too?" Lydia slammed her fat file shut. She began stuffing it back in the briefcase, obviously disappointed in me. "Jane? She's just another cog in the corrupt machine that put me in prison in the first place. That's why I came to you. I thought you could help me. You know what I'm talking about—you get it. I know you do!" Thunk-clack-thunk—that wretched briefcase was shut, which was a relief. She reached out and touched my arm briefly, and I thought she was close to tears. "Please help. I'm the victim here, Dr. Adshead. There's nothing wrong with me—it's him. We have to . . . we just need to make sure the truth comes out. Save all those other women who might suffer in future from his terrible abuse and unkindness."

It was extremely alarming that she had managed to hide the truth of her distorted thinking from every professional who had seen her since her arrest, including me. In fairness, the psychiatrists who had examined her for the prosecution at her trial had flagged some concerns. Unfortunately, Lydia's ever so normal performance and her notable good behavior in prison were taken as signs of a reformed offender, another example of how deceptive face value can be, even for someone trained to look below the surface and highly attuned to risk. I had failed to comprehend that behind Lydia's monochromatic facade lay her "true colors," an inner emotional life rich with vivid feelings like paranoia, fury, and outrage. I now thought Dr. W might be in real danger from her.

Lydia's successful performance was an important reminder of how mental disorder can sometimes be a chameleon, hiding in plain sight. Ever since her arrest she must have been planning to return to her object of obsession at the earliest opportunity. No matter that he didn't want her, or that his charges had sent her to prison for two years; her delusions were deeply entrenched. I had to think she was likely to seek reconnection with him soon, even as an adversary. I breathed a sigh of relief when she left, with a barked "Think about it, Dr. Adshead" rather than her habitual "Bye for now" exit line. As soon as she was out of sight, I went online to see if Dr. W had a website and whether it listed his address. I was glad to see there was a contact form instead, a precaution he might have taken in light of his experiences with Lydia. I called Jane, her probation officer, and we shared our dismay and concern. Jane said she would confer with colleagues and the police to formulate a plan of action. Meanwhile, I pictured Lydia fuming at home, hashing through her files and scribbled notes, tapping away at her keyboard in frustration as she scanned the internet to try and find Dr. W.

I would later hear that Lydia went to Dr. W's old office, located in a community health center. The young woman who worked at reception explained to the ordinary-looking middle-aged lady who asked to see him that he'd left months ago. Lydia insisted the receptionist was lying and pushed past her, throwing open the door of what had been Dr. W's office. She was furious to find it empty and launched into a bitter tirade, accusing the receptionist of hiding him and of being his lover. The terrified woman barricaded herself in the bathroom and phoned the police, while Lydia began to tear books from the shelves and upend furniture, smashing a glass vase in her fury.

The police came quickly, and she was arrested. A swift assessment was made by the local psychiatric service, determining that she was in an acute psychotic state. I have to say I felt mightily relieved when I came to work the next day and heard she was in custody. As sad and alarming as it was to hear of Lydia's breakdown, the remarkably quick action taken by the professionals, with no harm coming to Dr. W or his family, was a good outcome. Due to the history of threats to Dr. W, the on-call forensic psychiatrist for the locality thought the risk was such that Lydia needed detention in a secure psychiatric hospital rather than a recall to prison under the terms of her probation license. At least in a secure hospital she would have access to some therapy, though I did not know if it would help her.

I must admit that the more I learn about stalkers, the more I am struck by the obdurate quality of their obsession, the sheer heft and immobility of that "boulder" in their consciousness. People like Lydia occupy an elaborately created parallel universe, where they are fighting for something they never had. I am coming to think of them as psychologically deaf, because they can't hear rejection. Plain language like "I'm married, I'm never going to be with you" or "I don't want you near me" would be hard for someone whose ears were open to ignore.

I thought that Lydia might continue in her delusion indefinitely, in order to keep unresolved distress and grief at bay. Sadly, I doubted that she would be able to use therapy that helped her explore the meaning of her actions, nor would she countenance the reality that her late father would never apologize for what he did to her. If she ever became aware of the full implications of what she had done, and what that meant for her future life prospects, she might become suicidal. Paradoxically, it could feel safer to stay in her fantasy world, where she was a well-bred and empowered professional, the daughter of an "excellent man" who just had to find a way to convince the world that she was right and everyone else was wrong.

Like me, the reader may feel the pain of her story and of all that she had lost more than Lydia ever will. My brief interaction with her happened over a decade ago, and it is likely that she is still in the secure unit, preoccupied with writing her papers and drawing her color-coded charts, absorbed in the conspiracy that is now her life's narrative.

SHARON

"Thank you for coming to see me today—may I call you Sharon?" She didn't look up from her mobile phone. "Whatever." I was aware of an anomalous mix of feelings toward her already: sympathy, irritation, and sadness. She was nineteen, that liminal age where the girl and the woman jostle for position, and she was in danger of losing custody of her baby son. "I'd like to start by explaining how we—Sharon?" I was addressing the top of her head, a white parting zigzagging through dark roots. "I know this may be a bit hard for you, but could you put the phone down so that I can explain what we need to do together?" We were meeting in a local community center, in a room which I used mainly for seeing people involved in the medico-legal cases that I took on from time to time. Other therapists used the room too, so there was a generic setup, with comfortable armchairs, a couple of small tables with lamps, and the inevitable box of tissues. There were a few pleasant, anodyne framed pictures on the pale-green walls, as well as a clock facing my chair that told the time accurately, unlike most clocks in NHS settings.

After I left Broadmoor in 2013, I continued to work as a forensic psychiatrist, providing consultations for different mental health teams in female prisons and the probation service, as I've described, but I always tried to make space in my schedule to carry out psychiatric assessments for the family court, which deals with the care and protection of children, among other family disputes. I'd been asked to assess Sharon, and she'd clearly come reluctantly. Her moon-shaped face, curtained by lank orange-blonde hair, was

215

distorted by a scowl, her voice low and sullen. "How long's this gonna take?" She gave an exaggerated sigh, but at least she set her mobile phone aside. I felt like sighing too.

The situation was pretty serious. Thomas, her thirteen-month-old son, had developed a mystery illness during infancy which no one could explain. Sharon had been unwilling to work with health care professionals toward a resolution, complaining instead that they were somehow at fault. She had become increasingly aggressive and uncooperative, to the point where social services feared that she could not safely look after Thomas. They had applied for a care order, meaning that he was temporarily removed into foster care, and the family court had ordered a psychiatric assessment of Sharon in order to assess whether he could safely be returned to her care. Unlike criminal courts, if there is a risk of harm, family courts do not wait for proof of an offense; child safety is paramount, and the state moves quickly to protect its smallest citizens.

I tried to frame our task for her, emphasizing that I wasn't there to decide anything or take a side. "My job is to be neutral, help the court see things from your perspec—" But she cut across me. "I don't want to be here, you know. I'm a good mum, no matter what they say. The social's been in my face half my life, and what fucking good are they? I can look after Thomas just fine. It's those doctors—they don't listen, they don't care, they don't do anything!" As her voice rose, I heard a note of fear. "Now they're practically saying I'm a child abuser, aren't they? Taking him away from me! I'm a good mum, nothing like my mum, that's for fucking sure. The doctors are the guilty ones, not me." She sat back, and now I could see her eyes brimming. I pushed the box of tissues toward her, and I thought I heard a muffled "Thanks" as she blew her nose.

Her phone buzzed with a text, and she immediately went to reply. "Sharon?" I resisted an impulse to grab the device and set it out of her reach. "Gotta keep it on in case it's about Thomas, you know? I'll put it on vibrate." She was offering me a truce of sorts, and I took it gratefully. "So how do we come to be meeting?" I asked. She grunted, looking at the ceiling. When she'd arrived that morning, she'd flung herself into the chair and draped her legs over one arm, as if to signal her disdain for the process by not facing me—or not facing what we had to do together. I thought her aggressive presentation was a defense against feeling small and vulnerable. She was young David, confronting the evil Goliath of the family court and social services, a victim of the malignant over-reach of the nanny state. "My little boy was sick. Really, really sick, for ages. I tried to help him, and the doctors were crap. When I complained, they wanted to get back at me, so they lied to the social. The end." I made some notes, then looked up at her. "Get you back? How do you mean?"

"Duh. They didn't like me—or Thomas—because I called them out, didn't I? And you know the rest." She raised bitten finger-nails to her mouth and gnawed at the raw edge of her thumb. I wasn't discouraged; I thought she was showing some insight. She was probably right that the medical teams hadn't warmed to her. I made another note, aware that she was craning her head to see. I turned the pad toward her. "You're welcome to read it." She shuf-fled in her chair to sit normally and frowned, trying to decipher my scrawl. "I thought, with a shrink, isn't everything I tell you meant to be totally private, just between you and me?" I explained that the court needed to know what we had talked about so that they could better understand her point of view, which meant I had to get things down accurately. "Right," she said, sounding dubi-ous. I took inspiration from her smartphone, balanced precari-ously on the arm of her chair. "I need to take a clear photograph of your story, without any filters or Photoshopping. Does that make sense?" She rolled her eyes but nodded as if she understood.

I knew the basic contours already from talking with her lawyer and reading through the legal files they had provided. Sharon was a single mum who lived in public housing on the outer fringe of west London. Her parents were both dead; her mother had been in a car accident when she was small, and her father had died of an illness a few years later. As a consequence, she was fostered from the age of thirteen, and five years later, soon after being discharged from the care system, she had become pregnant. There were no details about the father in the documentation I had seen, but some medical notes that were included indicated her pregnancy and labor were normal.

Within a month of her son's birth, Sharon started to appear at her local doctor's office, expressing concerns about the baby's health, as often as two or three times a week. It's not unusual for first-time parents, especially those without family around them, to be peppering GPs and nurses with queries, but Thomas was found to be in good health every time. His height and weight were at the high end of the average range and none of the symptoms his mother described were evident upon examination. A health visitor (a visiting nurse) had been to see her at home and given her helpful pamphlets about breast-feeding and such, with advice on how to join mother and baby groups. That hadn't been enough for Sharon, and she began taking her son to different hospitals' emergency rooms on a regular basis, looking for answers to her continuing concerns. She described some alarming symptoms with great urgency; one nurse noted that she wept and said she was "desperate." But several different physicians at various hospitals were unable to detect anything—the baby always appeared to be in good health.

Late one night, when Thomas was about twenty weeks old, Sharon brought him in to the emergency room, saying he had a high fever and "might have sepsis." She described how other doctors had told her that he had "something wrong with his kidneys" and gave the junior doctor on duty a urine sample she said was Thomas's, claiming her health visitor had advised her to collect the sample if symptoms continued. It was bright red. Further tests were run on the baby. The senior pediatrician who was called to review the case found that the kidney scans were clear and the baby seemed comfortable. A new urine sample was taken and no blood was seen; the notes referred to "a perplexing presentation."

After making a call to Sharon's GP, the pediatrician heard about the history of frequent visits and false alarms at the emergency room and took the view that the case needed a review by the child safeguarding lead. This is a hospital staffer who is specifically assigned to coordinate safeguarding procedures for vulnerable patients, including contacting social services, if necessary. The dominos fell, one after another: a child protection investigation was opened, the local authority got involved, care proceedings were opened in the family court, and Thomas was temporarily removed to foster care. A court-appointed guardian would represent his interests while a psychiatric assessment of his mother was set in motion.

By this time, I had been providing reports for cases in the family court for more than a decade, including while I was still working at Broadmoor. The work drew on my increasing interest in early child development as it relates to risk, but my study of medical child abuse had begun many years earlier, not long after I became a forensic psychotherapist—partly prompted by my own experience of motherhood and what it did to my mind. Like many women, I found that maternal instincts did not switch on like a light, and I did not always find being a mother comfortable. I was used to being a competent caregiver at work, but sometimes I felt like an incompetent one at home, and this made me anxious.

I was interested to discover more about the causes of the kind of maternal anxiety that led to extreme behaviors, and together with some colleagues I embarked on research which was as enlightening as it was difficult. In the course of our work, we gained access to some disturbing covert surveillance footage from a 1980s child protection investigation, featuring a group of mothers caught in the act of stopping their children's breathing while in the hospital. Those videos were not easy to watch, but they offered a rare chance for a forensic psychiatrist to see violent offenders in action. Most of the women had no "bicycle lock" risk factors for violence and appeared to be the most caring of mothers, other than when they had their hands over their babies' noses and mouths. We concluded that the common denominator between women like this and violent offenders was their early attachment patterns, with high incidences of childhood abuse, neglect, and loss.[1]

Since then, I've seen more mothers like them, such as Sharon. Each case I've worked on has been unique, humanly rich, and always poignant. All of the women appeared to be making up stories about their children's ill health or actively making them ill and lying about it. At the same time, they were baffled by the idea that they could harm the child, as if this were out of their psychological sightline. Nearly all of them used one phrase over and over: they "just felt something was wrong." This unusual parental behavior was commonly known as Munchausen's syndrome by proxy (MSBP). The current official term is medical child abuse causing a child to have factitious or induced illness (FII). Munchausen's is a name appropriated in the 1950s by British doctor Richard Asher from the fabled Baron von Munchausen, a character who went around telling fantastic stories about himself. Asher used it to describe patients who gave false or exaggerated accounts of their illness. Subsequently, it was recognized that people might also do this "by proxy" with their children (or another vulnerable person in their care), giving rise to the term MSBP.

What usually happens is that a caregiver, nine times out of ten a mother, tells health care professionals that her child is ill when they are not, lying about or magnifying their symptoms. The most severe cases tend to involve children younger than five, no doubt because they can't protest or contradict their parent. GPs and pediatricians have to take such parental accounts at face value—and, indeed, are trained to do so—which means it can take some time before the truth emerges. Like Sharon, mothers may seek out many different doctors and different hospitals, reporting different symptoms. Eventually, when it becomes clear they are fabricating or even causing a child's symptoms or injuries, social services will be alerted.

Some of the mothers present themselves as anxious but brave, heroic caregivers who are just trying to advocate for their children. Others are demanding and accusatory, insisting that the doctors are wrong, that the child's tests are not normal and that more must be done, always demanding new and better investigations. Some will use social media to depict themselves as gallant fighters against the medical system. Even if the child gets better, there are mothers who come back to report a whole new set of symptoms, and so the cycle begins again, until a professional becomes suspicious enough to investigate. With all the smoke and mirrors involved, that can take months or even years.

Medical child abuse remains as controversial now as it was when the term was first coined, with critics variously questioning whether it can be conclusively proven, linking it to systemic misogyny or labeling the very idea preposterous, with all the fervor of those who question the American moon landings. It is hard for any culture to accept that mothers would harm their children, but there is enough good-quality data to show that it happens, even if it is rare. What the numbers actually are is another matter, since this kind of data is challenging to collect and verify, as we see with other kinds of abuse. One UK study conducted in the 1990s found an average of around fifty cases per year;[2] more recent overviews in the US suggest a similarly low incidence relative to population size.[3]

The biggest worry are those cases where someone actively induces illness in a child who may have an existing physical health condition. Every branch of pediatrics has a horror story to tell about this: the mother who put feces in an intravenous line; the mother who withheld or tampered with life-saving medication or oxygen supplies; the mother who used a ball-peen hammer to create "inexplicable" hematomas on the legs of her disabled son. Although this kind of behavior is uncommon, child protection professionals are attuned and reactive to potential signs. They are also trained to know that it can be a progressive behavior. A baby like Thomas might be in good health, with various tenuous symptoms, for a period of time, when the immediate danger is low, other than the risks posed by unnecessary medical interventions and highly anxious parenting. But if the child's mother or other caregiver does not get the medical attention they feel is needed, this could escalate into them impulsively inducing more alarming symptoms. In view of Sharon's history with Thomas, and the increasing frequency of her hospital visits, social services felt compelled to take action.

Sharon did not respond well to their intervention and was difficult and obstructive, refusing to let social workers touch her son or see him alone, or canceling appointments at the last minute. Social work is an invaluable but thankless job, among the most challenging of front-line services, and particularly so in child protection. Much as in the prison service, and in general health care, I've seen that people working in social services are functioning within an overwhelmed and underfunded bureaucracy, and mistakes can be made. If this leads to cases of child abuse being missed or misread, they will face an inevitable wave of media coverage and scapegoating. This is one reason why family courts have such a vital role: they are protecting parental interests as well as those of the children, and every case involves close scrutiny of all the evidence. In my experience, family courts are scrupulous about this and will seek out whatever independent opinions may be required; it is not unknown for a judge to hear from more than ten different experts in a given case.

As my session with Sharon neared its end, I realized I had no information about her childhood, which meant I couldn't explore any possible problems in her early attachment. As is often the case, the social services records were lists, not narratives, primarily data about her son and his health, with almost nothing about Sharon's past. I asked about her deceased parents, but she was not forthcoming. "What's this got to do with anything? Look, all I need is for you to tell the judge I'm a good mum!" When she'd gone, I reflected that she had unconsciously said something important about her own need to be a good mum. I thought she was expressing another layer of need too: she seemed to need her son in order to be an adult; without him, she reverted to being a distressed and frustrated girl, one who was probably quite fearful.

I submitted my report soon after that meeting. Under the UK's Children and Families Act 2014, care proceedings have to be handled within twenty-six weeks; in the past, backlogs and delays had meant the average was at least a year, which was rightly seen as untenable. I concluded that Sharon suffered from extreme anxiety but had no other mental illness, and made a recommendation that she have therapy, if possible. If she were willing to accept that help, I thought there was a good chance her anxiety might improve. I was not being wildly optimistic when I gave that opinion: I'd seen cases where women like Sharon had changed their minds for the better.

I doubted I would see her again and assumed that was the end of the story for me. But it was only the end of the beginning. Sixteen months later, Sharon's legal aid lawyers emailed me, asking if I would see her again. Since our last encounter, she had attempted to remove her son from foster care without permission; meanwhile, her alcohol and drug use had escalated. Eventually, the family court had been persuaded that Thomas should be adopted; this is always a last resort, so the judge must have considered permanent separation from Sharon to be "in the child's best interests." Her lawyer told me that soon after this judgment, Sharon had really gone off the rails. She was homeless on and off and was thought to have a meth addiction, but was refusing any treatment or housing assistance. About a year ago, she had met a new partner, Jake, a young man about her age who was well known to the police and the local addiction support team. She had become pregnant again, and the midwife who booked her into the prenatal clinic contacted social services because of the history with Thomas, her substance abuse, and because she could see that Sharon had a recent black eye and bruises on her arms. I feared I knew where this story was headed. Sure enough, social workers made plans to remove the baby into foster care straight after the birth.

This process is certainly not unique to the UK; most countries with organized legal systems have similar laws about the termination of parental rights, due to the reality of substance abuse, physical abuse, and neglect.[4] Striking a balance in terms of rights versus risk is not straightforward in the family realm, and advocates of maternal rights have increasingly protested about the infringement of civil liberties, particularly in the US. Removing a child from their parents in this way is not a common occurrence in the UK, but it is legally supported in the context of child protection legislation, and is done only when there are real safety concerns. The decision is usually taken months in advance, and the mother (and father, if around) will be fully aware and legally represented; there is no element of surprise. But the social work team in Sharon's case guessed rightly that this removal would be difficult, and it was. While some parents manage to keep it together in these circumstances, generally because their lawyers have advised them to cooperate if they ever want to regain custody, Sharon and Jake had to be restrained as their son was taken from the delivery ward.

Given her history, the judge wanted a review of Sharon's mental health, and I was instructed to see her again. When I read the notes, it appeared that, sadly, she had not had any therapy or help since we last met. This was unsurprising to me, and a familiar catch-22: local mental health services wouldn't get involved with her because Sharon had no severe mental illness diagnosis, while maternal mental health providers said they could help only if she was still looking after a baby. I knew that a few boroughs in London had specialist therapy groups to catch patients like Sharon; I'd set one up myself many years earlier and had seen how helpful they could be. But this option wasn't available to her either.

The lack of access to care in cases like this is so maddening and frustrating, for at least two reasons. First, within the landscape of offending in general, it is unjust that those who might benefit most often cannot get the most basic treatment. It is especially galling in the case of someone as young as Sharon, whose problems were potentially treatable and who might well bear more children. Meanwhile, other abusive people, including those in prison, are regularly offered interventions to look at the harm they do—indeed, they are expected to engage in treatment programs if they want probation, as I've referred to in cases such as Ian's and Lydia's. Why not abusive mothers who have had their children removed? It could be an automatic adjunct to care proceedings. Maybe this is how a culture that places so much emphasis on mothers being "good" pretends that bad ones don't exist.

Second, if Sharon didn't get the care and treatment she needed, I felt pretty certain she'd continue to get pregnant over and over again, in a chaotic and unplanned way. The risk to her babies would persist, and the trauma of the court's intervention might repeat again and again. She wouldn't be alone in this: about a fifth of all cases where children are removed from their mothers are recurrent care proceedings, with many of these "repeat removals" involving mothers who had been in the care system themselves as minors.[5] I am aware of one local authority that took nine children away from the same woman, due to her continuing risk. The tragic impact on her and the children, as well as the stupid waste of taxpayers' money and the court's time, could have been averted with therapy and possibly some long-term contraception, if she had been willing, but no help was available. On a positive note, there is now a wonderful charity called PAUSE, launched in London in

2013, which is filling important gaps in supporting women whose children have been taken into care.[6] It has expanded over the years, but it is not available everywhere.

When she burst into my office for our second meeting, Sharon wasn't tearful, distracted, or full of teen attitude; she was enraged. She refused to sit down when invited and instead paced the floor in the small space, desperate to unload her frustration. "It's like this is a fucking police state, the bastards . . . Everyone's against us!" A red flush crept up her neck and her eyes blazed. I let her go on. "Jake says they're trying to wear us down, you know, and we have to fight. You have to help us. My lawyers said you would help." I raised my eyebrows but chose not to comment on that. Instead, I asked her, "How does Jake feel about the baby?" Sharon sat down abruptly. I saw that her phone was glued to her hand, as ever, but she focused on me, her anger still at boiling point. "You think he doesn't want him? He was gutted when they took him off us. You should've seen him—I thought he was gonna kill someone." I told her I was just curious to know if he was excited about being a father, if he would welcome a chance to help her raise their son. "He's chuffed," she said quickly, "chuffed to bits. Comes from one of those big Irish families, so he's really good with little ones—loves his mum and all that." Perhaps she thought that all she had to do was become a mum and she'd be loved by him too. She wouldn't be the first woman to make that mistake.

Her lawyer had told me that Sharon was willing to cooperate, but I found she was still reluctant to answer my questions, and much like the last time, mostly eager to bad-mouth various officials and medical professionals who had been "useless" and lied to her. There was one moment when she seemed to open up, after I asked her what she and Jake had named the new baby. She didn't respond right away but swiped at her eyes with the back of her hand. Then she busied herself sending a text and pretended she'd forgotten my question. I felt a wave of great sadness and hopelessness come over me.

"Sharon? Do you want to tell me his name?" I asked quietly. I was thinking of stories like Charlotte's and all I had learned about how significant choosing a name is, for yourself or for another person. "Whatever," she said brusquely. "This is a bloody police state, you know. Taking someone's baby away just like that for no reason." She was dry-eyed and cold now, her rage depersonalized: this terrible thing had happened with "someone's baby," a child she could not even name aloud. Perhaps that was a kind of self-protection in case she never saw him again. "Jake says this is all a big conspiracy," she added. "He says they hate us for putting up a fight."

I asked if she felt safe where she was living now, with Jake. The words had barely come out when she interrupted, demanding to know what "they" had told me and whether "they" had "made shit up again" about Jake hurting her or hitting her or "whatever." I said we didn't have to talk about it if she didn't want to, and she nearly spat at me. "It's all crap. Don't believe a word of it." I thought it was time to diffuse the atmosphere a little and suggested she might need a little break. "Yeah," she grumped. I was about to get up and open the office door for her, when I realized what she meant. "Too right I need a break—we both do. Me and Jake, we're tired of all these people and all your questions and all this shit. He's our baby, and they're not having him—we'll get him back! I'm going to . . . I mean, we're gonna get our own flat and all. The council will give us a nice place, Jake says, if we get our baby back. Write that down. Tell 'em. That's what I need. A flat!" She wagged her index finger at my notepad. "Go on, get that down."

I did as she asked and included every word she'd said about her hopes and plans in my report. I came away thinking that her fight to be seen as a mother was as important to her as being in a relationship with this nameless baby boy. It seemed to me that she was not suffering the loss of her children so much as the loss of her social identity as a mother. So much flows from this—practical things like help with housing, as she'd hinted, but also a flow of cultural sympathy that accompanies a swelling stomach or a baby carriage, in the home and in the community. She was smart underneath all that swagger and swearing; she knew that motherhood brought status. She'd had it before, and she wanted it again. This made me even more curious about her own experience of being mothered, but much as I tried, Sharon still refused to go near any questions about this, and I couldn't force her. Sadness remained with me as I wrote my report and recommended again that she be offered therapy by someone competent to help her. I thought it was unlikely that I'd be needed in court or that I'd hear the result of the judge's deliberations, and so it proved.

When my phone rang three years later, I had to struggle to recall where I'd heard the lawyer's name before. Then the penny dropped: it was Sharon's legal aid lawyer, asking me to see their client once again. Sharon was pregnant for the third time and back before the family court. Social services were considering an application for another prenatal care order, but she wanted to be allowed to keep this baby when it arrived. I couldn't disguise my heavy sigh down the phone, but the lawyer interrupted me with a fervent "She's come a long way, Dr. Adshead." I murmured a polite "I'm sure," which sounded so doubtful that we both laughed. We joked that I was Eeyore to their Tigger in this case, but they wouldn't let me off the hook, arguing how important my expert input would be to the judge, given that I had a baseline for comparison, having seen her twice before. "Tigger" told me that everyone—the social workers, her guardian, and the judge—thought Sharon was doing well, but the court really wanted to know from me, "Can we trust the change we see?" I wanted to be useful to the court—and I admit I was curious to see this change that others had observed.

She was five months pregnant when she came to my office for the third time. There certainly was a physical difference: she had the fabled second trimester "glow" that some women experience; her skin looked healthy and her hair, now a natural brown, was thick and lustrous. A pleasant young man about her age dropped her off, introducing himself to me as Simon. He kissed her affectionately, saying he'd be back to pick her up when we were done. She stretched out her hand to shake mine, thanking me for seeing her again. This was even more remarkable than her physical transformation. She seemed to read my mind. "Bet you didn't think you'd see me again, did ya? Bit different this time, right?" It was indeed, I said, adding that as I recalled, she'd been very cross the last time we met. She nodded and gave a rueful smile. "Yeah, I'm sorry about that . . . Third time lucky?" Then she launched into a speech which sounded a little prepared but genuine. She told me she was grateful the court had asked me to evaluate her again, and she wanted to explain how much things had changed so that the judge would give her and Simon a chance with this baby. As she spoke, I noticed she was resting her hands on the baby bump, as if holding it in place. She followed my gaze. "Oh, we felt it move this morning, little kicks, you know? Maybe it'll happen again." I smiled, as you do when a pregnant woman shares that kind of intimacy, and it was easy to forget her history for a moment and feel warm toward her. Then she looked up at me, her face turning serious. "I do understand why everyone's so worried."

As we talked for the next few hours, it was the linguistic shifts I noticed most, even more than changes in her appearance and tone. There was a spontaneity and coherence to her speech and, notably, a total absence of swearing. Coherence in this context does not mean elegant prose; it refers to communicating with meaning in a reflective way. I often give trainees the example of the man who had killed some of his family members, and when I first spoke with him about it, he said, "It's all been a terrible misunderstanding." On its own that's a graceful and well-composed sentence; in the circumstances, it was jarring and bizarre, the words of a man who had no coherent story to tell and who was living in a parallel reality.

Sharon was now able to look at her past and acknowledge that other people had a right to hold a view that was opposed to her own. It was evident that she'd moved out of a distorted reality and denial into a more "live" frame of mind, where emotions like humor and regret could exist. I wasn't surprised to find that the big development in her life between this pregnancy and the loss of her last child was that she'd finally made it to the top of the waiting list for therapy. Within the NHS, a GP will refer you for psychological therapy, and you will be assessed and put on a waiting list. It can easily take two years to get to see a therapist, which is clearly a damaging and dangerous state of affairs, even if it gets little public attention relative to the outcry over waiting lists for physical health needs. Therapy waiting times got much worse in the wake of the front-line service cuts that followed the global economic crisis—unfortunate timing for Sharon. But this has been a problem for most of my career; the difference is that before the restructuring of the NHS, when norms from the world of business were imposed across the board, the medical professionals (as opposed to accountants) who ran mental health services had more flexibility. In cases judged to be sensitive or urgent, we could bypass rigid queuing systems, and we also had more clinicians available, many of whom were highly experienced. I can recall some gifted semi-retirees I worked with in my early years, brought in to support therapy clinics in the community; today, "efficiency standards" (code for "younger, less trained therapists cost far less") make that impossible.

The group for mothers that Sharon had finally joined had been set up by her local mental health service, and it sounded much like the one I'd run years earlier. I was so pleased by this news and encouraged her to tell me more. She admitted that when her social worker had first announced the "good news" about a place coming up in group therapy, she had not been keen at all, mainly because she hadn't known what to expect. But this social worker, Lisa, "really got me," Sharon explained—I noticed this was the first time I'd ever heard her say something positive about any professional trying to help her. More than that, she sounded affectionate.

Lisa was just a few years older than Sharon, and she'd been supportive in helping her to get away from Jake, who'd become increasingly abusive to her after they lost their son. Sharon had found new housing and a program to help her with her substance abuse problems, with Lisa's encouragement and assistance—"Like a friend, you know?" It occurred to me that this might be the first true friend she'd ever had. Sharon had met Simon not long before the place in therapy became available, and with Lisa, he'd encouraged her to attend. "They ganged up on me," she laughed, "and finally I gave in." She had to go for an initial assessment by a lady therapist, she explained, and she felt understood by her. That positive interaction had helped her to take the plunge and begin going to the weekly group. She wasn't the only one there who'd lost two babies, she told me, and she leaned in then, lowering her voice a bit. "You'll never believe it, but one of them had FIVE! Five in a row, taken away."

"What did you feel when you heard that?" I asked. "It was f—" For a minute I felt sure she was going to swear, but she stopped herself and found the word she wanted. "Amazing." "How so?" I asked. She described how the mother of five had talked for ages to the group, describing a terrible cycle of pregnancy and care orders and courts and police, beginning when she was just sixteen. Finally, she'd broken down, "crying her eyes out like a baby," and admitted that she just didn't like being a mum. "I couldn't quite hear what she'd said at first, and then she said it again, louder: 'I don't wanna be a mum, I don't *like* being a mum.' Just like that, right in front of everyone. Amazing." She shook her head, eyes shining as she relived the moment. "What happened then? How did people respond?" I asked. Sharon grinned. "People hugged her. It sounds crazy, I know, but it was good. We told her she was brave for saying it, you know? Then everyone started clapping. Seems funny, I guess, cheering someone for saying that, but it made sense, I swear." It did, I agreed. Recognizing reality is worth celebration, anytime.

I asked if she wanted to tell me anything else about the group. "Like what?" A vestige of her former suspicion flitted across her face. "Anything at all," I said. She thought for a moment. "It was good to know I'm not a freak. I mean, nobody's just born a good mum." I thought that never had a wiser thing been said, and I told her so. "Thing is," she went on, "I lost my mum and all, so young, and then when I had Thomas . . ." She faltered as she said his name. It seemed to me she was as moved by compassion for her younger self as she was by the thought of the little boy she'd lost. Her next words could have applied to either or both of them: "I wish it hadn't been that way." She reached for a tissue and blew her nose loudly. "It's just that . . . you don't have a clue how to be when a baby comes, you know? And it's so hard to tell anyone. You feel—" Here she corrected herself with an effort, switching to the first person, demonstrating that this was *her* story. "I mean, I felt,

I don't know . . . Every day, the baby was just crying and crying, and even if I fed him and changed him, he just cried and nothing I did would settle him. It was so hopeless and nobody seemed to get it and I felt so . . . trapped." I was trying to write down every word as she spoke. She waited, as if politely allowing me to catch up, or maybe it was just to take a moment to compose herself. Then she came close to an admission of past guilt, even if she swerved back to the second person. "I guess . . . you do anything you can think of to get some help. You're desperate."

I spoke carefully, knowing this was difficult. "Sharon, you didn't want to talk about your childhood when we met before. Do you think you could tell me a little more now?" She stared at the floor for a bit, then looked up into my eyes. "I had to talk about all that in group, so it's not as hard now. But not easy." I told her to take her time. She began with her father, who she said was an alcoholic; she thought maybe both her parents were, but she couldn't remember much about her mother, who died several years before her father, when she was seven. "How old were you when your father died?" She shrugged, and again I saw a flash of the angry teen. As the pain surfaced, so did the old anger. "Whatever. Thirteen? He was really sick, his liver packed up. But he kept drinking, or tried to. I looked after him for a while. It was f— It was horrible." I was sure it was. Liver failure can mean a slow, painful death—not pleasant for a young girl to see. I did not like to imagine that traumatized young teen, trying to cope alone. "He died after I went into care. I didn't see him again." She said this without emotion, almost shrugging it off. Maybe it had been a relief.

"And your mum?" I prompted her, hoping she was prepared to go further. Sharon exhaled, then crossed her forearms low over her body, as if cradling her baby to protect it from some oncoming threat. She kept her head down, so that I had to strain to hear her. "I can't remember much, but . . . there was an accident . . . I was with her. It was night. I don't know why, but the car flipped over, our car . . . I was trapped in there with her. I think she died while we waited for help to come." She went on to tell me that the emergency services had taken hours to arrive, or so it had seemed, and she had to be cut from the wreckage.

She suffered only minor injuries in the accident and was soon released from the hospital. Grieving and doubtless in need of treatment for the trauma she'd experienced, it sounded like Sharon had not received any such assistance. Instead, she went home and tried to help her dad, who, she said, was "worse than useless"; in the following years, he dissolved his grief in alcohol. Eventually, she confided in one of her teachers about this, and social services intervened to move her into foster care. Between the ages of twelve and sixteen she thought she had probably had six or seven different placements. "Then, when I left care, well, I was an orphan by then, wasn't I? I just wanted my own home and family, soon as I could, and then, with Thomas . . ."—she faltered there, but gulped in a big breath and went on—". . . I just knew something was wrong with him, and nobody was listening to me." An echo of her old refrain, I thought—was she going to revert to old Sharon? Instead, she looked me in the eyes and said, "I couldn't do it. I couldn't take care of him, and it's true, I did do all that stuff they said I did to him—put blood in his urine, all that stuff. It was true."

I had to ask about her second child, the baby she'd had with Jake that had been taken away in the hospital. "Stephen," she said. "But I don't know what they call him now. They say he is loved and cared for now with them, with his new family. I just hope maybe that he—maybe both boys—will come looking for me when they're big, and I'll get to explain that I was just . . ." She paused and then blurted, "I was just *fucked*." In spite of the heavy atmosphere and high emotion we both laughed when she said it. It was a relief. "I mean, I won't put it like that exactly—but I want them to know that back then, I was a mess." I gave her a thumbs-up for the amendment, and she smiled wanly and went on: "It wasn't that I didn't love them, and I need them to know that . . . I just wanted to give them what I never had. But that's another thing I got from the group, you know? How can you give anyone what you never had?" And then the tears came out and she sat there sobbing, hugging the new life in her belly and shaking as she wept. I pushed the box of tissues close to her and waited, thinking of Wordsworth's "still, sad music of humanity," the sound of lament.

I thought she might be equating mothering with mourning

and could not know if she was crying for her lost boys or for her mother. Her mother's early death had robbed her of a parent and a role model, but also of care and attention, which she then felt compelled to seek out in other ways. Her chronic fear that her baby might die, however unfounded, was graphically real to her. This might explain why medical reassurance had not helped her, and why she went from doctor to doctor and made all those panicked trips to the hospital. The emergency room was a place she associated with the pain and loss of her own traumatic childhood event, but also with rescue. The false narrative she'd created for Thomas was part of a cover story about her fear of being trapped and an unbearable longing for care.

Sharon was talking about the maternal group therapy again, and how deeply it had changed her perspective. "Day one, I couldn't believe it, people were saying things out loud exactly like what I'd been thinking all my life, reading my mind or something. Telling the truth, no matter how bad it was. I realized . . . we all wished things had been different, and maybe we'll never be okay with what happened in the past, but at least . . . I'm not alone." We both sat with that idea for a quiet moment and then, to my surprise, she burst out laughing. "Alone! As if." Her hands were pressed to her stomach. "There's the kicking again!" She bent her head and spoke to her bump: "All right you, that's enough dancing!"

There was so much love and care in her body language and words that my final question might have seemed redundant, but I wanted to hear her response. How was she feeling about the new baby? If she'd given me an automatic, beaming "marvelous," I would have worried. I was reassured that she admitted to me she still had plenty of concerns about what would happen when it was born. She was realistic about the ongoing involvement of "the social" and was determined to work with Lisa and with Barbara, the unborn baby's court-appointed guardian *ad litem*, an older woman who had been helpful and kind and "seemed to know a lot about how babies feel and think."

Our meeting was drawing to a close. Sharon took out her phone, which reminded me that she'd not felt the need to fiddle with it during our session. She sent Simon a text to say she was done, and before she rose to go, I asked if she had any questions for me. She thought for a bit, nibbling her thumbnail in silence. "Are you going to write this down?" I set down my pad and pen on the table between us. "I worry," Sharon then said, "that I'll always be anxious about my baby's health, that I'll never feel safe with her or that she's going to be okay. D'you think that's true?" It was her first mention of the new baby's sex. "Her?" I asked. "Yeah, this one's a girl." She smiled.

She was posing such an enormous question to me, and the answer I could provide seemed so small in response. I told her that all parents worry about their children, especially their health, but she must remember that what went on in her mind wasn't necessarily the truth of the matter. As Kipling wrote, our feelings can deceive us, whether they are of triumph or disaster. This is why we need friends, families, and advisers of different kinds (including therapists, sometimes) to help us test reality and explore our emotions. Without that counterweight we can easily get overwhelmed. I told Sharon she could always seek out help, now that she knew its benefits. With a little grunt she eased her bulk out of the chair, thanking me again, before hurrying off to join her partner. I'm glad to say I've not seen her since.

I felt hopeful for Sharon as I sat down to prepare my third—and final—report on her. I outlined how unresolved grief and PTSD had disorganized Sharon's mind since childhood, affecting her mood regulation and her relationships with caregivers. But her problems were treatable, and she had got help. I wrote that I felt privileged to have borne witness to her progress, and I made the point that cases like hers testify to the fact that people can and do change their minds, if they get help, and that it need not take years for therapy to make a difference.

Privately, even though I had no evidence for it, I thought having a daughter might help Sharon to have more compassion for the part of her that still felt like a small, vulnerable girl. We are not Madonnas, those of us who bear children, and we are all works in progress. To prevent the cycle of pregnancy and care orders that Sharon had been through, professionals need to reach out to mothers, and not necessarily after they've already lost a child. There could be untold benefits to identifying those pregnant women who might struggle with motherhood and providing them with some therapy, along with their birthing classes and folic acid, as early as their first prenatal appointment. I'm certain the family courts would see their workload diminished and countless lives would be enhanced or even saved. I understand that enacting a measure like this might not be politically convenient or cheap, but as Walt Disney would say, this is the "work of heart."

SAM

The Thursday Group was just getting going when Sam joined in the conversation. He'd been with us for a few months but had said little so far. He tended to gaze past whoever was speaking, as if focused on something we couldn't see. Tall and thin, he was in his early forties but had the gangling quality of a pubescent boy and would sit hunched in his chair or stretch his long legs out to their full length in front of him, big feet crossed at the ankles. Conscious or not, the effect was of a barrier.

After three years' absence, I'd been asked to come back to Broadmoor as a part-time therapist, mostly to do some training, as well as covering absences. One of the reasons I had agreed was that I would be involved in group therapy. While I was training, I'd learned from Murray Cox, both directly and from his published work, about the importance of group therapy for offenders with mental illness. Not long after I'd started training as a group therapist, I'd attended a conference and visited a psychiatric hospital in Connecticut, where I observed American colleagues working in a therapy group for people who had killed a parent. I'd come back fired up by what I'd seen, with a new understanding of how valuable it could be for people to help each other find words to talk about their similar offenses and explore the impact on their families. It took some time but eventually, in cooperation with several colleagues, we did establish group therapy in the hospital, specifically for people who had killed members of their family. These groups had continued and expanded over time, and today I was working with some other therapists who were running one.

Group therapy is the "real McCoy" for a forensic psychothera-pist. It can be more rewarding than working individually because there's such a different dynamic; for one thing, I'm not the only person trying to understand what's going on. There are always two therapists in the room (sometimes three), plus the four or five patients working with us. The patients become one another's experts, in a sense, once the group gets established—the guiding principle is therapy "of the group by the group." I have read that early pioneers of group therapy in the US were known as "con-ductors," which seems a perfect analogy, including the fact that they keep the group "in time." This also reminds me of a com-ment about psychopaths I heard many years ago: that they "know the words but not the music" of emotional encounters. Therapists facilitating a group are not fellow musicians, yet we have author-ity and we guide them, while they create something which can be multilayered and strangely beautiful. As in many orchestras, a flattened hierarchy emerges over time, which only improves the result. I had always loved working with these groups and missed them when I left.

"I'm telling you, his wife's gonna find out any minute" . . . "Yeah, that neighbor will grass them up, you just know it" . . . "Remem-ber last week, he saw them in the pub . . ." Three of the men in the group, Tim, Benny, and Kaz, were talking about a television program they'd all watched the night before. As in most long-stay residential settings, custodial or not, TV is a social unifier between people who may have little in common beyond their identity as patients or inmates. In a secure environment, communal viewing also enables people to share different opinions and even to argue safely. In our group sessions, conversations about TV seemed to allow the men to ease themselves into the work. Usually their talk was of sports, particularly football, but they also liked to watch dramas, with crime being the preferred genre; I remember when *Dexter* (an American program about a forensic expert by day who becomes a serial killer by night) was a favorite.

As the chitchat went on, Sam looked restless, but he appeared to be listening. Kaz now deliberately tried to include him. "You been watching, Sam? This woman . . . she can't see what's in front of her face . . . thinks the sun shines out her husband's arse." Benny added, "It's all too lovey-dovey for me . . . there's no marriage like that." Sam cleared his throat, seemingly about to respond. He opened his mouth, but no words came. We all sat waiting, not breaking the moment. Those of us who had been in the group for longer than Sam, therapists and patients alike, recognized the change of atmosphere that can precede disclosure of an important thought.

I let the silence linger a little, then said quietly, "Sam?" He pushed a thick hank of dirty blond hair off his forehead. "I was just . . . I was going to say . . . my mum and dad were together nearly forty years. Childhood sweethearts. Never looked at anyone else, I reckon." His voice was flat and nasal, his tone impersonal, as if he too were commenting on characters in a drama. Tim, sitting opposite him, looked doubtful. "How can anyone know that for sure? I mean, people lie all the time . . ." Kaz cut in again, loud and confident in his opinion: "Some people just love each other, you know." Both comments were revealing of the speakers, but at this moment, I was focused on Sam's reaction. His face was hard to read. "My mum was nearly part of my index, you know." I noticed that he used the familiar jargon as a way of keeping the nature of his offense at bay, which wasn't unusual for people who were new to therapy. He went on, "I nearly . . ." His eyes met mine and he stopped. I nodded encouragement. "Nearly . . . ?"

He broke eye contact with me, looking down at the floor, and muttered, "I was in a hole. I had to dig myself out." One of my colleagues spoke up, her soft northern lilt coming in like a harmony. "How did you dig yourself out, Sam?" He threw her a sideways glance. "It was . . . I was ill." We waited, but he had nothing more. This was the first time he'd spoken about his offense, the murder of his father ten years earlier. I said that what he'd told us sounded important and perhaps we could come back to it later. His contribution then sparked a thoughtful conversation among the other three men about their own parents' relationships, and their various emotions thickened the atmosphere, just as a piece of music can.

As the end of our group's hour approached, Sam stood up abruptly, shoving his chair aside. "It's time to go." My colleague said Sam was right, it was time, but we all wanted to acknowledge what he'd shared earlier with us. "It felt like you took a big step today, Sam." I thought he might respond to her, but he was spent, done for the day. The men filed out to join the waiting nurse who would escort them back to the ward. I saw Kaz touch Sam on the shoulder as they went and heard him softly say, "Well done, mate." Sam didn't respond, but he didn't pull away; that was a good sign. I hoped he would feel brave enough to tell us more about his parents in subsequent sessions, but I knew it might take some time.

We cannot insist that people attend any type of therapy in a forensic context. The group was not right for everyone; I recall one man who adamantly refused to join when we invited him, insisting, "I didn't kill anyone. You can dig my brother up and ask him if you don't believe me." Resistance can also come from a fear of the unknown, which is an ordinary kind of human anxiety that we all know. Another patient I had approached to join the group asked nervously, "Can you tell me what I'll know at the end?" Most offenders will come to realize that talking about their offense with a therapist demonstrates a willingness to try and reduce risk, and some will agree to attend a group to tick that box, to go through the motions. But this is where our group really came into its own. More like an essay than a multiple-choice test, the agenda was set by the group members, and the right answer, or the socially desirable thing to say, was not obvious. Those people who just wanted to tick a box soon dropped out when they realized they would be faced with people like themselves who knew what it was to kill. In Sam's case, once he had stabilized following his prison transfer, with the help of medication and some time, he had agreed to attend the group. He had expressed some reluctance but chose it in preference to one-on-one therapy. Colleagues told me he had admitted to killing his father but had never talked about its meaning for him. He had spent years in a kind of mental isolation, which must have been painful. As a colleague of mine observed, insanity is building your own castle in the air and living in it; we're offering to take down the drawbridge.

I recall some anguished professional debate at the outset about what we should call the group. The first proposal was the blunt title of the Homicide Group, but some people felt that "outing" people's histories in this way would be difficult and could put patients off joining. The therapy group at the hospital in Connecticut for people who had killed their parents had a poetic name, selected by the members: the Genesis Group. I recall thinking at the time what a hopeful choice that was. Its gifted "conductors," my American colleagues Marc Hillbrand and John Young, have long been inspirational writers on the theme of hope in forensic settings.[1] But there were plenty of other therapy groups in Broadmoor with explicit titles—from Sexual Offenders Group to Leavers Group—and so we agreed on the Homicide Group. Later, as demand increased and we began to run two weekly sessions, this evolved into the Thursday Group and the Friday Group. I reckon the ten years or so that I spent involved with these groups were some of the best of my professional life, thoughtful, challenging, moving, and not without humor.

Early on, we could see that things functioned best if we restricted the groups to four or five men at most, as opposed to the ten or fifteen that were more common in group therapy. There was something important about it being a "family-sized" unit. We also decided to have at least three therapists involved on rotation so that we could keep continuity through sickness or holidays. Security concerns required two of us to be in the room at all times, but it soon became clear that our safety was not an issue. Nobody was there to make trouble.

I've said that the people I work with are like survivors of a disaster where they are the disaster, and much like other survivors they can struggle with the language needed to describe unspeakable memories. Unlike with trauma survivors, we do not ask them to process painful memories by rehearsing every last thing that happened in great detail. Rather, we invite them to deepen their understanding of what they did by articulating their story aloud to the group and being willing to hear others do the same. Sometimes they've never been asked to speak in this way, outside of a specific legal framework which focuses on motive, method, and developing a defense. Being a member of a group like this can reduce their emotional isolation, and they can learn from one another how to live with their changed identities.[2] No one is suggesting to them that the past doesn't exist. British psychoanalyst Caroline Garland puts it bluntly: this recovery process is about "getting on with it, not getting over it."[3]

After the group session is over, the therapists always sit down together over a welcome cup of coffee and make notes on the themes discussed, and share and reflect on what we've experienced. On the day that Sam first mentioned his parents, one of my colleagues asked if we knew whether he had spoken to anyone about his mother before or if she was still in contact with him since his conviction for the murder of his father. As it happened, I told them, I had met with Sam's mother, Judith, in the past, as part of my medico-legal work. I knew she was still in touch with her son and visiting him regularly. It's understandable that some family members will cut off contact in cases like this, unable to find a way to be with the perpetrator, but I'm always moved when people can continue to care for their relative and stay in their lives. It is usually the mothers who are the ones to stand by their troubled "child," whatever their offspring's age and no matter what has happened.

When Sam's criminal trial was over, Judith had brought a negligence case in civil court against the mental health services trust that was looking after Sam at the time of the murder. I was asked by her lawyers to assess whether she had suffered mental health problems as a result of the trust's failure to warn her of Sam's release and the tragic consequences. This was well before I came back to Broadmoor and met Sam, who had served a few years of his prison sentence before his mental health deteriorated and he was transferred to the secure hospital for treatment. I remembered Judith's case well, as it raised significant ethical issues about confidentiality and risk. It had been publicly reported, so I was able to give my colleagues some background about what had happened and how it might bear on what Sam had said in the group session that day.

Sam was one of a subset of chronically mentally ill young people, usually male, who are revolving-door patients in our mental health services. The cycle begins in early adolescence, when psychotic symptoms first emerge, typically hallucinations or delusions and other types of reality distortion. Sometimes medication is helpful, sometimes it's not; it can stop hallucinations, but it cannot erase grief or fear, as the author and mental health nurse Nathan Filer has described so movingly.[4] Teenagers in particular can be reluctant to take their "meds" due to unpleasant side effects or because they are in denial that they have a problem. Some, including Sam, will turn to drugs and alcohol to ease psychotic symptoms and cope with painful feelings. Widely available substances like skunk (high-potency cannabis) or cocaine only worsen their mental state, causing a paranoia that may lead to acute mental crises and periods of involuntary detention in a hospital. There they may be violent to professionals, with mental health nurses most at risk of assault. It's ironic that the few times I have been assaulted in my long career were in general psychiatric wards, and not in prisons or high-security units. In Sam's case, he did try to assault his caregivers on a few occasions, but his target was his family, which is unsurprising;[5] as we've seen, much violence is relational, whether or not the perpetrator is mentally ill.

When his sister and his peers were heading for university or finding jobs and having romantic relationships, Sam was left behind. If anyone had been studying his progress on a map, as meteorologists might track an extreme weather event, it would have been plain that he was gathering force out at sea and might wreak havoc when he made landfall, with his family as the almost inevitable target. "Almost" is the operative word: just as hurricanes can change course or fluctuate in intensity, averting catastrophe, so can acute mental states, with some intervention. But Sam could not or would not get the help he needed, and his episodes of violence escalated until they "peaked" with the murder of his father.

I explained to my colleagues how Judith and I had met some three years after the tragedy, since this type of civil litigation takes far longer to come to court than criminal cases. This was not a big coincidence, as they knew: I work in the only high-security hospital in the region where Sam's offense occurred and where his prison was located, and I also take on some legal work from time to time, as I have described in Sharon's case. Some overlap is uncommon, but it can happen. I'd been asked to see Judith because of my experience working in trauma clinics and interest in the impact of murder on families. Her legal team were particularly focused on evidence of her long-term trauma; recent research by American colleagues had suggested that people bereaved by homicide could have intense and atypical grief reactions that persisted for years, resembling symptoms of PTSD.[6] My job was to hear Judith's story, examine her medical records, make a diagnosis and comment on treatment. I never saw Sam as part of this work, nor would there have been reason to do so. Unlike in a general psychiatric setting, where we have the usual hour (or fifty minutes), I could take all the time we needed. As I recalled, it was a thoughtful interview and I had the impression of a woman with real dignity and grace.

I remembered her as a slight woman in her sixties, with pallid skin almost the same color as her short hair. She was Englishly stoic at first, then tearful and in pain as our interview progressed. She told me she had worked in the HR department of an accounting firm for many years, before her husband was killed. Ever since then, she had been signed off work by her doctor, and the resulting loss of income formed part of her injury claim against the hospital that had been looking after Sam at the time of the homicide. She went on to tell me how she and her husband Ralph had met in their late teens and fallen in love. They had always wanted two children, and Sam was the younger, born when his sister Caroline was three. Judith smiled fondly as she recalled what an easy baby he had been and how happy he was as a little boy.

But the smiles receded when she described Sam's transformation during puberty. At first, she and Ralph had thought his "acting up" was just typical adolescent boy stuff, but he became more and more unhappy and agitated as he moved through his teens and started to be aggressive toward them. All adolescents struggle with their parents to some extent, experiencing the internal tug-of-war between need and separation, but those feelings are much aggravated by mental illness, and Sam was beginning to exhibit signs that would eventually lead to a diagnosis of schizophrenia.

His parents were not quick to grasp that possibility, and when the school suspended Sam for smoking cannabis, for a while they decided that must be the problem. He was increasingly confused and frightened, and appeared to be talking and listening to "voices."

Auditory verbal hallucinations (AVHs) are probably one of the most familiar symptoms associated with psychotic illnesses. It's a fascinating phenomenon, and not well understood. It's not the case that AVHs are always an indicator of enduring mental illness, and they can be positive and comforting in religious contexts or when people describe hearing the voice of a deceased loved one (there's been some interesting work on this by a group called the Hearing Voices Network). One time, Judith had asked Sam what the voices sounded like. She admitted to me that she imagined they might have different accents or genders, a common misconception she'd picked up from seeing lurid films about people with "multiple personalities." "They sound like me, Mum," her son had told her, staring at her as if that were obvious. Other patients of mine have described to me a series of inchoate mumbles or whispers that are hard to discern, which could explain why people experiencing AVHs may appear to be concentrating intensely as they struggle to hear. However, in severe mental illness, most patients say that the voices are nearly always negative and might include opaque commands like "You know what you have to do." It's also common for the voice to speak in the third person, as in "Sam's going to die soon" or "Everyone hates Sam." Despite some famous cases of violent offenders claiming they heard the "devil's voice" (or God's) telling them to act, it's comparatively rare to hear a specific order like "Kill yourself" or "Kill them," and of course, people don't always do what these hallucinatory commands tell them.

Judith and Ralph took Sam to their GP and described what was happening, which eventually led to an appointment with the Child and Adolescent Mental Health Services (CAMHS), where Sam got some support from a specialist team for young people with psychosis. But he was reluctant to take prescribed medication, complaining that it made him feel nauseous and "numb," including a loss of libido that felt both unfair and alien to a boy of his age. After he turned eighteen, he came under the aegis of the adult mental health services and his parents were no longer updated about the details of his care, which would be considered a breach of confidentiality since he was no longer a minor. But he was living in their home, and they were in a constant state of worry. He would get into highly paranoid states and sometimes accused them of plotting against him. On one occasion he had torn apart his sister Caroline's room, looking for something he said she had stolen or hidden from him, smashing her things and terrifying her to the point where she decided to move out and live with friends, which her parents encouraged. When Sam "came to," as Judith put it, he was acutely distressed by what he had done and unable to explain himself, which was immensely frustrating. This kind of episode is typical of a "psychotic break," in which the sufferer is disconnected from reality by their paranoid beliefs.

Sam could also be tearful, hopeless, and needy. Judith's eyes welled up as she recalled how he would come to her and sob that he had nothing in his life and how much he wished he was "normal" like his peers and had a girlfriend or plans for his future. With his parents' encouragement, he would occasionally try to work with rehabilitation services in the community, but his symptoms always returned and he'd revert to being paranoid and surly, especially when he was smoking strong forms of cannabis, such as what's called skunk in the UK. A pattern of relapsing psychotic episodes took hold which became increasingly difficult to tolerate. It sounded like Judith and Ralph's love for their son was unflagging throughout this period, even when he became violent toward them. Judith called the police on one occasion, when Sam hit Ralph and nearly broke his arm, but they hadn't wanted to press charges. Their hopes were raised when Sam got a specialist placement in a rehab hostel, where there was occupational therapy and other interventions available to help him. For a while, things improved, but he would turn up sporadically at the family home to ask for money or complain about life at the hostel, and after some tense and frightening standoffs, Ralph and Judith were persuaded to take out a restraining order against him.

This brought them a little peace, Judith said, but less contact with Sam meant almost no news about his condition. He was going in and out of the hospital, they knew, after losing his place in the hostel, and he had spent some time living on the street, which made his parents feel guilty and worried. Now and then, when he was an inpatient, they would be invited to participate in case reviews at the hospital, but if Sam refused to have them there, they had to leave. They let the medical team know that they would continue to support him as best they could, but they could not have him back in the family home because of the violence. I had the impression that they had been caught in a middle ground between acceptance of their powerlessness and an unwillingness to detach fully from a son they had already lost many years ago.

Not long before the murder, they had written to his consultant detailing the history of Sam's abusive behavior toward them and asking if he needed long-term care in a psychiatric hospital, although they knew they had no role in that decision. There was little to no chance that would happen. It is not widely understood that the old system of asylums or long-term care for the mentally ill is long gone in the UK (and also around the world); in the NHS, the average length of stay in a psychiatric unit bed is three weeks. Following the anti-psychiatry movement of the 1970s, and as part of the general antigovernment zeitgeist of the era and the austerity that followed, Britain and most social democracies adopted the idea of social integration of mentally ill and learning-disabled people, transitioning to a system of "care in the community." This meant that the burden of care fell on the family, since community services were (and remain) drastically underfunded. This is yet another manifestation of the disproportionate and misguided emphasis our society places on physical health over mental health, and possibly the gravest example.

A dear friend of mine who experienced the tragic conjunction of her husband's serious cancer diagnosis and her teenage son's developing symptoms of schizophrenia similar to Sam's described to me the stark difference in their experiences as patients, and the hollow meaning of "care in the community" in practice. Health service providers rallied around her husband, with fulsome provisions for treatment and assurances that these would be available for as long as he lived, for which the family were grateful. Meanwhile, her son, whose mental state was disintegrating fast, had almost no options for treatment, and those that arose were limited and ineffective.

Judith's experience was not dissimilar, and it was exacerbated by the fact that she felt unmoored from her son's care in his adult life, when she was no longer privy to most of the details of his diagnosis or treatment. Her language had begun to falter as she recalled for me the last few occasions when she had seen Sam, perhaps two or three times in that final year before the murder. He had turned thirty, she said, though he always looked young for his age. She worried about him being so shaky and sweaty, which she was told was due to his meds, and it was heartrending that he always seemed so sad. Her composure returned when she began to describe the homicide itself, I noticed, probably because this was a narrative she would have had to revisit many times over for various professionals.

She described how Sam had arrived at the house one night when they thought he was still in the hospital and let himself in through the back door, which they had left unlocked. Ralph had been washing dishes after dinner; she was in the utility room just off the kitchen, doing some laundry, when she heard shouting—Ralph's raised voice and Sam swearing at him, demanding money. She ran in and saw the two men struggling together, locked in a fight. She had gone to dial 999 (the UK equivalent of 911), when, to her horror, she saw Sam grab a rolling pin from the jar of utensils by the stove and aim it at Ralph's head. She dropped the phone and tried to intervene, but Sam swatted her away with great force and she hit the wall and fell to the ground; she heard her arm break with an audible crack. She also banged her head hard and blood was dribbling into her eyes. But she did see and hear Sam kicking Ralph viciously, over and over, as he lay unconscious on the floor. "I think I passed out then," she said tonelessly.

Sam ran away from the scene, but he was picked up by the police almost immediately and confessed to the crime. He was soon charged and remanded to prison. He went on to be convicted of murder, receiving a mandatory life sentence in prison.

This was a little surprising to me, given his psychiatric history, which might have suggested the lesser verdict of manslaughter, but the two psychiatrists who assessed Sam for the trial did not agree about whether he was unwell at the time of the killing. The jury had clearly preferred the evidence of the psychiatrist for the prosecution and found Sam guilty of murder, which meant that there was only one sentence the judge could pass.

Judith's testimony was also relevant; she had heard Sam demand money from his father, and the prosecution emphasized Sam's history of being abusive and violent to his parents when he needed money for drugs. The mental health history in this case was not wholly ignored by the jury, but it is complex to distinguish between sane and insane motives in a case like this, and you never know how a jury will decide. If Sam did become mentally unwell in prison, he could get some kind of treatment, and if his condition was bad enough, he would be transferred to a secure hospital. Ten years after the murder of his father, this is what happened. As part of his treatment, and with his agreement, he started work in our Homicide Group.

Judith's negligence case looked simple on paper: the hospital trust had a duty of care to Sam and breached it by failing to assess his risk properly. They had compounded this by allowing him community leave from the ward when they knew his behavior could be dangerous. They did not warn his family that he was allowed out, nor that he had absconded. That breach had caused harm to both Sam and his family, and therefore they ought to be able to claim damages in respect of that harm. The hospital's position was that they had no legal duty to Sam's family, only to their patient. They pointed to the fact that the criminal court had concluded he was not mentally ill at the time of the homicide. It was not their legal duty to prevent him from harming others, and under the Mental Health Act they had an obligation to care for him using "least restrictive practice." At the time of the homicide, Sam had been assessed as being of minimal risk and was on an open ward, where community leave was both normal and inevitable as part of the treatment protocol. It was true that he had gone AWOL, but that had happened with him during other hospital stays without his seeking out his parents or doing anything harmful to anyone. The medical team had no way of knowing he would go home or try to hurt his parents, and there was no legal requirement to contact them when he was found to be absent. In fact, to do so would have been a breach of Sam's right to control the disclosure of his private information, a familiar concept we all know as "doctor–patient confidentiality."

There is a general consensus in the medical profession that in certain circumstances, such as when a serious enough risk of harm exists, it is justifiable to break a confidence. The question in Sam's case was whether this was one of those instances, and whether there had been a proper process of looking at the risk and potential harm of not disclosing. I thought his caregivers could have justified disclosing to his parents that Sam was at liberty, and I had a number of pieces of evidence to support this. I also maintained that respecting patient confidentiality has never been synonymous with absolute secrecy.[7]

Probably the most famous example demonstrating this is *Tarasoff v. Regents of the University of California*, wryly known as "the case that launched a thousand writs."[8] Tatiana Tarasoff was a student at the University of California, Berkeley, who was murdered by Prosenjit Poddar, a fellow student who had become depressed after he tried to pursue a romantic relationship with her, which she reportedly rejected. Notably, this is one of the first recorded cases of "stalking behavior" (before it was known as such) as the precursor of a fatal assault. Poddar sought therapy for his depression, and when he revealed to the campus psychologist that he was having thoughts of killing Tatiana, they were so concerned they notified the campus police. Poddar was briefly questioned and detained, but he appeared to be rational and promised to leave Tatiana alone. After he was released, he terminated therapy at once and never went back. Three months later, he went to the young woman's home, where he shot and stabbed her to death.

The lawsuit her parents subsequently brought against the university and its employees alleged that they had failed in their duty to protect Tatiana and claimed that the psychologist should have breached Poddar's confidentiality and warned their daughter. The suit was initially dismissed for "lack of cause," but the Tarasoffs persisted, all the way to the state's Supreme Court, which concluded that the university was immune from the lawsuit but that the Tarasoffs' claim could succeed against the individual psychologist, who had failed in their "duty to warn" the potential victim. There were vociferous protests from the psychiatric community, which argued that patients' trust was essential, and people would be put off if they thought their information might be shared with third parties. Unusually, the Supreme Court reviewed its decision, but the second verdict supported the original view, with only slight modifications. It stated that if a therapist believes their patient poses a danger to a third party, then they "bear a duty to exercise reasonable care to protect the foreseeable victim from that danger" and that "therapeutic privilege ends where public peril begins." A wave of similar *Tarasoff* laws followed around the US, and even though American law is not operative in the UK, many cases relating to confidentiality here have referenced *Tarasoff*, and the GMC swiftly adopted guidelines about disclosures "in the public interest." Even now, *Tarasoff* continues to be an important benchmark in the international discourse about confidentiality.

In the opinion I wrote about Judith's case, I argued that the team looking after Sam had not followed established guidance about confidentiality or properly considered the risk to his family. I was not saying that they were bad people or bad doctors, only that they had made a mistake, as we humans do. They had not fully considered the circumstances in which they could breach confidentiality and had made a faulty risk assessment when they allowed a patient like Sam to have community leave and failed to inform his parents. The result was tragic not only for the victims, but also for Sam.

After submitting my report, I had to meet with the medical expert for the defendants. Dr. B and I agreed on the basic facts, namely that Sam had been mentally unwell but had been doing better in the lead-up to the homicide, as borne out by the fact that he had been moved to an open ward and granted some leave, prior to his "escape." We disagreed about the risk he posed to his family. Dr. B said there was no prior evidence of any danger, whereas

I referred to his parents' letter to the consultant, which outlined several examples of historical violence toward them and suggested that Sam needed to be held in long-term care. I did concede that he was not known to have made any threats to his parents in the last few months before the homicide, but it was arbitrary to base the risk assessment only on that period rather than on the whole back-story of Sam's life and illness. His parents were named as identifiable people in his circle who could be seen as "at risk," and that was enough to justify at least a discussion about warning them, using both the GMC and similar NHS guidelines as professional cover.

Dr. B felt differently, saying there was not enough evidence to support my contentions and justify information-sharing, and he believed the hospital would have been subject to complaints and even legal action by Sam had they gone ahead. I responded that the medical team looking after Sam had involved Judith and Ralph in their clinical case reviews in the lead-up to the homicide. When Sam had not returned to the hospital from leave at the agreed time, alerting his parents might have helped prevent or reduce the risk of harm to them—I was thinking of that unlocked back door at their home. We were able to agree that it *was* usual practice to involve the immediate family in community leave decisions; it was just that Dr. B suggested it was also reasonable practice *not* to do so. We set out our views in a joint statement and waited to see what would happen next. Either the case would go to trial or, more commonly, the litigants would reach a financial settlement on an undisclosed basis. Judith's lawyers accurately predicted that the case would proceed due to its potential wider import; it might set a difficult precedent if it were settled out of court—and who knew how many similar suits would follow?

On the day I was called to testify, I donned my court suit, of the same black, severely cut style favored by lawyers. Expert witnesses spend a lot of time and effort on creating their court "look," and there are even expensive professional development courses that give guidance on how to do this. It would be foolish to pretend that appearances don't count. I have found that blending in with the sober courtroom costume is a way of communicating that

I understand my role in context, which is to assist the court by showing where my opinion fits with the legal questions. Although I had been retained by Judith's team, my duty was to the court, not "the cause." It was the judge that mattered most; their understanding was paramount.

There is a lot of waiting around in court, but finally my turn came. I stood and took the oath. There are secular versions these days, but I chose to use the traditional language, "so help me God." The job of the counsel for the hospital was to challenge my conclusions and undermine my arguments, in the nicest possible way. Good lawyers don't get excited or make dramatic gestures and statements. The best ones gently but firmly take you down a line of argument that, if you're not careful, can lead to you contradicting your own opinion or saying something you don't really mean. The counsel for the hospital trust began, "Dr. Adshead, isn't there a public interest in keeping patient confidentiality? If so, why do you say it should have been breached in this case?" She went on in this vein: "You state that the plaintiff should have been told about her son's community leave, but on what grounds?" "You accepted that there was no evidence that the patient posed a risk to his parents on the day in question, is that correct?" "And you accepted that the medical team held a view that was within the bounds of reasonable medical practice?" "If your more extreme view was accepted, then no psychiatric patients would have a claim to confidentiality. Isn't that discriminatory, and might it not cause some people, or their carers, to avoid seeking necessary medical assistance at all?" This went on for a few hours, which wasn't bad— I've known experts to be questioned like this for days.

Her parting shot was to draw attention to the fact that I was a forensic psychiatrist and had been working in Broadmoor for most of my career. "You haven't practiced much as a general psychiatrist, Dr. Adshead, have you? In fact, you've worked mainly with highly dangerous mentally ill people, many of whom have committed terrible and violent offenses, correct? Surely that has an effect on your perception of the degree of perceived 'risk'"— at this point, she allowed herself a little "scare quotes" gesture for the benefit of the judge. All of this is the usual stuff of cross-examination. My job is to stick to my view and explain that while counsel's questions may be interesting, they don't undermine my opinion. I try not to appear dogmatic and remain equable at all times, even in the face of more provocative questioning, but we don't always know how we come across in court. The outcome of a case can depend on how the judge is feeling that day, and how anxious they are about how the case appears to the public eye.

I felt for the psychiatrist who had made the decision to give Sam community leave, even as I recognized that more weight ought to have been given to their duty to warn. All psychiatrists have to make risk assessments of their patients, knowing that once in a great while things do go badly wrong and those outlier cases will draw a lot of public attention and professional censure. It has not happened to me yet, but people I've known well have been at the center of such calamities and I have seen the toll it takes on them. The stories always start in such ordinary, uncontroversial ways. I remember years ago, when one of my own general hospital patients went missing while on leave, like Sam had. He was being treated for mental illness and had a history of violence, but at that time, he appeared to be making good progress. The clinical team had been in agreement with me that he could have community leave, and when the nurse informed me that he hadn't returned on time and they were calling the police, I was deeply alarmed. "This is how it begins," I remember thinking, with a terrible knot in my stomach. I braced myself for the emergence of news of the worst kind—as well as the juggernaut of condemnation that was going to follow.

As it happened, the man was found and returned to the ward before anything happened. But I still remember vividly how shaken I was, knowing full well that if he had taken drugs and perhaps got into a fight where he landed an unlucky blow, the morning papers would have been busy branding him a "monster," and along with his victim and their family, I would have been connected with the tragedy for evermore. It was hard not to feel vulnerable and ashamed; if it had gone wrong, there would have been a mandatory inquiry into my role, as his responsible clinician, in the decision to allow him to leave secure care, and the press would have read this as incompetence or worse. If the inquiry had found that I had made a mistake, I would likely have been reported to the GMC and would have faced both losing my license to practice and a potential civil action. I knew of one case like this where the victim's family had made death threats to the psychiatrist involved, with a devastating impact on the doctor and their family. In another instance, a photo of the psychiatrist involved was splashed all over the national papers, under headlines like "Appalling Blunder," and they were branded as "The doctor who let killer out of hospital" and "put killer's rights before public safety."

Judith lost her case against the hospital. The court found that the team treating Sam had no duty to prevent harm to her or Ralph, and while a mistake may have been made in his risk assessment, the duty to care for Sam had not been breached. I wasn't surprised; the law always prefers certainties and clear evidence that can be analyzed and tested. Such a framework doesn't allow much room for addressing questions of duty between humans in close relationships, where there is always some emotional ambiguity and a shifting moral horizon. I understood that the court was ultimately not prepared to touch the difficult question of third-party duty of care, but I did question why there was no recognition that the harm he did to his parents would affect Sam's own health dearly for years to come. When I encountered him in the hospital, long after this verdict, he was only beginning to grapple with the implications.

As I've described throughout this book, in order to reduce people's risk, therapists need to help them talk about their history and what happened when the "bicycle lock" clicked open for them; in our Homicide Group, this meant the moment of fatal violence. Only by describing this could members of our group take agency for their actions, which is usually marked by a move from a passive to an active voice in their self-narratives. That progression was first described to me when I was training with Murray Cox, my mentor, who loved the metaphor of the dark lamp (as I mentioned in the Introduction) and paid such exquisite attention to language. He described how a patient moves from "I don't know what you're talking about" to "It wasn't me" to "It was me, but

I was mentally ill at the time" to "I did it when I was mentally ill," until they finally land on "I did it." Cox called this coming to terms with one's actions a *"scala integrata."* Today, when I work with trainees, I describe this process as a *via dolorosa*, where every mental footstep is painful and sometimes all a therapist can do is be a companion on the journey.

After the Homicide Group session where Sam had first mentioned his parents' long marriage, he thawed some more and was able to talk about them more freely, when prompted by the dynamic in the group. On one occasion the men came in talking about the reality TV show *Big Brother* and their dislike of the idea that viewers were watching for people to fail, judging them in order to vote them out. This led to a fascinating discussion of how they each felt about the lack of privacy in prison and the hospital. Kaz joked that the female therapists were like Big Sisters, not only watching them all the time, but scrutinizing their every word. Before I could explore that comparison, with its authoritarian and punitive connotations, any further, Sam joined in. He talked about how as a teen he used to feel as if he were "behind a glass wall," constantly watched and worried over by his hyper-anxious parents, who treated him like he was a baby all the time. The way he told it, it seemed as if they were neither his parents nor his victims but people he didn't know, members of an anonymous audience. But gradually, as he went on, I sensed he was moving along Murray Cox's *scala integrata*: he was beginning to take some personal responsibility.

After nearly a year, he arrived at a point where he no longer referred to his offense as his "index" but was able to say, "When I killed my dad . . ." It is always quite a moment when someone manages this transition, and I remember well the day it happened. He started by describing the morning of the day of the murder, a cool day in October, a decade earlier. He recalled his relief when he managed to get away from his nursing escort after they left the hospital grounds to go to the corner shop. He said he walked quickly at first, looking back over his shoulder, then broke into a run to put as much distance as he could between him and the hospital. After a while, he realized he was approaching the area where his parents lived. He wasn't ready to go there, so he made his way to an abandoned building down by the river where he knew a few guys. He was sweating and desperate for a drink, and someone gave him a lager and a pill—he wasn't sure what it was. He'd lost some time, maybe passed out for a bit, he told us. When he woke, there were sirens, police, flashing lights, and the others were scattering in all directions. He was disoriented and afraid, but he got away without being caught. He turned toward his parents' house. Sam paused at this point, I remember, and answered the question forming in my mind before I could ask it: "I don't know why . . . I guess it was home." It was late by that time, he said, and he slipped around the back of the house. He saw through the window that his dad was making tea in the kitchen and his mum was in the utility room doing some ironing.

He said he stood outside watching for a while, "like it was a movie or something," and I pictured him out there in the cold night, observing the domestic scene within. I imagined a view of Judith and Ralph chatting in pantomime, she perhaps enlisting his help in folding some sheets. I could understand how their homey companionship might have seemed to Sam as remote and exclusive as anything Hollywood could manufacture. He didn't elaborate on what in particular irked him about the tableau through the window, but he told us he got cold and started to feel angry. He approached the back door to look for the spare key under the planter, but then tried the door and found it was open. At that point in his tale Sam paused to take a deep breath, and we all sat quietly, waiting for him to go on, sensing that the next part might be hard for him and for us. As so often happened in that group, I felt the awesome responsibility of bearing witness to horror. Eventually, after we had held our silence for a few minutes, I thought he might feel he'd said enough for one day. Nonetheless, I asked, "Sam, do you want to say any more?"

"I want a drink," he blurted, abrupt and loud. At first, I thought he was talking about now, but no, he was back in that garden at home, speaking of himself in the historic present. His eyes were unfocused, fixed on the blank white wall behind my head. "I need money. I need to get some coke. I'm sleepy, I'm cold . . . I'm afraid." He furrowed his brow and wrapped his arms around himself as he said this, his voice tense and low. "I think someone's followed me, man. The police are after me, I have to get inside, hide my face. I can't see my mum and my dad . . . There's my dad." He swallowed hard, then went on: "He's looking at me like I'm the worst thing that's ever happened to him . . . He's not best pleased. I mean, he looks fucking terrified, and I'm thinking, 'That's not right, you shouldn't be scared, you should be glad to see me, I'm your son.'"

His speech was accelerating. Everyone in the group sat perfectly still, letting the story flow into the space between us. This quiet collaboration of listeners, like a silent orchestra following a lone oboe solo, their bows or instruments poised in midair, is quite remarkable to experience. In a group like this, after years of practice, I know when to set aside my conductor's baton and let things flow. "So Dad's saying, 'Sam? What are you doing here? You're meant to be in hospital.' And now I'm thinking, 'That's not much of a welcome, is it? Hasn't even asked how I'm doing or anything.' I'm fucking angry, and I'm thinking, you know, 'He's probably the one that called the police on me.' And then he says, 'Sammy'—like when I was a teenager, that babyish stupid nickname—'Sammy, I think you should go.' And I'm thinking, 'Man, that's it, even my dad hates me now.'"

I didn't take my eyes off Sam, but I heard one of the other patients let out a sort of half gasp, releasing a little bubble of the tension I expect we were all feeling. Sam bent over in his chair, elbows on his knees, rubbing at his face with his hands as if to scrub away his features. I thought he might be working up the courage to keep going, and I was filled with a sense of sadness and dread that was almost theatrical, like that feeling of watching Medea or Macbeth, when you know what's coming and whisper to yourself, "Oh no, don't do it . . ."

After a bit, Kaz leaned over and said, "You okay, mate? Need some water?" Sam nodded, and one of my co-therapists got up, went to the water cooler, and passed him a cup. He downed it in a gulp. Then he looked up at the ceiling, then over at the clock on the wall, which never told the correct time—anywhere but at one of us. "I don't think I can say any more right now," he said hoarsely. Tim spoke up: "You only have to say what you can—we've all been there." And then Benny, another patient, added his two cents: "It took me years, man. Don't worry, we know how it gets too real." I was touched by their support, and maybe Sam was too, because he was able to continue. I noticed he moved into the past tense at that point, as if he needed a little distance in order to get to the end. I made a particular effort to commit his language to memory, but there was little danger I'd forget its devastating and simple eloquence.

"So that was it. That's when I killed my dad. I don't remember it all, but I know I started hitting him, grabbed something and started bashing him. And then Mum was there screaming at me, and I pushed her away and she hit the wall with sort of a cracking sound . . . and then there was nothing but me hitting my dad. And then no sound. It was like the world fell away. I was frozen there, standing over him, and he was lying there in this puddle of blood. I remember I looked around and thought, 'This is it, this is the end of everything.' " Sam dropped his head into his hands then, and I let a pause linger to see if he had anything more to say, but he was silent. Then I looked around the group and asked if anyone had anything they wanted to say to Sam. Nobody spoke. "Perhaps the rest is silence," I said. Not all revelation needs a response, and maybe no words matter when someone describes how they have shattered their world.

Later, after the session was over, I suggested to my colleagues that the fact this had all played out in his childhood home made things worse for Sam, as if the past were his only safe place and now even that was closed to him. We talked about the "bicycle lock" combination that had clicked into place that night, all those risk factors lining up, and if the final "number" was the look of fear in his father's eye—or just an intolerable feeling of not being the person he wanted to be.

I've often thought about Sam and Judith since then, and whether his final fatal violence could have been averted. I still share my colleagues' and the courts' concerns about the protection of patient privacy, but I think we need to approach the question of confidentiality in a new way. Mental illness is a family affair; can we make risk management more of a cooperative effort between all those affected by it? This case forcefully brought home to me that for all the lip service paid to care in the community for the mentally ill, it still seems to be nobody's job to look after their caregivers and family. In an era when privacy and personal information have been monetized to such an extent by social media and marketeers, perhaps we could create a counterweight in the realm of health and safety. It isn't always necessary to treat privacy like Gollum's "Precious," and certainly not in cases like this.[9] There need not be a competition between people like Sam and his parents about who owns or has access to his medical information.

In the absence of such cooperation, Sam's parents were landed with a new identity that they never chose, as victims of his violence. And now Sam himself is defined as a member of an extremely small group of people who have both a mental illness diagnosis and a homicide conviction, a complex identity that resonates with pain. How is he meant to go forward? I was heartened recently when one of our Homicide Group members diverted from the usual banter about escapist television programs and announced that he'd been reading a good book, given to him by a fellow patient. He smiled at me and said, "It's right up your street, Dr. Gwen. It's by a man called Viktor Frankl who was in a concentration camp, and it's all about finding meaning in places like that . . . or places like this."[10] He gestured widely with his arm, taking in the drab meeting room and the little circle of men and staff, as well as the whole institution.

I had never mentioned Frankl to the group by name, but that patient was spot-on: the premise that all suffering has meaning *was* right up my street, wherever that is. I always stand in awe when someone takes ownership of a life-and-death story and there arises a shared sense of hope that radiates outward, allowing meaning and purpose to come from catastrophe. In this way, as one of my patients in the Homicide Group pointed out, people who have killed can make something of themselves, even if they face many years in prison, "otherwise two lives are lost rather than one."

I thought of Judith, faithfully visiting her son for years after the loss of her husband, and how the difficult work Sam had undertaken in our group might lighten her load because it had eased his pain more than any medication. I have spoken about how a new thought can provide hope, opening a new door in the mind. This is not a special insight of mine; hope is well known to be vital to well-being, and to all kinds of recovery. It is considered the main curative factor in group therapy, because once you step through that door, you realize you are not alone. Hope relies on this kind of connection. Grasping this is not only necessary for our patients, or for those who work with them—it is profoundly important for everyone.

DAVID

I share my private consulting room on rotation with other thera-pists. It is a pleasant spot, warm and light, and I like it because it is such a different environment from the prison and the hospi-tal. There are soft furnishings, the walls are not painted a uniform dirty white, and above all there are no locks and no alarms, no constant anticipation of danger. I've reduced my workload these days, but I continue to work as a therapist in secure settings within the NHS a few days a week, alongside some writing, teaching, and medico-legal work. Very occasionally, I will see a private patient. Like most NHS doctors, I do not have a private practice as such, which I'm aware is a contrast to the situation in the US, where most psychiatrists and psychotherapists are sole proprietors of a private therapy business who may also be affiliated with a hospital or other institution. In the NHS, we aren't prohibited from having private patients, but there are only so many hours in a day, and it is my preference to work within the state-funded system with those who do not have the resources to pay for private help.

My new patient was a family doctor in the nearby town who had been referred to me by a colleague. I had agreed to meet him because if I do offer private therapy to anyone, it will usually be to fellow medical professionals, as it can be so hard for them to access help, for a whole range of reasons which I will describe. I'm not offering long-term therapy, and I make that very clear to them up front. I will give an assessment and do a limited number of sessions, then guide them to someone else, if necessary. I've chosen to work in this way because I'm accustomed to having firm boundaries between my forensic work and my off time. As I've described, I am always grateful for the high walls of secure institutions, which create such an unambiguous line between my job and my private life, helping me to leave work behind at the end of each day. If someone is agreeable to the idea of short-term therapy, I find a few sessions are often enough; as one surgeon who came to me put it, he had felt "mentally messy," and a handful of hours together were sufficient for him to clear his head.

I heard David before I saw him that morning. The window of my room overlooks the parking area and I had been sitting quietly, expecting his arrival, when the sudden slam of a car door outside made me jump a little. As hurried footsteps crunched across the gravel, I gathered he was finishing a phone call—not a pleasant one, by the sound of it. After a moment there came a muffled rumble of the same voice at reception, one of those baritones I associate with singers or soldiers. Closer now, I heard a snapped "No need, she's expecting me," immediately followed by three quick raps on my door. He came in before I could rise from my chair.

"David X," he announced, thrusting his hand out to shake mine. He wasn't a big man, but his presence filled the small space. He had a strong handshake and a professional smile that didn't make it to his eyes. His clothes suggested he had paid attention to his look: he wore a crisp white shirt, and a patterned silk handkerchief peeked from the pocket of a smart blue blazer. A high forehead was crowned with a mass of curly salt-and-pepper hair and his head seemed too big for his body. The double meaning of "big head" occurred to me later, and I wondered if this initial association was a response to something "bullish" in David's presentation of himself to me at this first meeting.

"What brings you here today?" I asked him, as I picked up my notepad and pen, adding, "I'm going to make a few notes just so I don't forget the important things. Is that okay?" He waved his hand to signify not just assent but the irrelevance of the question. He was a doctor too; he knew the drill. "What exactly did Giles put in the referral?" I sensed an antipathy in his tone which might have reflected a difficulty in swapping over to the patient's chair— or perhaps it was just anxiety about what his GP might have said.

These first minutes with a new patient are always full of cues, and it can be frustrating that there's no time to process them in the moment. His GP had mentioned depression, I told him. David shook his head: "No, I wouldn't call it that, actually. It isn't my mood, it's my sleep. Quite simple really: I'm having trouble sleeping and the SSRIs [referring to a category of antidepressants] he gave me didn't do a thing." I asked how long he'd had the problem. A few months, he told me, "or maybe a year." I frowned inwardly. That's a long time for anyone to be sleep-deprived, and it made me think that David's issue might be complicated. "The referral mentioned something about troubles at work too. Is that related to the lack of sleep?" David looked blank for a moment, then, to my surprise, he laughed, a harsh, dry chuckle. "Had to say something, didn't he?"

He gazed at me as if seeing me for the first time since his arrival. "I asked Giles to refer me to you in particular, Dr. Adshead. Heard you on Radio 4 on my drive into town one day. Bit of a celebrity, aren't you?" In recent years I've done a few public lectures, mainly about working with homicide perpetrators, and once I was "on the radar" of a few people in the media, I began to be invited to join panel discussions from time to time, talking about forensic work. I don't mind doing this, but it is an unexpected side effect of my job, not something I pursue. Comments like David's didn't really invite a response, but his need to say it suggested he might be nervous and could also be attempting to use mild flattery as a way to establish a connection. I wondered too if it mattered to him that "his" psychiatrist had some public presence or was well regarded.

He was saying, ". . . and who doesn't have troubles at work, eh? I mean, look at what we do and under what pressure. The NHS has gone to the dogs, and we're left to clean up the mess. Thank God I'm retiring soon. Takes a special kind of nerve, this job, wouldn't you say? Think about it: we're extraordinary. We have to be." He crossed his legs and gave me what I'm sure he thought was a winning smile, and again I had that sense of him wanting to flatter or charm me, positioning "us" as special because he needed to be. There was something controlling about all this, and I found myself recoiling inwardly from him. Of course, I knew that was clinically significant—something about his psyche was tweaking something in mine. Another reason I have such a limited private practice is that I like to discuss reactions like this with thoughtful colleagues who share an experience of the patient and can help me reflect. In an institution like Broadmoor or a prison, even working within the probation service or with the courts, I'm connected to others; in private practice I'm on my own. I was able to keep a neutral expression while still communicating interest and warmth with my body language, eye contact and careful listening and questions, but throughout I was aware that I was wishing I could get away from David, and curious as to why.

I wondered if it was because he didn't really want to be there—if, despite his genial presentation, he was feeling as I did. Why did we both want to get out of the room so badly? Probably we had touched on feelings and thoughts that were troubling to us both. As put off as I was by his manner, I would later reflect on what he had been saying about the NHS, and whether that had disturbed me. He was correct in saying that the health service has been sorely battered by years of cuts and restructuring, and faces an uncertain future, which is upsetting to anyone working in the field. I also had to wonder whether he was tweaking some concern I had about my own future, given our similar ages, as well as our shared profession. It can be discomfiting to be made to think about how little time lies ahead of us compared with what is behind.

There's truth in that old saying that doctors make bad patients, especially when it comes to mental health. This is a worry because rates of depression and substance abuse are higher in our field than in other professional groups, which contributes to an increased suicide risk. I have worked with doctors in general practice like David who are required to be all things to all people, with a huge workload. They truly can't afford to be "mentally messy." Mess is anathema to most doctors; our training emphasizes scientific rigor and the need to be in control. Strength and dependability are highly prized; we are taught that like a ship's captain, we are expected to be at the helm, not leaving the deck until the job is done. As a junior doctor I quickly learned never to call in sick, which would have amounted to letting the team down or risking being seen as weak. As the American poet Anne Sexton once observed of doctors, "they are only a human / trying to fix up a human."[1]

I've had an interest in the psychological needs of doctors for a long time, partly because I am a physician who's had to struggle with the mess in my own mind, and I know how difficult it can be to ask for help or carve out time for self-care. I've had at least ten years of therapy, partly as a requirement of my original training, but also to help me to make sense of who I am and some of the difficulties I've faced in my life. I've struggled with depression, and in 2010 I trained in mindfulness-based cognitive therapy (MBCT), which is often used in the treatment of chronic depression. Mindfulness is a meditation practice based on Buddhist traditions, and I wish I'd come to it much earlier, as I've found it to be so helpful both personally and professionally. Reasoning that these practices might also benefit other doctors, I've since become involved with a few like-minded colleagues (one a Buddhist monk as well as a psychiatrist) in organizing annual "Mindfulness for Doctors" retreats.[2]

My interest in working with fellow doctors also extends to those who get into real difficulties as a result of their struggles, to the point of transgressing rules or norms. I'm intrigued as to what makes colleagues who are by definition pro-social, helping and cooperating with others for a living, decide to "break bad." Over the years, I've seen how different stressors affect doctors' mental health, and the way their professional and personal identities merge in what is necessarily a performative job. It is no surprise that they are the embattled protagonists of so many television dramas.

I was able to witness the consequences of some of my colleagues' developmental struggles early on in my career. Soon after qualifying in forensic psychiatry, in the mid-1990s, I did assessments for the UK's medical licensing and regulatory body, the GMC, and sat for a time on their Fitness to Practice panel. The GMC has the power to suspend doctors from working or have them "struck off"—the rather brutal phrase used to describe revoking their license. During this period I was fortunate to get a scholarship to travel to the US and study at firsthand the therapies our American colleagues were developing to help medical professionals. The groups I observed on my trip were made up primarily of practitioners who had lost their licenses and needed to remedy this by completing treatment programs. I remember being astonished at the thousands of dollars they had to pay so that they could return to practice; back then, as now, there was some free psychiatric support within the NHS for medical practitioners, although not the long-term therapy that some require. Most of all, I recall that across many different backgrounds and specialties, there was one common thread: they never wanted to ask for help until it was too late. For some doctors (and I think I may have been one of them once), choosing to study medicine in the first place seemed to be a way to avoid vulnerability, as if somehow being a doctor and a patient were mutually exclusive.

There is also a practical reason for doctors not to seek help with their mental health: it can impact on their license to practice. These days the GMC is primarily an agent of public protection and is highly reactive to any suggestion that a doctor might not be "a safe pair of hands." This shift in emphasis was driven partly by the case of Dr. Harold Shipman, who in 2000 was convicted of killing fifteen of his elderly patients. His case drew huge international attention, especially as it closely resembled a similar case in the US from around that time, involving physician Michael Swango. Both men were dubbed "Dr. Death" by their national media. In the UK, a high-profile public inquiry would go on to find Shipman responsible for more than two hundred murders. History shows us again and again how black swan events can lead to disproportionate fear, and after Shipman there was a significant backlash against doctors.

With all of these stumbling blocks, it is small wonder that many doctors won't raise their hand for assistance. But in this case, David had gone to his GP and asked to be referred to a therapist; not just any therapist, but one he'd decided was suitable for him, for whatever reasons. Having made it this far, here he was telling me that he was just tired, not depressed. His manner was upbeat, his presentation calm. Since he was denying any illness, I thought we would need to get out of the medical narrative and into his experience as a person. I fell back on my favorite question: "If this were a story, where would it start?"

David sighed and glanced at his watch, as if wondering if he really had time for all this. It seemed important to me to let the pause extend into a silence that he would have to break. After a minute or two, he began by explaining how, two years earlier, his long marriage had ended. When his wife left him, he began to have dreadful nightmares, which became worse over time, until he was getting only a few hours of sleep a night, at best. "No rest," he said, shaking his head, "no rest." He admitted this had made him "a little short-tempered" at work. "You know how that goes, everything grates on you. And our wretched admin woman, Helen, she's always on at me, asking me for my paperwork and all that admin rubbish . . ." He appealed to me as a colleague. "Don't you just hate it?" I didn't reply, although I do dislike paperwork as much as anyone else. "Then, you know, one thing led to another." He didn't elaborate, leaving me to wonder what constituted "one thing" and if his troubles at work were limited to a single female colleague.

I was curious too about how much she and others might have put up with from David before they complained; the esprit de corps among medical professionals means it can take a while to use up goodwill. It crossed my mind that his patients may have begun making complaints as well, and perhaps the therapy wasn't David's choice after all. I asked him directly if that was the case. He insisted it wasn't. He had come to see me because he knew he had to get over the end of his marriage, he said, and get rid of the damned nightmares, which were surely connected. "Oh? Can you tell me what they're about?" I asked. He parried. "Never remember them. I couldn't say. Sorry to disappoint you, Doctor." People's memories of dreams are variable, and as I noted in Tony's case, the interpretation of them associated with traditional psychoanalysis is rarely part of my work. I was more interested in the fact that David "couldn't say." What was muting him? I made a note, then asked what he did when he couldn't sleep or woke from a nightmare. "I just try to shake it off, as you do. Get up, get myself a drink, go online—wait for the dawn."

Our time was nearly up, and David wanted to know where we would go from there. I suggested we meet for six sessions over the following six weeks and then review. We set up a regular day and time to meet, then he stood to leave, thanking me for my time. "In your expert hands, I'm sure I'll make great progress." Did I detect a hint of sarcasm? He was on his way out before I could respond. I glanced at the clock and saw that he had effectively terminated the session a few minutes before time. I had a feeling of being dismissed like a junior cadet by a superior officer.

The following week he did not appear at the appointed hour. I waited in my office and even went to the window to watch for his arrival, but there was no sign of him. "He rang and said something came up," our receptionist reported. That was interesting. I thought he wasn't working at present—"on leave," according to the referral note—so it wouldn't be a medical emergency. It was more likely that having begun the process, some reluctance had arisen about engaging with the work of therapy. But he was right on time for the next session, even a few minutes early, breezing in with smiling apologies and an explanation for why he'd been absent. He was a keen golfer, and just as he'd been leaving the club last week to meet with me, he'd run into our local MP, an acquaintance of his, who had asked him to join his table. The MP was having coffee with—and here David dropped his voice and almost mouthed the name—the deputy prime minister of the day. I think I was meant to be impressed. "I couldn't very well beg off, could I? 'Terribly sorry, chaps, must go see my therapist.' Anyway, I'm here now. What's the plan, Doctor?" I think I had the passing impression that he was a little too hearty, as if he'd been drinking, but he was so lucid I didn't pursue it.

I suggested we might use this session to talk about his life history. I wanted to know about his childhood, his growing-up story, but instead he responded by starting in the recent past, at his silver wedding anniversary. He described throwing a lavish party ("Cost an arm and two legs, let me tell you") at the golf club's smart restaurant, with dinner and dancing—"Black tie, the works." He mentioned two grown-up children, who came for the event with their young families. There was a daughter who lived in Wales and a son up from Cornwall, but he revealed nothing more about them or the grandchildren, not even giving me their names. He did comment in passing that "they adore Connie," his wife. I thought I detected a note of sadness there, something of *Twelfth Night*'s Sir Andrew Aguecheek and his wistful "I was adored once too."

David described in detail the elaborate party arrangements, the speeches, the fine French wine that he'd ordered, and the Tiffany necklace he had presented to his wife in front of the crowd. "It all seemed, you know, tickety-boo. Happy families. Then . . . boom." A few weeks later, Connie packed her bags and went. He snapped his fingers: "Just like that." "I'm sorry—do you mean she left you without explanation?" He looked away, then shrugged, telling me his wife had just suddenly announced one day that she wanted to go and live in Cardiff with their daughter, to be with the grandchildren. "It was fine," he said. "Fine," I reflected back to him, unconvinced by this innocuous little word that so deftly closes down emotional conversation. "Look, there wasn't anyone else, if that's what you're thinking. On either side. Nothing like that. We'd grown apart, probably." I just nodded, waiting for more. He stared at me, somehow conveying anger that I wasn't responding. Then he shifted position, clasping his hands behind his head, extending his legs, and looking up at the ceiling. "What else can I tell you?" Now he sounded rather bored. I asked if he wanted to say a little more about his children—what did they make of the split? "I couldn't say." That phrasing again. What was preventing him from saying more? Did he know?

There was something worrying about the picture that was emerging. A man in his late fifties who is approaching retirement is already statistically within a higher risk group for suicide, whether or not he admits to depression. Some doctors become so identified with their work that retirement is tricky; it can seem like not just the end of a career, but the death of a part of their self, which is possibly why so many carry on well past the normal pension age. It was important to be forewarned and stay mindful of what a loss of identity might feel like. Good mental health also depends on community, and David sounded socially adrift in the wake of his divorce. His club might be a convivial setting, but golf isn't a team sport, and he appeared to have no relationship with his children or their families and may have alienated at least some of his work colleagues.

I imagined him at home after Connie departed, a lonely man with a pressured job coming in late, knocking back a few stiff drinks in the hope that they might help him to sleep, then drifting around the echoing rooms looking at framed photos of a life lost to him, before a slow climb up the staircase to bed and a struggle for respite, only to be plagued by indescribable nightmares: a dark and pitiful nightly sequence, repeating on a loop. Sometimes I have had to stop myself from filling in gaps like this, even though such images occur to me quite naturally. I have learned that picturing a life that is not my own, although a component part of empathy, can also stop me from hearing or noticing what is real. But if I never did it at all, that might be worrying too. How does one step into someone else's shoes and not imagine where they walk?

I thought I'd better ask David for the name of someone close to him that I could speak to if necessary—a trusted friend perhaps. This isn't an unusual request to make in cases involving depression, and it only happens with the patient's permission. He brushed me off, but he knew my professional duty, so when I pressed him gently, he grudgingly agreed that I could speak to his GP and practice manager if it came to it, "which it won't." He couldn't even muster the name of a close friend. It was an emotionally bleak landscape, and I had the sense of some deeply buried distress. But as our session ended, David assured me that he was "in fine fettle," urging me "not to worry, my dear." He left the room with a cheery "See you next week," and I could have sworn he winked at me.

The next time we met he appeared dressed in casual gear, face flushed, sporting a polo shirt with the collar up, very pleased with his golf game that morning. His ebullience subsided when I asked if we could go further back in his history, to his early childhood. "Ah, we're into Freud territory now, are we?" Making exaggerated air quotes, he gave me what I imagined were the only lines of Larkin's poetry that he (and many others) knew by heart: " 'They fuck you up, your mum and dad . . .' "[3] He broke off, grinning, as if expecting a gold star from the teacher. I said nothing. "Freud, Jung . . . it's not real science, is it, Dr. Adshead?" I wondered why he wanted to belittle the profession. I know there are some doctors who still view psychiatry as a Cinderella specialty, but it is unusual in a GP since their work is so entwined with mental health. I decided to treat his comment as banter and allowed myself an eye-roll, as if pretending to be insulted on behalf of all psychiatry. "Tell me about your parents," I prompted. He threw up his hands in mock surrender and began.

His narrative was brief and to the point, more professional bio or newspaper profile than memoir in style. He was named for his father, who was also a GP. His mother was a nurse. "Usual thing. Runs in families, doesn't it? Same for you?" I noted how he felt an immediate need to change course and start a different conversation, something more mutual and less like doctor and patient. Mildly, I reminded him that we were there to talk about him, not me. For a second, I felt a pull to use his first name and was aware of something maternal in that urge. It's always an interesting moment when therapist and patient move to the use of first names, if that happens. We weren't there yet; in fact, he continued to address me as "Doctor" to the end, although it always had a mocking quality, I thought, in line with his snarky attitude to psychiatry.

David went on, describing how his father had set up his consulting room downstairs in their family home. He recalled how the children had to tiptoe around and be quiet during office hours: "Seen and not heard." Technically, his father was always at home, but . . . And there David halted, unable to articulate something. "He was . . . there and not there, you know?" It was the first time I thought he'd said something with some personal truth to it. I recorded those words on my notepad, sensing they had an emotional complexity which would only later be revealed. David raised his eyebrows when he saw me taking notes but made no comment.

He went on to talk about his mother working shifts at a nearby hospital and how the children were cared for by a succession of nannies. What were they like? "Super," said David, adding that he felt "lucky to be looked after by such gorgeous young creatures." I mindfully suppressed a wince. He was the eldest; the four children were each separated by a year or so—"Close in age, if not in life, I'd say." Again, this had a more personal ring to it and that rueful sort of Aguecheek tone I'd noticed earlier. He described being sent off to his father's Catholic boarding school at eleven, where he did well in his studies and excelled at tennis, becoming captain of the team, just as David Sr. had been in his youth. I commented that it sounded as if his mother and father were somewhat absent from his childhood, but he balked at this, insisting that they were excellent parents, "top notch." He added that his father had coached him at tennis and golf in the school holidays (neither of them team sports, I noticed), and there was a family holiday to St. Ives each summer. Picture perfect. I imagined David Jr. all those years ago, coming home during school breaks to find the nanny busy with the little ones, having to rummage around in the kitchen for a cold supper, padding about in his socks so as not to disturb the patients below, and staying up late to study "real science" at his desk in order to become a true replica of his father. How else would he get parental attention, between the younger children and the stream of needy sick people downstairs?

I was thinking how familiar his story was. In the 1970s, American research into vulnerable doctors found that the majority tended to be firstborn children who had complex relationships with their parents.[4] I had seen this in other doctors who had come to me, and there was always that same emphasis on strength and normality, on achievement and action. I thought David's whole presentation had a contemporary, almost millennial twang, carefully curated, ideal for Facebook and Instagram. Here's David in school uniform, and there he is holding a tennis trophy, his proud dad's arm round his shoulders, and that's him with his adorable younger siblings, all arrayed in stairstep formation, squinting into the sun on the beach in Cornwall. Happy families. It was not that I thought he was lying, but rather that this was a kind of cover story culled of any blurry, painful, or unflattering moments.

He continued with a similarly jolly account of medical school in London, giving no sense of the usual messiness or uncertainty of student life. He had met and married Connie, who was training to be a nurse. He described her as "a looker, back in the day," adding that she was "a good girl" and "did what she was told." He seemed oblivious to how derogatory that sounded. I made notes as he went on to talk about the births of his son Tom and daughter

Lucy. "How were they, growing up?" I asked. He said something vague about how they'd been "fine" and had "done well enough in life."

Group animals, like humans, need to be able to read the feelings of their fellows, that process of "mentalizing" another person. David seemed to have little capacity to think about others' emotional experience, and once again I marveled that he was a GP, given their need to be particularly thoughtful about human relationships. As he presented this restricted and rather offhand view of his marriage and family, I remembered how he had also dismissed a (female) work colleague and how he had been making those little digs about my work ever since we met. If he minimized the feelings, beliefs, and experiences of others so easily, he might also be doing the same with his own. Given his other risk factors for suicide, that worried me. Moreover, if he couldn't allow himself to be vulnerable, to make that shift from doctor to patient, I doubted if I could help him.

At our six-week review, we agreed to continue our sessions. I wouldn't normally have done this—as I have said, I tend to limit my private sessions. But I felt we hadn't really begun, as if he'd been treading water thus far. When asked how he was doing with his sleep, he shook his head, repeating his original complaint—"no rest"—as if that were a final verdict. I again tried to draw him out on the reason for his lack of rest, asking him about his nightmares, but he changed the subject, veering off to talk about work and how he planned to go back soon after his "little break" to "serve out my time." To my ears, that casual use of the idea of a prison sentence was particularly intriguing, but he didn't mention it again.

Our weekly discussion consisted mostly of him telling me about his thoughts (though less about his feelings), always peppered with little jibes about therapy clichés and comments about how "you shrinks do go on about the past." I thought wistfully of my work in places like Broadmoor with patients who, for the most part, recognize that they need help and are willing to put the work in. I never thought David's resistance to therapy was personal; on the contrary, I had no sense of an attachment to me—or to anyone else. At times I found him both wearing and unpleasant, and as always, I had to note that as interesting and move on.

Sometimes people who interview me will ask how I combat my negative feelings about patients, an idea which suggests emotions require action. I know that the opposite is true: "feelings aren't facts," as I often repeat to trainees, and they will pass. There's no battle involved, other than the mindfulness required to keep presenting a neutral expression and posture. In fact, I think I welcome any strong feelings I may have because they can be so revealing of the other person's state of mind, as illustrated in so many of these stories. I'm sure my adverse emotional reaction to David was actually part of the reason I broke my usual rule about only seeing private clients for short-term work. He wasn't overtly nasty, nor did he appear to be depressed, but I couldn't shake the feeling that there was something darker here behind his "performance." Given what I'd experienced with other patients, including women like Lydia and Zahra, I was worried that he was blocking me from seeing something important. I noted that he missed the odd session too, without any prior notice, or would arrive late without much explanation, actions that could signal aggression.

On one occasion he was on time but in a temper, talking about a row with Helen, his (long-suffering, as I imagined her) office administrator. He was back at work now and blaming her for whatever had happened that day, suggesting she was "chippy" because she was unmarried and middle-aged, "past her prime." The same might have been said of him, I thought but did not say. I was so aware of identifying with Helen and trying not to feel outrage on her behalf that I almost missed a significant and apparently offhand comment that it was David's birthday that day, and his children hadn't been in touch with him. I resisted a passing urge to say, "I can't imagine why not," and simply asked him how he felt about that. "I'm not upset, if that's what you're getting at," he said. "Upset?" I asked. David raised his voice at me, which he'd never done before. "Oh, come on, Doctor. You know what I mean. I won't be crying myself to sleep tonight. I'm not *sad* about it." He gave the emotion great emphasis, as if it were ridiculous.

"So," I asked, "if not sad, then what do you feel?" He told me he was angry that "after all I've done for them," they "couldn't be bothered" to call and wish him a happy birthday. "How hard would it be?" And then he was off on a rant: "I worked to give them all that I had, more even—the best schools, tennis lessons, the lot. Lucy was never academic, but I wanted Tom to go to medical school and he had the brains for it, but what did he do? Drama and *media studies*, of all things, and now he plays the piano in pubs and clubs for a living, teaches a bit on the side. What a bloody waste— I gave him everything. I can't fucking believe it." He paused for breath then, his face flushed with feeling.

These were painful emotions, right up at the surface where we could see them, presented in more emphatic words than I'd ever heard from him. It was a long speech for him too, and although it seemed as entitled and demanding as usual, I thought I heard an agonized longing for a son who would be like him. I would tread with care in my response. "David, are you angry that your son didn't want to go into medicine, after you followed your own father into the profession?" He shrugged. "I couldn't say." I tried not to let that catchphrase irritate me and went a little further: "Do you wish you'd been closer to your own father?" But even as I said it, I thought it might be off the mark. David smiled in a way that was downright unpleasant. "You people think you're so clever. Well, I'll have you know, Dr. Adshead, I was perfectly close to my father, and he was proud of me. And rightly so. He was just a country GP, never built a successful business as I've done, never published." The dialogue had taken a wrong turn, just when I'd thought we were getting somewhere. My heart sank as he spent the rest of the session telling me about his latest article in the *British Medical Journal* and reviewing all his other professional achievements.

I was beginning to think that David could not—or would not—use what I had to offer. Success in therapy, as we've seen in other cases, means accepting that something about your mind and beliefs may have to change. His mode of engaging with me had a narcissistic quality, though I wouldn't say he had a personality disorder or any other kind of mental illness. Rather, he was dismissive and grandiose, with a way of dealing with others that made it hard for him to ever allow himself to be vulnerable. This is common enough among people in leadership roles in a competitive and capitalist society like ours, particularly in males, when they have the added challenge of dealing with cultural ideas of masculinity that define strength as never showing weakness. But as every one of the foregoing stories attests, vulnerability is absolutely essential to the therapy process. The more open someone is, the more possible it is for them to reach an acceptance of their self and change their mind for the better. I feared that David might not get there.

I also suspected that he had not always performed his self to other people in this way. Rather, his experience of childhood loneliness and emotional neglect had led to a tendency to avoid painful feelings, so much so that, as he reached adulthood, he taught himself to keep the ordinary human griefs and difficulties out of his psychological line of sight, or his "inscape," as Victorian poet Gerard Manley Hopkins so eloquently put it. It seemed doubtful that more tolerance and perseverance on my part, for some indeterminate period, were going to alter his defenses.

I invited him to review things again, to reflect on his work with me thus far. He seemed to find this process uncomfortable and again made noises about how he was "fine" and he "couldn't say." But I pushed a little, to try and get a response: "I'm aware that you're still having nightmares. I understand you're still not happy at work and counting the days till retirement. What is our work together doing for you, if anything?" David acted as if affronted, accusing me of trying to get rid of him. Perhaps he was more attached to me and the work than I had realized. I picked up my notes and turned to the line I'd written down early on, when he told me he experienced his father as being "there and not there." I asked if it was possible that was happening with us now. "You come, you talk, but I feel as if there's much you can't articulate, as if you are also 'here and not here.' Can you help me to understand what that's like for you?"

Sometimes the mere suggestion that therapy is not infinite can prompt people to reassess and bring out new thoughts, which is the essence of change. David did not respond to my question immediately. He sat quietly, hands in his lap, and took a few slow, deep breaths, as if self-soothing. After a while, in a low voice, he asked what I meant. What was it I thought he wasn't saying? There was still a tinge of the bully there, a little challenge in his tone. I told him I had no clue. He smiled. "Well then" — as if the matter were settled. I waited, listening to the clock measuring the time remaining, until another question came to me. He had told me some time ago that he had no idea why his wife had suddenly up and left him. Was there anything more to that story? Long experience had taught me that you never know what might happen in therapy, and I did have a concern that asking this might anger David. I wasn't entirely sure it was the right course of action, but he had led the way, so I took the plunge.

David appeared to arrive at a decision, slapping his palms on his knees. It looked like he was about to get up and leave. This was so unlike my work in forensic settings, where patients will rarely terminate a session — or if they do, it is often a sign of progress, showing they might be getting in touch with healthier ways to express "upset," as I'd seen in cases like Tony's or Zahra's. Then David spoke, leaning forward, close enough that I could feel the warmth of his breath, his eyes locked onto mine. "All right, Dr. Adshead, I guess I'll tell you." He relaxed a little, settling back in his chair again, and after a moment he proceeded to explain to me that his wife Connie had always been "uptight," what he'd call "a classic English prude," if I knew what he meant. I didn't nod, but I guess he thought I understood. One day, he told me, Connie "lost it" when she found he had been watching some porn on his computer. She'd gone to look up something in their household accounts, "or so she said," and had stumbled on a site he had accidentally left open.

Any psychiatrist will perk up their ears at things that occur "accidentally." Carl Jung used the word "synchronicity" to describe these kinds of acausal "meaningful coincidences." I made a note of it for later. "That set her off," David was saying, rolling his eyes skyward. He described how Connie started crying, then there'd been a terrible argument and she'd packed a suitcase and driven off to their daughter's house, "making a big drama out of nothing." He crossed his arms over his chest and glared at me as if I were his histrionic spouse. "The end," said his body language.

"How long have you been looking at pornography?" I asked. He waved his hand, telling me it had been "years." I waited. "Several years, okay?" "Since . . . ?" He allowed that it might have started when his children were small, when his wife became "obsessed" with them, his tone pathologizing her maternal interest and hinting at unfair neglect of him. That would have been at least twenty years ago, I calculated. "Would you call it a habit?" I asked. David snorted. "It's a hobby! Something everyone . . . I mean, come on. It's not like it was back in the day, top-shelf-at-the-newsagent stuff—it's everywhere. Free, all over the internet, 'Hot Teens,' 'Wet Schoolgirls,' that sort of thing, popping into your inbox at all hours." He paused, perhaps becoming aware of some change in the air or tension between us, and added lamely, "It's not illegal. Everyone does it."

Now I had a problem. David was describing an activity that could potentially have a criminal aspect, and I needed to know more without sounding like an interrogator. I asked if he was aware that what he was suggesting had serious implications—he could lose his license or even go to prison.

"Who's going to know?" he shot back. "I'm no fool. I'm careful about it, you know, and I only use my home computer. So." I was concerned that he might be using pornography that was illegal. As an experienced health care professional, David must have realized that if he confided to me that he was downloading child pornography, this was a crime that I would have to tell somebody about. Confidentiality between doctor and patient has its limits, even outside of secure institutions, as we've seen in the case of Sam and his parents; this is essential in the context of child protection. In the US, doctors are mandated by law to report any possible risk to a child, and even in the UK, where it is not mandatory, there is an expectation that doctors will act without compunction to protect children in danger. This is implicit in any case involving the downloading of child pornography, and in this particular instance it was exacerbated by the fact that David was a family doctor. I'd never found myself in a situation like this before, and I knew I would need to seek advice from trusted colleagues about the next steps. I was sure doing nothing wasn't an option. David was looking at me, tapping his fingers on his knee, as if irritated, waiting for my lead. He seemed as uneasy as I was about the turn this session had taken.

I reminded him of my professional duty, adding that of course I wanted us to think it through together and consider what we might do next. He frowned. "So, Dr. Adshead, if I told you—which I haven't, by the way—that I was downloading violent, sadistic pornography involving minors, you'd have to report me? Is that it?" By now I was familiar with the games he played and how he liked to provoke a reaction, so I didn't give him a direct reply. Instead, I asked, "Where do *you* think we go from here?" He looked crestfallen, as if he would have preferred an argument. Then he lapsed into a protracted silence, lasting several minutes at least. At one point, he dropped his head into his hands, raking his fingers through his hair as if to comb out his thoughts. It was the longest silence there had ever been in our work together.

When he finally looked up at me, his face was serious. He cleared his throat. "Right. Well then. That's what I've been doing. That's why Connie left me." I encouraged him to go on, to say more. He spoke slowly, with pauses and halts to find words to say the unsayable, and I didn't interrupt him. Initially, his porn "hobby" had been a means of retaliating against his wife when she was neglecting him, but then it became a private way to de-stress himself. He would wait till she and the children went to bed and then go into his study, which he said he kept locked, "of course," as if protecting his children in this way were evidence that he was somehow a good father. To me, it sounded more like consciousness of guilt about his activity.

He found a whole world online, and for years he carried on looking at "pretty ordinary" porn—women with big breasts, people having sex in various positions, "nothing odd or kinky." At some stage, and he couldn't quite pinpoint when it was, he found himself drawn to websites that advertised girls in school uniforms and the like. They were young, but not children. They were having sex with actors playing teachers and dads, men his age. I wondered if it affirmed his sense of self to watch vulnerable girls apparently enjoying sex or being degraded by men much like him.

The story got darker, and I was reminded of the progressive quality of any addiction, that relentless search for greater highs, for more oblivion. He described moving from one "class" of website to another, invited by fellow travelers into a world of cruelty and sexual exploitation involving children, even toddlers. It was hard to hear, but I imagined it was harder to say. His gaze stayed firmly on his hands in his lap as he described what he'd seen and how this habit had increasingly consumed all of his leisure time. In the last ten years of his marriage, he and his wife grew further apart, living almost separate lives. A few years before she left, Connie seemed to suggest she was aware of his "hobby," but he denied it.

When she finally found the evidence on his computer, it was just before their silver anniversary, and she told him she didn't want to go ahead with the party they had planned. She wanted a divorce. But they made a bargain: the social event was important to him, a landmark, so Connie agreed to participate in this public lie, if he accepted that afterward she would be leaving him and their marriage was over. Otherwise, she would tell their children and the police about what was on his computer. He agreed, but he still thought she was overreacting.

A painful, heavy atmosphere had settled in the room. I took some time to think, feeling conscious that the end of our session was in sight and we needed a plan for managing what he had just told me. As if reading my mind, he glanced up at the clock. "Are you going to contact the General Medical Council?" He sounded weary, his normal bluster gone. I didn't reply immediately. "I will answer that, David, but first, can I ask why you're asking?" He looked confused. "My career will be finished . . . everyone will know." Then his tone became more aggressive and familiar. "Look, Doctor, my problem was no rest—which, by the way, you've not solved—and now what?" With rising agitation, he heaved himself out of the armchair, glaring down at me, accusatory, back in command-and-control mode. "Are you going to make me out to be some kind of pedophile?" He didn't wait for an answer. "If you repeat what I've told you in confidence, by God, I'll sue you in every court in the land. I've got some powerful friends, you know. I can make life difficult for you."

"Will you sit a moment, David?" This was quite a disturbing turn, but I tried to keep my voice as level as I could. I was aware of the irony of longing for Broadmoor again, not only for the fellowship of colleagues and the clear boundaries, but for the sense of safety and ubiquitous security. There were no alarm bells within arm's reach in this space. He snatched up his coat and moved to the door. "I'm off. You won't be seeing me back here again in this shithole, you useless . . ."—he struggled to think of the right insult—". . . shrink. What a joke. Pointless, I knew this was pointless." He strode out, and moments later I heard his car door slam and the squeal of tires as he drove away.

My body was shaking, as if I'd been in a car accident or narrowly escaped one. I didn't know what David was capable of, but the sense of threat had been tangible. I tried to control a rising nausea with mindful breaths, sitting there for some time, knowing I had to make sense of what I'd heard and formulate a plan. Nobody likes to get another person into trouble, and David was in for a world of trouble if I reported this. But he had left me with no choice; by bringing his offending to therapy, he had put me in the dual role of investigator and bystander at a crime scene. As my physical anxiety subsided, my main worry was not for myself but for him. I thought he might become suicidal upon realizing what he had done; there was no closing this Pandora's box. He had just committed professional suicide in front of me—and he must have known it. Was that what he'd wanted from the outset, and it had just taken time to get there? Maybe he had merely needed to get his offense off his chest and genuinely thought that confidentiality rules protected him or that there was some gray area in the law. But that felt far-fetched to me for someone of his intelligence and experience.

In another era, psychotherapists might have been expected to keep these kinds of disclosures secret, but as I've described, our society—including the GMC and the justice system—now puts great emphasis on protecting people from care providers, and of course anything related to the potential or actual abuse of children is seen not only as evil, but as a safeguarding emergency. I didn't think David posed any risk to children, but I knew that wouldn't matter in the minds of others. If he had been relying on the idea that he had done nothing wrong because he had never actually come into contact with a child, as some pornography users will argue, then he would find out how mistaken he was. Downloading child pornography has long been unequivocally seen as a criminal offense which supports the abuse of minors through encouraging the production of such images. There has also been an increasing amount of virtual child pornography (VCP, the computer-generated, highly realistic imagery that is also used by producers of adult porn) over the last decade, with some users claiming that no harm was being done to anyone if the "actors" were not real. Thankfully, this disturbing idea has been met with a raft of criminal legislation in most jurisdictions, much of it also applicable to cartoon and drawn images. Of course, VCP does grave damage because the proliferation of all this material, however it is generated, normalizes child abuse.

Users like David are also quick to insist, "It doesn't make me a pedophile." As I've defined the term in the story of Ian, that is correct but irrelevant; most adult men and women who download child pornography are not exclusively or even primarily sexually attracted to children. It is believed that the majority of them, as with CSOs like Ian, are married to other adults, often with children of their own, whom they may or may not abuse. Getting detailed and accurate data on this is always challenging, but international law enforcement bodies know enough about the industry and its profits to extrapolate that there are tens of millions of these consumers worldwide.[5] The uncomfortable truth is that this audience must include a significant proportion of people just like you and me, including secret users among our friends, families, neighbors, and educators—and yes, even our health care providers. Considerable study of the connection between watching porn online and "contact offenses" has been made in recent years, suggesting those who do move from the virtual to the actual are more likely—but not exclusively—to be those who have exhibited prior criminal or antisocial behavior. One German project aimed at prevention and treatment took the name *Dunkelfeld*, venturing into the "dark field" of undetected and unprosecuted child exploitation behaviors.[6]

Sitting in my office after he stormed out, I recalled how David had originally come across, with his Facebook-friendly childhood, wonderful parents, and success at work. Yes, he was bombastic and grandiose, but so ostensibly "normal," to use that well-worn word again. He was a family man, a golf-playing doctor in suburbia, for heaven's sake; there was nothing obviously extraordinary or dangerous about him. He practically embodied the idea encapsulated in W. H. Auden's lines, written on the eve of the Second World War, that "Evil is unspectacular and always human, / and shares our bed and eats at our own table."[7]

I found myself thinking back to other encounters where I had missed something under the surface, with people like Lydia, who presented so well. I had to recognize that both Lydia and David were around the same age as me when we worked together, and had a similar racial, educational, and social background to mine. Also, both David and I were doctors, with a shared professional experience, to some extent, and both facing retirement. Despite all the training and experience I'd had, that bias held some sway: "normal" is self-defining, and they were "like me." At least with David I had sensed from the outset that there was something dark and worrisome underneath, and I had continued working with him for far longer than I ever intended for just that reason. My internal alarm had been ringing since the moment he first stepped into my office.

With the benefit of hindsight, I can also see that because I had spent so much time working with violent offenders, many of whose early childhood experiences were horrendous—people like Charlotte or Sharon or Gabriel—I had been inclined to discount the far more subtle adversity David had known. After all, having busy working parents, being raised by nannies, and living in lonely, high-pressure boarding schools—these things seem relatively harmless. They are familiar in our culture, and the vast number of British people who have similar experiences rarely break any laws, let alone turn to violence. At an advanced stage in my career, childhood narratives like David's have given me a renewed appreciation of the significance of early childhood trauma and its influence on our mental development, as well as on our propensity for violence. How subtle, how nuanced that can be; it does not require obvious early abuse. Experience of what might be considered a kind of "benign neglect," when found in combination with other risk factors, can also be predictive of violence or self-harm, or both.

I pictured again, as I do so often, the image of a bicycle lock, and lined up the other risk "numbers" that David had, including his gender, his social isolation, and perhaps also alcohol or substance abuse, something I had wondered about at times in the course of our work together and which is also disproportionately common in the medical profession. What was the "last number" that had sprung that lock open for him? What had been his equivalent of an innocent laugh from a girlfriend for Marcus or the simple phrase "so long" for Kezia? What did he see or think about in those moments before he had taken the decision to click on his first image of a little child being horribly exploited and abused—and then another, and another, on into the vortex? I will never know this because he "couldn't say," just as he couldn't talk about what his nightmares contained. I can still recall my early patient, Tony, and that description of his final, fatal look into the blue eyes of his victim, before he took his life and the boy was transformed in Tony's sleep into a ghastly Medusa head. I thought David would probably be contemptuous of Tony if he met him, and on the surface, nobody would see them as having anything in common. But I did. I'd come full circle to a man who exploited the young and vulnerable to avoid his feelings, and was plagued by horrors in his sleep; at least Tony had been able to tell me about his nightmares.

When I asked him early on what he did when his nightmares woke him up, David talked about getting out of bed and "going online." Much as some people dissolve their distress in alcohol, turning on a computer and watching someone else being tormented and vulnerable did something for David psychologically. Perhaps doing this made him regain a sense of power when those disturbing dreams rendered him weak with fear. This was not so different from the function of Ian's abuse of his vulnerable children, or what Sam had told the Homicide Group about his father calling him by a childish nickname and his need to assert himself as a man by overpowering his dad. If David were to go on and get treatment for his use of porn, much as with substance addiction he would be asked to abstain in order to understand what his "drug" had done for him and to help him find a healthier substitute. Some years ago, my patient Zahra had to learn to express her anger and grief without setting herself or anyone else on fire; David's route to recovery, if he chose to take it, would involve finding his own way to safely express those feelings.

As I sat calming myself with some deep breaths, I was reminded of David's distinctive line about his father: "He was . . . there and not there." I had remarked that this was a fine description of him too, as I experienced him in therapy. Now I wondered if he saw his offending self through this lens: if he was never "there," simply because he wasn't actually in a room doing terrible things to a drugged or restrained child, he might have persuaded himself for a long time that he was free to persist with his "hobby." At some point that rationale had worn thin, bringing him to my office. With a jolt I realized that if David had sought me out after hearing me discussing my work on the radio, then he may have chosen me because he knew I had worked with sex offenders. It was possible, even if it was unconscious, that he wanted to bring his offender self to therapy for detection.

I took legal advice and consulted with some colleagues, and then I called the GMC. They thanked me for my concern, took the details, and it was done. I wrote a letter to the GP who had originally referred David to me, saying that therapy had ended abruptly, with his problems unresolved. I heard no more from him. I didn't expect to hear from David again either, and nor did I. The GMC could involve the police, but a case against him might never proceed if he denied everything and destroyed the evidence. Or he might be criminally prosecuted and sent to prison, with a sentence of up to five years as a possible outcome. I thought this could be catastrophic for him. If he were identified as an offender, he stood to lose much more than his license to practice or his liberty; it might feel as if his whole history had been erased. His identity as a doctor extended far back into childhood, even to his birth, when he was named for his GP father.

I think I deliberately avoided trying to find out more about David's fate because I dreaded to hear what had happened. In theory, he had plenty of potential for recovery, but much would depend on what he wanted and whether he could even define it. He had often used expressions like "I couldn't say" or "I can't think" when I questioned him, like an actor with no lines or one who had gone blank, clues that had hinted to me of his underlying distress. If he could find a new vocabulary that would allow him to "speak his mind," there was a chance that he could change; he might even go on to have a restful retirement and a happier third act. Even the little he had revealed to me about himself was probably the most he'd ever shown anyone of what lay behind his facade. It was a start, the beginning of an essential dialogue.

I hoped that he would be able to seek help again one day. Hope is not fanciful or naive; it is a mature defense against sadness and loss. I had not relished working with him, but in the unlikely event he ever came back to me, I would welcome him and try again, and maybe he would allow himself to be vulnerable. I considered whether I had let him down; it was possible that in the absence of a supportive team around me to help me process my negative responses, I let him get under my skin, to the point where I wasn't as helpful as I could have been. The truth is, no matter how long I'm in this job, I'm still a human, with human likes and dislikes. All the training and experience in the world doesn't wash that away, and I don't think I'd want it to.

JAMAL

I stepped through the air-locked double doors that took me into "seg," the segregation unit at a male maximum-security prison. It looked just as you might imagine: a bare, long corridor lined with cells, which had small hatches set into their metal doors for serving food and communicating with the prisoners. The duty officer's station, positioned at the midpoint, glowed with the gray light of a bank of monitors for the CCTV feeds, adding to the sense of Orwellian gloom.

It was the late 1980s, and I was a young trainee psychiatrist at Broadmoor, at the start of my career. As part of gaining high-secure experience, I was expected to pick up my share of referrals to the hospital from prisons like this one. Today, I'd come to see a young man called Jamal, who had been held in seg for six weeks, following a series of disturbing and disruptive outbursts. In UK prisons at the time, keeping people in enforced isolation for more than seventy-two hours was not the norm; the average stay tended to last days rather than weeks or months. From 1998 onward, prisoners from maximum-security prisons requiring longer-term isolation would generally be sent to close supervision centers, or CSCs. These are five small specialist units in England and Wales, reserved for around fifty of the most risky and challenging prisoners in the system—a miniature British version of America's controversial "supermax" prisons.[1]

My task was to evaluate Jamal's mental health and decide whether he needed to be detained (or "sectioned," in the jargon) under Section 47 of the 1983 Mental Health Act, which licensed involuntary hospital admission for the treatment of prisoners. The regular psychiatrist at the prison had already signed off on the transfer, but the law stipulates that a second opinion is needed to confirm the patient has a mental disorder requiring treatment, and that was my job today, which meant I had to see Jamal in person.[2]

I was used to going into prisons by this time, because making assessments of prisoners' mental health needs is a significant part of any forensic psychiatrist's work. The prevalence of mental illness is extremely high in our male prison population, as it is in male prisons around the world. That fact does not validate the myth that the mentally ill are dangerous; rather, it indicates how stressful prison is and how vulnerable most offenders are.

Prisoners who did not have a history of mental illness or disturbance before their incarceration may develop serious problems afterward. It is not just the loss of liberty that causes their distress; it is the sense of being helpless and struggling with their new identity as an offender. Newcomers may be bullied by other prisoners and staff, and they can struggle to find their footing in unfamiliar, unpleasant surroundings, under rules that can seem arbitrary and unjust. In this environment, alone with feelings of guilt and shame, facing the fearful contents of one's own mind can feel excruciating, and prisoners sometimes find themselves, as Oscar Wilde put it so poignantly, "measuring time by throbs of pain, and the record of bitter moments."[3]

I was feeling a little nervous as I made my way toward the segregation unit. I'd been there a handful of times before to assess people, but usually with a colleague, not alone. I didn't fear for my safety, since working in Broadmoor had already taught me that nowhere was as safe as a place prepared for high risk. My anxiety was more to do with an earnest desire to get the assessment right, to be good at my job—a typical egoistic preoccupation of trainees in any field. Coming on my own, I also think I felt more aware of my identity as a stranger—not just any stranger, but a female one. In those days, female forensic psychiatrists were something of a rarity, although this has changed significantly over time; according to a professional census carried out in the UK in 2019, almost a third of us are women now.[4] There are higher proportions of females working throughout our prison and probation services too, making the sight of a woman in such surroundings unexceptional today. But at the time, I can remember being self-conscious about the noise my shoes made on those echoing metal stairs, a tinny, tympanic sound that seemed too feminine in this place of such constrained but intense masculinity. I endured the scrutiny of my clothing and appearance from the men I was dealing with in my work, staff and inmates alike, and sensed the gender paradox they were facing. I held keys that symbolized a control and a power they reflexively equated with maleness.

I have memories of times when I was told off by seniors for wearing "too short" a skirt or having "too many" buttons on my shirt undone, as if I had breached some unwritten rule about how I should look. Their comments also seemed to imply that I was subtly responsible for arousing desire in the men I'd meet at work. I tried not to take this too personally, partly because I was acclimatized to this kind of sexism after years of working in a male-dominated profession. I didn't condone it, but I didn't wish to give it more air. However, it didn't take me long to switch my skirts for trousers and start wearing flat suede boots that barely made a sound as I walked.

Some of the gendered response I experienced early on was reminiscent of the initiation rites of a closed order or fraternity. I remember one occasion when some male officers in the prison I was visiting had brief fun at my expense by sending me off to see a highly disinhibited man who could not stop exposing himself from the moment I walked into the room. I knew how to respond ("Mr X, don't do that"), and simply asked an officer to escort the poor man back to his cell, before arranging for a male colleague to see him for assessment. Looking back, I must admit that sometimes I did little to undermine sexist attitudes. I have a memory of arriving at the security lodge of a male prison one Monday morning after rather too good a weekend and joining in the officers' laughter after they did a routine search of my handbag and extracted a corkscrew I'd forgotten was there, dumping it on the table next to my wallet, car keys, a book, and a bikini.

The segregation unit was deep inside the labyrinth of red brick, set apart from the other blocks, far from the main entrance. It took quite some time to get there, laboriously unlocking and locking a succession of double doors and heavy gates as I went along, careful to ensure I opened and shut them quickly. I knew that if I dawdled, a piercing siren would begin to wail, which would be both disconcerting and embarrassing. In my mind I was rehearsing the details of the case. Jamal was serving a life sentence for a gang-related homicide, with a minimum of twelve years. He had been only a few years away from a first parole application when he began his disruptive and aggressive attacks on staff and fellow prisoners on the wing, apparently without provocation. The prison ultimately moved him to seg, where isolation had exposed and increased his mental distress. This was unsurprising; prison governors are damned if they do and damned if they don't when they consider whether to separate such inmates from their fellow prisoners. Human rights groups, such as Solitary Watch in the US, and the American psychologist Dr. Craig Haney have published substantial research indicating that the experience of being held in seg for any length of time damages nearly everyone to some degree.[5] By the time I arrived on the scene, Jamal's mental state had disintegrated so much that the staff could no longer handle him. He screamed abuse at everyone, seemed to be experiencing auditory and visual hallucinations, and had begun making "dirty protests," smearing excrement on his cell walls and throwing feces at staff.

There was the usual cacophony on the wings as I went through the prison: inmates banging against cell doors and walls with fists or heavy objects, prison officers thumping up and down those metal stairs in their boots, all punctuated by shouts, including the odd catcall or obscenity aimed at me when I passed by. The contrast as I stepped through the gates into seg was stark. There was a sudden hush, and the lack of natural light gave the unit a netherworld or underwater quality. I knew that the small number of men held there were isolated and medicated, and I was used to the difference in atmosphere, but today that quiet felt ominous.

I explained my purpose to the duty officer at the desk. He did not look happy and barely glanced at the paperwork I held out as he shook his head. "Not possible. Not now." I offered my warmest smile. "Not even a quick word?" He didn't thaw. With a look the jaded give the naive the world over, he jerked his head toward a couple of white hazmat-suited figures with mops and buckets, shuffling slowly outside the open door of one of the cells at the far end of the corridor. "We've just had to move him." He indicated a nearby cell.

"He's in there while they clean up." I understood what he was telling me: Jamal must have launched another one of his dirty protests that morning. Even so, I hated to waste the trip, and without an evaluation he would not receive hospital treatment. I ventured, "Might I try to say hello, see him for just a moment?" He relented with a theatrical sigh. "But talk through the hatch, would you? We can't open the door." I started forward. "Careful. He could have more shit to throw."

Instinctively, I wrapped my jacket tighter in a gesture of self-protection, reminding myself that it was dry-cleanable. Many people have worse jobs than mine, I thought, not least the men in those clammy white protective suits. I approached the cell door and knocked. No response. Another officer, younger and less forbidding than my Cerberus, leaned in and whispered to me, "Stand aside. I'll get the hatch." He shot back the flat bolts, and I peeked in.

The rectangular-framed scene was about as bleak as could be. There was a plastic bed with no bedding fixed to the wall of a windowless room of no more than eight feet by ten. Stark white fluorescent lighting illuminated a figure who was curled into the corner where bed met wall. He was a slight, naked man with olive skin, the curved and bony "C" of his spine painfully articulated due to the lack of body fat. His dark hair looked wet; they probably had to hose him down before moving him across. He was so diminutive he might have been a child. I stooped, bringing my face closer to the opening to make sure he could hear me, feeling like I was imposing myself on him. "Hello, it's Dr. Adshead? From the hospital? Here to see if I can get you some treatment?" Speaking in questions always communicates a measure of uncertainty—I think I was trying to gauge if he could even grasp the idea that help was an option in his world. "How are you doing in there?" What a thing to say. I changed position, trying to find a better angle, mindful that if the man within were to look my way, he'd see only a disembodied mouth, hovering in midair like something from a Samuel Beckett play.

A hand on my shoulder and a whisper close to my ear reminded me that I must take care, watch out for any sudden moves. Jamal might be concealing some shit in his hands, which were hidden from view. I drew back, my own hand instinctively covering my mouth. But I had to try again. "Mr. X . . . Jamal? Can you hear me? Anything you want to say?" At that, he lifted his head, and I tensed. The guard touched my shoulder again, but I shrugged him off and moved even closer, trying to get my face level with the prisoner's through that wretched hatch. If I could just establish eye contact, make some connection... And then I did. Jamal twisted toward me, his eyes locked on mine, body language suggesting he was opening up, relaxing a bit. "Good," I thought. "Oh, look, he's smiling at me." Only then did I realize with a jolt that he was baring his teeth.

Growling and hissing, his face reddened as he unleashed a torrent of abuse, a shrieked line of expletives merging one into the next: "Youfuckingcuntbitchshitfuckingasshole." The words flew at me with all the force he had, and he got the result he must have wanted. I flinched, hastily stepping back.

"I'd leave it there, miss, if I were you." The young officer made to close the hatch.

"Wait," I said. I was determined to make a dignified exit at least, so I leaned forward and put my eyes to the opening once more, to bid Jamal a professional farewell. "Goodbye for now, Mr.—"

My last sight was of him crouched on his haunches, saliva coating his lips, eyes narrow, nostrils flared wide as he prepared to launch himself at the door and at me. Fortunately, at that instant the officer moved swiftly to secure the hatch, metal scraping against metal. A fraction of a second later, Jamal's body made contact on the other side with a horrible thud, and although he was a featherweight, the reinforced door rattled with the impact.

I breathed out, trying not to look as shaken as I felt, and turned to leave. I'd seen enough. I paused to read my companion's name badge. "Thank you so much, Officer Y," I said, as if the visit had been a delight. "You've been ever so helpful." I signed out under the "I told you so" eyes of the duty officer and looked up at the CCTV screens behind him, just in time to see the cleanup team emerging from the far cell with their mops and buckets. Their shoulders were hunched and they did not appear to be conversing. I sensed a mournfulness in them, even under all that get-up. Not so much because of the task they'd just performed, but as if they couldn't believe that caring for another human had come to this.

I did not need years of experience to confirm that Jamal was acutely mentally unwell, and I got on with signing the forms that would see him admitted to the hospital. Beyond feeling sorry for him, I didn't think much more about the episode. Once Jamal received medical attention and was stabilized, he would likely be moved back to prison to serve out his sentence, hopefully without relapse. I doubted I would be involved; Broadmoor at that time housed a shifting population of more than five hundred men, and I had no reason to think that our paths would cross again.

One morning not long ago, I found myself in a planning meeting with some of my psychotherapist colleagues. One of them offered up a new idea, suggesting we start a group for male patients who were parents, helping them to explore their masculinity by talking about fathers and fatherhood. Group therapy was well established in Broadmoor by this time; we'd found that groups offered a reflective learning space for exploring shared experiences, good or bad, which was helpful in changing the outlook for a broad spectrum of patients. Some of our groups addressed mental health (such as the ones that focused on specific kinds of mental illness), specific offenses (such as the homicide groups), or future recovery and rehabilitation, like the Leavers Group, for men moving on from the hospital.

A few people on the staff voiced their doubts about whether a Fathers Group was necessary or valuable. I wondered if their doubts were driven by a discomfort with the idea that people who had done such terrible things and were so mentally unwell could also be parents just like them. I didn't have this doubt myself, even though I am a mother, because I'd seen how important it was for patients to have some other identity apart from being an offender. Something as ordinary as parenthood could give them a chance to connect to the wider community. I was glad when we were able to identify a list of some thirty men whom we could approach. Many of these fathers had been instantly and permanently cut off from their families upon arrest or conviction, particularly if their victim was within the family circle, as is often the case with homicide. But some had stayed in contact with their relatives, communicating by phone and by letter. A few were even receiving sporadic visits from their children, which took place in a child-friendly room, arranged and decorated to be welcoming, but with extra security. Other men had children they had never seen or who had been taken away from them early in life, by either the justice system or by the children's mothers.

We were struck by the range of issues and needs among the candidates. One older man was conflicted because he had been writing letters to his two grown-up children since killing their mother twenty years earlier, but now they wanted an in-person visit, and he felt he couldn't face them. A patient with paranoia had heard that his adult son, whom he had abandoned as a child, had just been arrested for armed robbery. He was fearful they would end up in the same prison after his discharge from the hospital and the son might try to harm him. There were many more sad stories, and we couldn't take them all on; to begin with, we had to narrow in on half a dozen people. We divvied up the shortlist, and I left that day with a clutch of names, feeling hopeful about the possibilities.

I had little success with my early candidates. Unfortunately, most of them were wary about joining, and I guessed it might be easier if I approached them again later, when the group was more established. But we did need some people to participate if we were going to get started. I felt a bit anxious as I went to interview Jimmy, the last man on my list. He was a fifty-three-year-old man who had been convicted of murder when he was eighteen. He'd been in prison ever since and was way over his minimum sentence; it seemed that his mental illness had hindered him from making any progress while behind bars. The referral to our proposed Fathers Group had come about because a social worker on his team had recently informed him that he had an adult daughter. Leah had been conceived just before his arrest thirty-five years earlier; her mother had never told him this, and until recently she had also kept his identity a secret from her daughter. The young woman was now interested in contacting him, and Jimmy's medical team felt the group might help him process his feelings about this, if he was willing.

Jimmy had been in Broadmoor several times over the years due to periodic bouts of psychotic depression and suicidality. In his medical notes, I read that he'd "come a long way this time." I also read that some on his team were unsure whether it was a good idea to "open this can of worms" regarding his newfound fatherhood. Other reports described a pro-social man who had been active in occupational therapy, particularly enjoying cooking. He was a ward representative at patient community meetings and was seen as being supportive to younger patients when they came from prison; I saw that one note described him as "fatherly" toward them, which I thought was a good omen. But his primary nurse, Will, had noted that he was "still somewhat fragile." Will said that since hearing the news about his daughter, Jimmy had become downcast and irritable, isolating in his room at times, which was not like him. Will's overview of Jimmy's situation only made me more eager to approach him about our Fathers Group. Yes, the sudden news of his parenthood was a stressor that might trigger unpredictable and risky emotions. But I felt that the group might be exactly the right kind of intervention for Jimmy, at precisely the right moment.

When I arrived on the ward mid-morning, the staff looked at me blankly. As happens sometimes, there had been a mix-up about my appointment time. Jimmy wasn't there; he was doing his ward job cleaning the kitchen and was "in a bit of a mood"—he might not want to talk to me. Undeterred, I decided to seek him out, making my way to the empty dining area. I looked through the glass panels in the kitchen door and saw a lone man carefully mopping the floor with an air of concentration. He had a bushy dark beard and a bald head, and wore tracksuit trousers and a plain black T-shirt that stretched tight across his protruding belly. He was not tall, standing perhaps only a foot above the height of the mop, and his overweight torso—almost certainly the result of medication and a lack of exercise—balanced like the letter "O" on stout legs.

When he looked up and found me there observing him, he didn't react, as if he saw nothing of interest. He maneuvered the mop to squeeze it empty of water and replaced it in its holder, before turning to make eye contact. He was waiting for me to approach or say something, so I nudged the door open and introduced myself, asking if he'd be willing to talk for a bit. His shrug indicated he was used to strange doctors turning up at odd times, expecting to speak with him at will, and was rather indifferent to such intrusions. "Will there be questionnaires?" he asked, his tone neither friendly nor rude. "If so, I'll need to get my specs." His eyes were dark, with thick eyelashes, and his skin was a pale brown. I wondered about his family origins and what part of England he was from; his accent suggested London, but I couldn't be sure.

I was lucky to find one of the nicer rooms on the ward empty. It had big windows facing the gardens, and two chairs were already set up in my usual formation, several feet apart, with one nearer the door. We took seats opposite each other, and he waited for me to begin, hands clasped in his lap. I started by explaining the idea of group therapy, but he interrupted me when I paused in mid-spiel: "I know about this. I went to a Friday Group last time I was in here, like, for people who killed a stranger?" News to me; I must have missed that in his records. I asked him how he'd found the group and whether it had been helpful. At this, he smiled at me, a lovely, gentle smile that went right up to his eyes, and I felt a sense of relief that something had relaxed between us. "I liked it a lot," he told me. "The people were nice, and we used to have coffee and biscuits there, and I made everyone a cake once." "What kind of cake?" I hoped my playful question might elicit a response that told me something about him as a person. Jimmy looked taken aback. "Um . . . chocolate loaf, I think, with some coconut in? I made it in OT [a reference to occupational therapy]. Why do you ask?" I assured him I just liked cake and cake-making, especially when chocolate was involved. "Huh," he said, not sure what to do with that. It was time to get to the point.

"Is it okay if you tell me a little about your daughter?" He nodded slightly, but then he twisted his body away and turned his head to look out of the window, as if to block me. I felt myself wanting to reassure him, but instead I sat there patiently, waiting. After a few minutes, Jimmy began to speak, describing his shock when his social worker came to see him with the news. Someone from social services in London had been in touch with her about a woman called Leah, who had only recently found out that Jimmy was her biological father. "Me. A father. All these years and I never knew." He shook his head, and it was hard to tell whether he was pleased or horrified by the news, or something in between. I decided it was too soon to ask and let him go on. He explained that all this Leah knew was his name and that he was in prison, and she had asked her social worker for assistance in finding him. They had made some inquiries and found out that he was in Broadmoor.

I felt like I was missing something important, and without thinking I asked, "Why did Leah have a social worker?" Jimmy turned to face me then, and I now saw he was trembling a little, possibly on the edge of tears, revealing for the first time the fragility his nurse had mentioned. Instantly, I regretted asking him a "why" question. I knew better than that, but the need to fill in that kind of narrative gap, fishing for it like a dropped jigsaw piece under the table, is strong in all of us. Jimmy kept his voice steady. "She'd been in care for a while as a kid. Same as me. Seems like she . . . this Leah, she stayed in touch with the social worker after that, and now she's, like, in her thirties, getting on with life and stuff, wanting to know about her dad. The dates, the timing in the letter . . . I mean, they say it matches up. I don't know. The social worker said I got some girl pregnant—the mum—not long before my index. But I don't know. I can't remember her. It was so long ago. And I mean, it might all be bollocks, right?"

This was encouraging, that he could share such a big emotional load with a stranger. I was interested that he said he couldn't remember the mother, although in fairness it was long ago, and he'd been through a great deal since. I told him I was glad he felt able to talk about this with me, adding, "Do you want it to be true? That Leah is your daughter?" He looked nonplussed. "I don't know." I pressed: "What does it make you think about?" At this he smiled again, a brief flash of white teeth. "This is just like how it was in that Friday Group—the therapists asked stuff like that all the time!" I smiled back. "It's true, therapists do ask those kinds of things, for sure." Then I put it to him that we'd really like to have him join our Fathers Group, if he was willing.

His response surprised me. "What time of day is it on?" I told him we were still working that out and asked whether there was a time when he couldn't make it. He explained that he was a Muslim and would need to schedule things around his prayer times; also, on Fridays he attended the prayers led by the visiting imam in our multi-faith room. No problem, I assured him; the day and time of our group could be scheduled around these things.

Not knowing before our meeting that Jimmy was a practicing Muslim had thrown me off. It is often the case that our patients' religious and spiritual identities are overlooked, even though we know that this aspect of their lives can be important in terms of recovery and rehabilitation. I had worked with many Muslim men over the years in Broadmoor and in prisons. Although this faith community constitutes only 5 percent of the general population in the UK, a recent Ministry of Justice report indicates that 16 percent of prisoners now identify as Muslim, up from 8 percent in 2002. What this means is hard to know. It would be easy to assume that this change somehow relates to the "war on terror" and the rise in religious extremism and terrorist-related offenses in recent years. But only 2 percent of the thirteen thousand Muslim prisoners currently incarcerated are serving terrorism-related sentences. One explanation for the increasing prevalence of Muslim prisoners is that imprisonment reflects socioeconomic conditions, and just under half of all British Muslims live in some of the most deprived areas of the country.[6] Another reason is that many non-Muslims convert while serving a prison sentence; the government estimates that circa 30 percent of prisoners identify as Muslim after incarceration.[7]

Some of the men I've met who converted inside have told me that they felt it was a way of leaving their old offender identity behind, and they had found the process of conversion to Islam to be relatively simple. Younger men have described to me how it offered them a different way to "do" masculinity as they moved out of adolescence. It also allowed them to trust in something or someone other than themselves, perhaps for the first time in their lives.

In some cases, Islam had replaced a faith tradition that they felt had failed them, either because their faith community had shunned them when they offended or because its leaders had hurt them. There were too those who were survivors of abuse and neglect in (mainly) Christian care homes. Islamic prayer and study practices also provided a certain rhythm to their days, a welcome alternative to the deadening and unstructured boredom of prison life. For nearly everyone I've talked to about this, their choice represented a positive solution to distress and despair, as well as an investment in a better future. Of course, not everyone turns to organized religion as a response to distress and crisis, but even a brief study of the place of religion in world history demonstrates how spiritual transformation often comes about when people feel that their worlds are falling apart.

I was curious whether Jimmy's Muslim identity had been lifelong or not. "Jimmy, were you raised as a Muslim?" My question provoked a rather odd reaction. Immediately, he stiffened and frowned, folding his arms over his chest. His previously friendly demeanor was gone. "I don't know." His voice was toneless now. "Don't know? Or don't remember?" He lifted his head. "I don't really want to talk about this, if you don't mind. It upsets me." I shifted in my chair, wondering what was happening. Something was buzzing at the edge of my consciousness, some little memory mosquito that wouldn't land.

I apologized for raising a subject that was upsetting to him, especially as we were just about to part. "You don't have to answer now if you don't want to," I reassured him. "We can come back to it, if and when the time is right for you." Jimmy nodded, accepting my apology. "It's just . . . I really don't know much about my childhood. I think I was in care a lot—like her, like Leah . . . I do know I converted to Islam in prison, a long time ago. Changed my name to Jamal for a while, but then went back to being Jimmy." While I was trying to digest that hefty biographical wedge, he suddenly stood up. "Is it noon? I have to go for *dhuhr*—my prayers." We agreed to meet again, one-on-one, to talk a little more together before the group started, and he left quickly, without looking back. I sat there thinking, "Jamal. Jamal. I know that name." Of course, I must have met more than one Jamal in my long working life, but there was something about this man . . . and now he'd left me in his own uncomfortable place of not knowing.

It took another meeting with him and a couple of hours reviewing his electronic records for the penny to drop. Jimmy was the Jamal I'd seen in seg all those years ago; I even came across a scanned copy of my own report, pausing over my once-neat signature on his original Section 47 paperwork. I recalled how nervous I had felt that day and thought back to those mournful men in the cleanup crew charged with scrubbing down a shit-smeared cell. Most of all, I remembered how disturbing it had been to realize that the raw-boned child-man was not smiling but baring his teeth at me. Marrying that discomfiting image with the round, middle-aged Jimmy with the nice smile was confusing.

I felt certain he would have no recall of our brief encounter, and I was right. When I told him at our next meeting that I now realized we had met before, many years earlier, it was his turn to be taken aback. He had no memory of ever seeing me. I couldn't blame him; after all, to him I had been just a brief, disembodied mouth, hovering in a gap in a thick cell door. And when people are in psychotic states, their minds are disorganized by intense emotions and even alterations of consciousness, which make it difficult to form or retain memories. I recall one man I worked with some years ago who had killed a stranger while in a psychotic state. He told me that he only realized what he'd done two days later, when he was sitting in the pub reading about the case in a local paper. He finished his pint and immediately went and turned himself in to the police.

I pieced Jimmy's early life together from the various records, taking some time to access old reports from thirty years ago. Back when there were more resources and time for social workers and psychiatrists to talk to people, they took better and more extensive histories, so there was a lot of information for me to digest. I learned that Jimmy had been born to a fifteen-year-old single mother with a drug habit who went on to have three further children over the next six years. Social services had inevitably got involved, as it became clear that his mother (barely an adult herself) could not care for any of her children. Jimmy bounced in and out of foster care throughout his childhood, and then started to get into trouble from his early teens. Arrested on a murder charge just before his eighteenth birthday, he had a short stint on remand in a young offenders institution, before his conviction and subsequent admission to adult prison.

I scrolled through the trial transcripts, reading about the homicide. One night, the gang that Jimmy ran with was confronted by a rival bunch of drug dealers who were trying to make inroads into their territory. There was a midnight brawl in the city center, and when shots were fired, a thirteen-year-old boy from the other gang was killed. Jimmy was one of three gang members charged with joint-enterprise homicide for the murder of the boy. It seemed to be an open-and-shut case; Jimmy was still holding the murder weapon when the police arrived. Curious to see young Jimmy, and wondering if I'd glimpse something closer to the Jamal that I'd met long ago in seg, I clicked on a video file from the trial records containing surveillance-camera footage from the crime scene. The picture quality was poor. CCTV has been around for decades but only came into common usage in public spaces in the UK during the 1980s, in response to a rise in crime. The technology back then was pretty low-grade, and it was hard to imagine that this material had been much use to anyone in court. I played the brief clip a few times and could discern only that there were some slight, hazy figures coming together in a gray muddle, moving and merging like amoebae under a microscope, then becoming a pulsing blob which suddenly broke up with a couple of white flashes of gunfire. Then came a rapid dispersal of shadowy shapes, human smoke drifting off in all directions, leaving behind an amorphous lump on the ground. It looked more like a rock or a blanket or some discarded rubbish than someone's young son who would never become a man.

I began to see some similarities between my own life story and Jimmy's over the three decades since we first met, which I found both disconcerting and moving. We had both spent our adult years in custodial settings, like prisons and secure psychiatric hospitals; we had both explored how faith might inform a person's identity and their relationships, he through Islam, and I through a deepening experience of Christianity. I'd had a close relative who had converted to Catholicism and ultimately entered a monastery, where, just like Jamal, they had acquired a new forename in accordance with sacramental tradition, as a symbol of a new life in faith. And Jimmy and I had parenthood in common too, with grown children who might want to ask us questions we couldn't answer, although I had enjoyed the blessing of living with mine for all their years and witnessing their remarkable process of growth.

We had several more individual sessions together in preparation for the Fathers Group, and Jimmy seemed to welcome them, always showing up on time and always responsive, although his mood was sometimes low. His conversation was still punctuated by this idea that he "didn't know" much about his early life. "My illness . . ." he would say, ducking his head. "I can't remember." But one day, he did manage to tell me a little about his mother. We'd been speaking about Will, his Scottish primary nurse. "My mum was part Scottish, I think," he said. I let that rest for a moment; then, since he'd invited her into the discussion, I asked, "What was she like?" I was bracing myself for a dismissive lift of the shoulders, but instead he surprised me with a few details, blurted out in a short list. "Blonde. Skinny. Lots of freckles, all over. Sometimes angry, sometimes soft." "Angry?" "About me, yeah." I waited for him to offer more, noticing the trembling in his hands again and the way he fought to keep his voice steady. "She didn't want me. I was an accident. I'm a bad seed, she always said. A bad seed." He looked so vulnerable as he recalled this, as if his mother had sentenced him just as the judge had done. "Bad seed" is such a pernicious phrase, often heard in ill-informed debates about nature and nurture, as if humans can be flawed from conception and "born bad."

It was small wonder he might want to change who he was and become someone else's son—and Islam celebrates fathers as loving caregivers and providers, with a ready-made brotherhood forming a spiritual family. Jimmy dropped his head into his hands, rubbing his bare skull again as if to cleanse himself of the harsh words his mother had imprinted there, and we sat in silence together like that for some time. Though I knew this was something that the group might bring out and explore, I wished he would tell me if he knew or felt anything at all about his birth father. But he didn't—and I didn't prompt him. I would let him lead.

When I next met with Jimmy, I could see he was down. His body language was always expressive, but now he slouched in and flopped down in his chair, clasping his hands across his broad belly and staring down at his feet, barely responding when I greeted him. When he didn't say anything for several minutes, I simply asked if he'd like to pick up where we had left off last time; we'd been talking a little more about his conversion to Islam.

I'd heard how Jimmy had had a hard time in prison from the start. This was mainly due to his slight, boyish appearance, which made him physically vulnerable to those who wanted to bully or suborn others. Any resistance would lead to more abuse, and the prison staff either were too busy to notice or sometimes looked the other way. He had already told me that not long after his conviction he was moved to a prison where he was targeted as a whipping boy by some other young men. He didn't go into a lot of detail, but I got the impression that his tormentors were relentless, punching and kicking him when he went by, stealing his things, spitting in his food. One day they had torn apart his cell—"ripping up my stuff and taking a shit on the bed"—while he was out for a brief period of exercise in the yard. An older man called Abdullah, who lived three cells down from him, had intervened, helping Jimmy restore order to his cell and telling the others to stand down—enough was enough. "And did they?" "He was a big bloke, he had some respect," Jimmy explained, with a touch of pride.

"Abdullah sounds kind, from what you were saying last time. You said he helped you?" I detected a softening in Jimmy then, as if the memory was warming. "Yeah. He thought I was one of them at first, I guess." "One of them?" "You know, a Paki or something. But I told him I was Italian." I raised an eyebrow. "I always said that as a kid, like when people tried to bash me around for being a Paki, you know?" Such a casual addition to the catalogue of maltreatment he'd experienced in childhood. "And after he befriended you, did Abdullah invite you to convert to Islam?" Jimmy looked a little affronted. "It doesn't work like that, Dr. Gwen. It's like, you have to ask for yourself when you're ready. That's what Abdullah said. He just took me along to see the imam with him. Talked to me, introduced me to his mates." I was mindful that Jimmy's usually patchy long-term memory seemed much sharpened when talking about this important relationship.

"I could tell him things, and he never got mad or said I was wrong or bad," he went on. "At first, I thought that was kind of, like, crazy. He was just always peaceful, always on about accepting things as they are and Allah will protect you, stuff like that. So after a while I felt like I could tell him . . . I mean, I wasn't sure, but I think my dad wasn't Italian. Maybe he was a Muslim. Algerian or something, I heard my mum say that one time. But I didn't want to be like my dad." This was such an important turn in our conversation that I made a real effort to hold myself entirely still, my expression sympathetic and interested, while inside I was willing him on to try and say more about this father whom he'd never mentioned till now. "I said to Abdullah . . . that thing she always said, you know? I'm a bad seed. And he told me . . ." He trailed off, perhaps trying to recall the man's exact words. I let him search, and eventually he said, "Abdullah told me, 'In the eyes of Allah there is no such thing as a bad seed. There's only bad soil, and faith and love can help us to grow, like water and sunlight.'" His delivery was matter-of-fact, but hearing him repeat that simple metaphor about the power of nurture moved me. It sounded like it had meant the world to him, and I recognized it as a kind of distillation of so much that I'd learned over the years since we'd first met.

This introduction to Islam would have a profound and lasting effect on his life. Being a member of any faith group can be a protective factor in people's mental health, in or out of prison, although obviously it is not a guarantee of either good mental health or non-offending. Those who are suspicious of organized religion often point to the way it is used to justify antisocial acts, including violence and cruelty. Some atheists might go further and suggest that faith is prima facie evidence of irrationality, if not madness. But philosophically, faith rests on reason and doubt, not the psychotic certainties attending some kinds of mental illness. For Jimmy, his introduction to Islam had provided an exit route from the chaos, loneliness, and pain of his life up to that point, and it had been good for him, at least initially. He had found a ready-made, protective social group, the first family he had ever known.

On his twenty-first birthday, he converted, making the declaration of faith called the *shahada*, affirming that God is the only deity worthy of worship and Muhammad His Prophet and messenger. He would also choose his new name, although that was more of an expectation than a requirement, Jimmy explained to me, but "it felt like a new start, and I wanted to do what he wanted." "Abdullah?" I clarified. "Yeah. I mean, I believed, but I also wanted to, like, make him happy and proud, you know?" This sounded very like many a son and his father, I thought but did not say.

Instead, I asked what had made him choose the name Jamal, thinking of how important names had been to some of my patients, like Charlotte, who left her nickname of Charlie behind, or Gabriel, so proud that his name signified "strength." But perhaps Jimmy had not chosen his Muslim name at all. I suddenly thought I might be projecting my knowledge of the process a nun went through before her first vows, how the whole community prayed for discernment in choosing a name for their newest member, which was conferred in a ceremony of rebirth and commitment. But Jimmy was adamant he'd picked out his own, and he'd chosen Jamal because he'd discovered when studying the Quran that it signified beauty. "Or handsome. And I thought, I want to be called handsome every day, you know?" He broke into his broad, beautiful smile, and it was like spring sunshine.

After conversion, Jamal devoted himself to study and prayer and stayed out of trouble. He was serving a life sentence, but with good behavior he would have been on track to do the courses he needed to complete and apply for parole. He might have emerged before he was thirty, with his whole life before him. Tragically, that's not how it panned out. Instead, Abdullah was released after a few years, and Jamal was moved to yet another prison. This meant the loss of a hard-won sense of security for him, and he became paranoid. He was increasingly hostile and assaultive, launching what he saw as preemptive attacks on others without warning or provocation. He began to talk about being possessed by a djinn, a spirit in early Arabian and later Islamic mythology who can be summoned by a sorcerer. He stopped eating after accusing prison staff of tampering with his halal meals, even though they came in sealed packets. He had ended up in seg, and his first referral to Broadmoor had been made, which was where I'd come in.

In the ensuing years, he had shuttled back and forth between prison and hospital, in a process of escalating aggression and mental decline that hampered any chance of him progressing through the prison system, let alone being paroled and released. He was one of those unfortunates who got "stuck," serving nearly three times the length of his original tariff. Many such prisoners serve their sentences several times over; I know of one case in which a man served twenty years for an offense with an eighteen-month sentence.

After the 9/11 terrorist attacks in the US, there was a ripple effect both there and around the Western world that led to increased Islamophobic attacks on prisoners. This perhaps reflected an unthinking fear response that was rife in the world outside, recalling Auden's wise observation that "those to whom evil is done do evil in return."[8] Worn down by ever more frenzied bullying from some of his fellow inmates, Jamal's faith wavered, and eventually he changed his name back to Jimmy, or as he put it, "I gave it all up."

"So how did you find your way back to Islam?" I asked. Jimmy put a hand over his heart, his face serious, and said, "I was lucky." Following one of his stints in the hospital, he was moved to a new prison, and by chance he heard news of Abdullah from a guy who used to worship in the same mosque as him. With the help of his offender manager, Jimmy was able to write to his old mentor, and they'd begun to correspond. "I saved every letter, you know." He sniffed, looking away from me out toward the perimeter fence, scanning the distant hills as if he might see his old friend appear on the horizon, walking toward him, waving in greeting. Then he added, so softly I nearly didn't catch it, "I miss him." I nodded, understanding without words.

The next time we met, Jimmy brought some of the letters along to show me. He became tearful as he talked about the gentle encouragement in those pages and how much they meant to him. I could see they were smudged and creased, with one or two pages nearly falling apart as he opened them. Clearly, he'd read and reread them many times, and now he handled them delicately, laying them out on the table like an antiquarian with a rare manuscript. I felt incredibly privileged when he offered to read some excerpts to me aloud, and I thanked him. He was wearing round NHS-issue specs, lending him an owlish look. He nudged them up to the bridge of his nose, then located the bit he wanted to share first. "'I believe in you, my son, and Allah does too, even if you do not,'" he read slowly. "See what I mean?" I asked him when this was written, trying to better understand the context of the message. "I don't know," Jimmy said, turning the page over. "There's no date." He thought it had come at a bad time for him, when he was feeling suicidal, as if his life were a waste. He had felt like that a lot. "It must have been after I stopped being Jamal," he said. "See?" He held up the letter to show me that it opened with "Dear Jimmy."

He had felt guilty about lapsing as a Muslim and had hated confessing to Abdullah that he was no longer Jamal. But Abdullah had never criticized him about that, writing to say that whatever his name, he was "a beautiful child of God" and his life would not be wasted if he used the rest of it for good. The other extracts

Jimmy shared with me that day went on in this vein, full of love, wisdom, and support. He stopped often, too choked up to continue. Yes, he had been suicidal at the time, yet he did not kill himself, and I gave silent thanks for this generous, good man whose letters had offered Jimmy a lifeline. If his life mattered to just one other person, then it could matter to him too.

Sadly, following that flurry of correspondence, the older man stopped writing, and Jimmy learned that he had died after a long battle with cancer. "He'd never said—not a word about it." I could see the grief remained fresh for him, perhaps not only for Abdullah himself, but for what he represented. Beyond a faith culture, comfort, and care, he was filling the role of Jimmy's absent father. In the wake of Abdullah's passing, Jimmy made a serious suicide attempt in prison, after which he was once again transferred to Broadmoor. It had taken him a long time to stabilize this time around, but once he felt better, he had asked to see the visiting imam, and slowly he'd restarted his prayer life. Lately, he'd been wondering if he should change his name back to Jamal, but it was confusing because now there was this daughter Leah, who knew about him only as Jimmy. "I don't know who I am," he admitted. This was the truest thing he'd said to me, and I told him so. Knowing yourself is a lifetime's work and a great challenge for everyone.

As we approached the date of the first Fathers Group meeting, Jimmy shared with me that he felt deeply worried about contact with Leah and what she would think of him if they ever met. I understood well the general parental anxiety he was expressing. That fear of being judged and found wanting, the risk of becoming the object of shame or blame for one's offspring are not unique to those who meet their children for the first time later in life, and it is daunting. King Lear aptly describes the particular pain of the thankless child as being "sharper than a serpent's tooth." I try not to offer easy reassurance to my patients, but I did point out to Jimmy that any potential encounter with Leah was in the future, and he would have time and space in the present to plan for it. He could use the Fathers Group to think about this. He was still anxious, though, countering that he knew his medical team were talking about him being ready to go back to prison in the near term, to begin the process of applying for his long-overdue parole. "I mean, what if I get out and then me and Leah meet up, and I'm, like, this . . . this . . ." I wondered if he would fill in the blank with a pejorative like "loser" or "convict" or "murderer," those seemingly indelible labels.

After a long silence, I decided to try something. "Jimmy, how do you think Abdullah would describe you today?" That stumped him for a while, and then he looked up at me. "I don't know." I wasn't going to let him off the hook. "Would you like to make a guess?" He looked down, frowning in concentration. Then he ventured, "I think he might say we're all children of God, so that's what I am." "Anything else?" "He'd probably say . . . I was born a good person and lost my way, but now I'm better, because Allah by His mercy helped me find my way back so that I can be helpful to others." I think that might have been a direct quote from one of the letters. As he said it, I noticed he straightened his shoulders slightly and sat taller in his chair, and I felt something lifting a little, like a light veil. We sat together for a while, and it was peaceful. I wished that Abdullah and Leah could see Jimmy now, thinking about them and their importance to him.

We were in the big meeting room where we had had the first of our therapy sessions, and now, just outside the window, a bird began to sing, loud enough to hear through the thick glass. We both turned to look at it, a gray-brown creature perched on one of the spindly branches of a newly planted tree. I wished, as I so often do, that I knew what type of bird it was. As if reading my thoughts, Jimmy said, "Do you know what that is?" I shook my head. "Same here," he said. "Don't know a bloody thing about birds." "There's lots we don't know, but we can learn," I said.

He watched the bird for a few minutes, hopping about busily to its own tune, and then said, "I have a thought." We both laughed, because this had become a kind of motif in recent sessions—his sudden announcements of new thoughts, like green shoots he'd discover at odd moments. He cleared his throat. "I don't know who my father is, but I got a new one." I thought of Abdullah, but he might well have meant Allah or the Prophet. "So, Leah, she never knew who her father was either, but now she does, which can help her." He was mentalizing her experience; this was significant and hopeful. Like his daughter, he had been fatherless and had spent time in care when he was young. In combination with other risk factors, that childhood experience and his sense of identity as a "bad seed" had contributed to a long history of using violence toward others to relieve his distress. But then he had found a friendship with Abdullah, which had given him a sense of being valued.

Identifying with Abdullah and his faith gave Jimmy a way to be a man who was hopeful and positive, in complete contrast to his mother's pessimistic vision of him. In my work, I've seen how people need to be given opportunities to change, which can come from a range of sources, including friendships, creative activity, and faith practices. All these things offer psychological solutions that far surpass the power of drugs or violence to relieve emotional pain. It was such a good sign that Jimmy was able to see that now. Whatever happened next between him and his daughter, I felt optimistic about his future. In the near term, he would benefit from joining our therapy group and would probably bring some useful insights to a discussion about identity and fatherhood that might help others.

As our final session drew to a close, I asked if he intended to go ahead with changing his name back again. He pondered that for a minute, then said, "Maybe whether I'm Jimmy or Jamal, it doesn't matter. Not to Leah. Maybe I can just be there for her somehow. I think that's what Abdullah would say." He paused. "That's what he did for me."

That was such a liberating and beautiful thought, a blossoming of understanding in him, that I could almost have joined the bird and burst into song. Instead, I thanked him and told him again I was so grateful to him for sharing Abdullah's letters with me, which was such a gesture of trust. I reminded him that the group would start soon, and I asked him how he was feeling about that. "I'm ready," he told me, his dark gaze level with mine.

That group was meant to start in April 2020, but as so often in my work, the best-laid plans went awry, this time thanks to a global pandemic. Jimmy's transfer back to prison was delayed, his plan to apply for parole put on hold. All group work was suspended, but we hope to start again soon. Meantime, he has not changed his name back to Jamal, but he does remain committed to his faith practice. Will, his primary nurse, let me know that Jimmy had been writing long letters to Leah, not to send, but to work out what he wants to tell her one day. And now another spring has come, and Jimmy, like all of us, knows more of himself than he did a year ago. What a world it would be if we could all appreciate that much.

CODA

The many life stories I have heard in the course of my work have given me an infinite respect for the mind's complexity. The deeper I go, the more I realize how unknowable it is, like the vast oceans or the universe itself. I hope that as this book ends, the reader will surface, glad of the fresh air and freedom, with a changed perspective on what we call "evil." It is really a term, much like beauty, that says more about the viewer than the object. Telling these tales of suffering and violence will have served a purpose if, next time you see a news item or a film about some "evil monster," it's possible for you to look at them with a new consciousness, knowing that we are all more alike than we are different. I am grateful for your willingness to give this time and thought, as I am grateful for the courage of the men and women who have shared their thoughts and feelings with me over a working lifetime.

There are few countries in the world where mental health spending is sufficient to meet the needs of the population, because governments are unwilling to prioritize it. I wish for my psychiatric great-grandchildren to look back on this period as if revisiting medieval times, shaking their heads at how our society and medical establishment put so much thought and money into advancements in cardiac care or laser surgery or the wholesale replacement of vital organs, and yet did little to help people heal or rediscover their minds, inside and outside of institutions.

Far more than punishment or sanctions, recognizing common humanity can change minds for the better. We need improved legislation and allocation of public resources, promoting measures that encourage pro-social attitudes and reduce childhood adversity. Among our interventions should be more and better help for people with addictions and the socially isolated, and assistance for parents with mental health problems; we also need greater investment in specialized psychological therapies for complex conditions. That bicycle-lock analogy tells us what the risk factors are, so now we need the political and social will to reduce their impact and even to abolish some of them. Yes, it will cost us time and money, but the rewards will be beyond price.

The work of inspirational contemporary thinkers like the American justice campaigner Bryan Stevenson, the teacher and philosopher priest Richard Rohr, and some religious leaders including Pope Francis reminds us that the struggle for peace, restoration, and empathy never stops and requires both solidarity and hope. There is so much good to be done, if we dive in with our minds open and our hearts willing. If the people in this book stay with you, in the same space where we conjure ideas of the devil, it is worth remembering that "there but for the grace of God" go any of us.

ACKNOWLEDGMENTS

The human mind is too complex to understand using only one way of thinking or one kind of technique. If raising a child takes a village, then changing minds takes many people working together in different ways. I am more grateful than I can say to those who taught me, supervised me, and worked with me in trying to help offenders change their minds and to articulate how that happens. They are more numerous than the stars in the heavens and too many to name, but those who shine in the context of this book are Sophie Lambert, Laura Hassan, and Kathy Belden.

Although most offenders are men, most men are not offenders, and Eileen and I want to dedicate this book to our favorite men. I thank my dear sons Dan and Jack, who daily demonstrate grace, kindness, and humor, despite years of (generally) benign neglect. I also offer this work in memory of my much-missed father, Sam Adshead, who always said to me, "Of *course* you can write a book." Eileen thanks her husband Greg for his limitless patience, wisdom, and generosity of spirit, and for embodying Thomas Aquinas's idea of love as "willing another's good."

NOTES

INTRODUCTION

1 Some more reflections on the idea of evil can be found here: G. Adshead, "Capacities and Dispositions: What Psychiatry and Psychology Have to Say about Evil," in T. Mason, (Ed.), *Forensic Psychiatry: Influences of Evil* (New Jersey: Humana Press, 2006), pp. 259–71.

2 From "Maggie and Milly and Molly and Mae" by e. e. cummings, in G. J. Firmage (Ed.), (1972), *The Complete Poems 1904–1962.* Copyright © 1956, 1984, 1991 by the Trustees for the E. E. Cummings Trust (New York: Harcourt Brace Jovanovich).

3 See Prison Reform Trust, *Bromley Briefings Prison Factfile: Autumn 2018* (London: PRT, 2018); Ministry of Justice, *Prison Receptions 2018* (London: Ministry of Justice, 2018).

4 It was nearly 5 percent in the PRT's 2018 studies, but the figures are rising annually. See the PRT fact sheet from April 2019 titled "Why Women/England and Wales" for more granular detail.

5 M. A. Cox, "Dark Lamp: Special Hospitals as Agents of Change: Psychotherapy at Broadmoor," *Criminal Justice Matters* 21, no. 1 (1995): 10–11.

TONY

1 K. Haggerty and A. Ellerbrok, "The Social Study of Serial Killers," *Criminal Justice Matters* 86, no. 1 (2011): 6–7.

2 Radford study: M. G. Aamodt, "Serial Killer Statistics," September 4, 2016, retrieved from http://maamodt.asp.radford.edu/serial killer information center/project description.htm.

3 C. Grover and K. Soothill, "British Serial Killing: Towards a Structural Explanation," *British Criminology Conferences: Selected Proceedings* 2 (1999): 2.

4 H. Cleckley, *The Mask of Sanity* (St. Louis: C. V. Mosby Company, 1941).
5 Hare's website: www.hare.org.
6 S. Yochelson and S. Samenow, *The Criminal Personality: The Change Process* (Lanham, MD: Rowman & Littlefield, 1994).
7 S. O. Lilienfeld, A. L. Watts, and S. F. Smith, "Successful Psychopathy: A Scientific Status Report," *Current Directions in Psychological Science* 24, no. 4 (2015): 298–303.
8 J. Bowlby, *A Secure Base* (London: Psychology Press, 1988).
9 R. J. Lifton, *The Nazi Doctors: Medical Killing and the Psychology of Genocide* (New York: Basic Books, 1986).
10 R. J. Morton et al. (Eds.), *Serial Murder Symposium 2008* (National Center for the Analysis of Violent Crime, Quantico, 2008).

GABRIEL

1 P. Taylor and N. Kalebic, "Psychosis and Homicide," *Current Opinion in Psychiatry* 31, no. 3 (2018): 223–30.
2 R. Rohr, *Things Hidden: Scripture as Spirituality* (Cincinnati, OH: Franciscan Media, 2008), pp. 24–25.
3 Federal judge T. Henderson in *Madrid v. Gomez*, 889 F. Supp. 1146, 1265 (N.D. Cal. 1995).
4 See valuable work by Lorna Rhodes (*Total Confinement*, University of California Press, 2004) and Craig Haney ("Restricting the Use of Solitary Confinement," *Annual Review of Criminology* 1 (2018): 285–310).
5 K. van Schie, S. C. van Veen, I. M. Engelhard, I. Klugkist, and M. A. van den Hout, "Blurring Emotional Memories Using Eye Movements: Individual Differences and Speed of Eye Movements," *European Journal of Psychotraumatology* 7, no. 29 (2016): 476.

KEZIA

1 G. Adshead, "Damage: Trauma and Violence in a Sample of Women Referred to a Forensic Service," *Behavioral Sciences & the Law* 12, no. 3 (1994): 235–49.
2 See K. Halvorsrud, J. Nazroo, M. Otis, et al., "Ethnic Inequalities and Pathways to Care in Psychosis in England: A Systematic Review and Meta-Analysis," *BMC Medicine* 16 (2018): 223.
3 J. Read, R. Bentall, and R. Fosse, "Time to Abandon the Bio-Bio-Bio Model of Psychosis: Exploring the Epigenetic and Psychologi-

cal Mechanisms by Which Adverse Life Events Lead to Psychotic Symptoms," *Epidemiologia e Psichiatria Sociale* 18 (2009): 299–310.

4 M. D. Enoch and W. H. Trethowan, "The Othello Syndrome," in M. D. Enoch and W. H. Trethowan (Eds.), *Uncommon Psychiatric Syndromes* (Bristol: John Wright & Sons Ltd., 1979).

5 See United Nations, *Global Study on Homicide 2013 — Trends, Context, Data*, https://www.unodc.org/documents/gsh/pdfs/2014_GLOBAL_HOMICIDE_BOOK_web.pdf.

6 D. Bhugra and M. A. Becker, "Migration, Cultural Bereavement and Cultural Identity," *World Psychiatry* 4, no. 1(2005): 18–24.

MARCUS

1 L. Dixon and K. Browne, "The Heterogeneity of Spouse Abuse: A Review," *Aggression and Violent Behaviour* 8, no. 1 (2003): 107–30.

2 M. Liem et al., "Intimate Partner Homicide by Presence or Absence of a Self-Destructive Act," *Homicide Studies* 13, no. 4 (2009): 339–54.

3 F. Pfäfflin and G. Adshead (Eds.), *A Matter of Security: The Application of Attachment Theory to Forensic Psychiatry and Psychotherapy* (London: Jessica Kingsley, 2003).

4 J. Bowlby, *Attachment and Loss* (New York: Basic Books, 1969).

5 Browning's poem can be found here: https://www.poetryfoundation.org/poems/43768/my-last-duchess.

6 One such study is M. R. Leary et al., "Interpersonal Rejection as a Determinant of Anger and Aggression," *Personality and Social Psychology Review* 10, no. 2 (2006): 111–32.

7 The full manifesto can be found here: https://www.documentcloud.org/documents/1173808-elliot-rodger-manifesto.html.

8 S. Maruna, *Making Good: How Ex-Convicts Reform and Rebuild Their Lives* (Washington DC: American Psychological Association, 2001).

CHARLOTTE

1 Prison Reform Trust, "Prison: The Facts. Bromley Briefings Summer 2019" (2019), http://www.prisonreformtrust.org.uk/Portals/0/Documents/Bromley%20Briefings/Prison%20the%20facts%20Summer%202019.pdf.

2 More details within the same PRT report. See also Baroness Corston's 2007 report on women in prison: https://webarchive.nationalarchives.gov.uk/20130206102659/http://www.justice.gov.uk/publications/docs/corston-report-march-2007.pdf.

NOTES

ZAHRA

1 T. A. Gannon, "Female Arsonists: Key Features, Psychopathologies and Treatment Needs," *Psychiatry: Interpersonal and Biological Processes* 73 (2010): 173–89; G. Dickens, P. Sugarman, F. Ahmad, S. Edgar, K. Hofberg, and S. Tewari, "Gender Differences Amongst Adult Arsonists at Psychiatric Assessment," *Medicine, Science and the Law* 47, no. 3 (2007): 233–38.

2 See the Ministry of Justice's quarterly "Safety in Custody" report (July 2020): https://www.gov.uk/government/statistics/safety-in -custody-quarterly-update-to-march-2020; also Maya Oppenheim's article "You Could See Their Distress" (2020) is just one of a vast body of reports on this sorry trend among women: https://www.indepen dent.co.uk/independentpremium/uk-news/self-harm-women-prison -gender-men-stats-a9332401.html.

3 G. Adshead, "Written on the Body: Deliberate Self-Harm as Communication," *Psychoanalytic Psychotherapy* 24, no. 2 (2010): 69–80.

4 Robert Frost, "A Servant to Servants," in Edward Connery Lathem (Ed.), *The Poetry of Robert Frost* (New York: Holt, Rinehart, and Winston, 1967).

5 F. Pfäfflin and G. Adshead (Eds.), *A Matter of Security: The Application of Attachment Theory to Forensic Psychiatry and Psychotherapy* (London: Jessica Kingsley, 2003), pp. 147–66.

6 D. Kahneman, *Thinking Fast and Slow* (New York: Farrar Straus and Giroux, 2013).

IAN

1 Jim Gilligan has written extensively on the topic of shame as a driver for violence, but you might begin with *Violence: Reflections on a National Epidemic* (New York: Vintage, 1997); also his ever-more-topical *Why Some Politicians Are More Dangerous Than Others* (Malden, MA: Polity Press, 2013).

2 C. Burns, "The Young Paedophiles Who Say They Don't Abuse Children," BBC online article, 2017, https://www.bbc.com/news/ uk-41213657.

3 https://www.csacentre.org.uk/documents/scale-and-nature-scop ing-report-2018/.

4 Break the Silence report: https://breakthesilence.org.uk/wp-content /uploads/2017/06/Statistical-Information.pdf.

5 A. Gewirtz-Meydan and D. Finkelhor, "Sexual Abuse and Assault in

a Large National Sample of Children and Adolescents," *Child Maltreatment* 25, no. 2 (2020): 203–14.

6 E. Chenier, "The Natural Order of Disorder: Pedophilia, Stranger Danger and the Normalising Family," *Sexuality & Culture* 16 (2012): 172–86, https://doi.org/10.1007/s12119-011-9116-z.

7 A. Bentovim, "Why Do Adults Sexually Abuse Children?," *British Medical Journal* (clinical research edition) 307, no. 6 (1993) 897: 144–45, https://doi.org/10.1136/bmj.307.6897.144; also J. M. Bailey, K. J. Hsu, and P. A. Bernhard, "An Internet Study of Men Sexually Attracted to Children: Sexual Attraction Patterns," *Journal of Abnormal Psychology* 125, no. 7 (2016): 976–88; K. Faller, "Why Sexual Abuse? An Exploration of the Intergenerational Hypothesis," *Child Abuse and Neglect* 13 (1989): 543–48.

8 R. K. Hanson, R. Gizzarelli, and H. Scott, "Attitudes of Incest Offenders," *Criminal Justice and Behaviour* 21, no. 2 (1994): 187–202, http://www.ncjrs.gov/App/publications/abstract.aspx?ID=148915.

9 Perkins's review of SOTPs: D. Perkins, S. Hammond, D. Coles, and D. Bishopp, *Review of Sex Offender Treatment Programmes* (Broadmoor, UK: High Security Psychiatric Services Commissioning Board, 1988); E. Welldon, "Group Therapy for Victims and Perpetrators of Incest," *Advances in Psychiatric Treatment*, 4:2 (1998): 82–88.

10 Canadian study: K. Baril, "Sexual Abuse in the Childhood of Perpetrators," INSPQ, Quebec, 2020, https://www.inspq.qc.ca/en/sexual-assault/fact-sheets/sexual-abuse-childhood-perpetrators.

11 E. Waugh, *Brideshead Revisited: The Sacred and Profane Memories of Captain Charles Ryder* (6th edition) (Harmondsworth: Penguin, 1981).

12 L. Shengold, *Soul Murder* (New Haven, CT: Yale University Press, 1989).

13 This is an ancient idea of shame and has also been widely attributed to Carl Jung.

LYDIA

1 W. James, *The Principles of Psychology* (New York: Henry Holt and Company, 1890).

2 Crime Survey data on stalking: https://www.ons.gov.uk/peoplepopulationandcommunity/crimeandjustice/datasets/stalkingfindingsfromthecrimesurveyforenglandandwales.

3 www.suzylamplugh.org.

4 J. R. Meloy, *Violent Attachments* (New York: Jason Aronson Inc., 1997).

5 D. G. Dutton, K. Saunders, A. Starzomski, and K. Bartholomew, "Intimacy-Anger and Insecure Attachment as Precursors of Abuse in Intimate Relationships 1," *Journal of Applied Social Psychology* 24, no. 15 (1994): 1367–86.

6 J. R. Meloy, K. Mohandie, and M. Green, "The Female Stalker," *Behavioral Sciences and the Law* 29 (2011): 240–54; also S. Strand, T. E. McEwan, "Violence Among Female Stalkers," *Psychological Medicine* 42, no. 3 (2012): 545–55.

SHARON

1 G. Adshead, D. Brooke, M. Samuels, S. Jenner, and D. Southall, "Maternal Behaviors Associated with Smothering: A Preliminary Descriptive Study," *Child Abuse & Neglect* 24, no. 9 (2000): 1175–83; see also G. Adshead and K. Bluglass, "Attachment Representations in Mothers with Abnormal Illness Behaviour by Proxy," *British Journal of Psychiatry* 187, no. 4 (2005): 328–33.

2 Report on this study: https://www.bbc.com/news/uk-england-london-37048581.

3 One such US study: K. Jaghab, K. B. Skodnek, and T. A. Padder, "Munchausen's Syndrome and Other Factitious Disorders in Children: Case Series and Literature Review," *Psychiatry (Edgmont)* 3, no. 3 (2006): 46–55.

4 American colleagues discuss this in C. Angelotta and P. Appelbaum, "Criminal Charges for Child Harm from Substance Use in Pregnancy," *Journal of the American Academy of Psychiatry and the Law* 45 (2017): 193–203. See my response from a British perspective in G. Adshead, "No Apple Pie," ibid., 204–7.

5 K. Broadhurst et al., "Vulnerable Birth Mothers and Recurrent Care Proceedings, Final Main Report," Centre for Child and Family Justice Research, October 2017.

6 https://www.pause.org.uk.

SAM

1 M. Hillbrand and J. L. Young, "Instilling Hope into Forensic Treatment: The Antidote to Despair and Desperation," *Journal of the American Academy of Psychiatry and the Law* 36, no. 1 (2008): 90–94.

2 G. Adshead, "Stories of Transgression," in C. H. Cook, A. Powell,

and A. Sims, (Eds.), *Spirituality and Narrative in Psychiatric Practice: Stories of Mind and Soul* (London: Royal College of Psychiatrists, 2016); also M. Ferrito, A. Vetere, G. Adshead, and E. Moore, "Life After Homicide: Accounts of Recovery and Redemption of Offender Patients in a High Security Hospital—A Qualitative Study," *Journal of Forensic Psychiatry and Psychology* 23, no. 3 (2012): 1–18.

3 C. Garland, *Understanding Trauma* (London: Routledge, 2002).

4 N. Filer, *This Book Will Change Your Mind About Mental Health* (London: Faber & Faber, 2019).

5 S. E. Estroff et al., "Risk Reconsidered: Targets of Violence in the Social Networks of People with Serious Psychiatric Disorders," *Social Psychiatry and Psychiatric Epidemiology* 33 (1998): S95–S101. Also "Raising Cain: The Role of Serious Mental Illness in Family Homicides," June 2016 report from the Office of Research and Public Affairs.

6 C. Heeke, C. Kampisiou, H. Niemeyer, and C. Knaevelsrud, "A Systematic Review and Meta-Analysis of Correlates of Prolonged Grief Disorder in Adults Exposed to Violent Loss," *European Journal of Psychotraumatology* 8 (sup. 6), no. 1 (2017): 583524.

7 G. Adshead and S. Sarkar, "Justice and Welfare: Two Ethical Paradigms in Forensic Psychiatry," *Australian and New Zealand Journal of Psychiatry* 39 (2005): 1011–17.

8 *Vitaly Tarasoff et al. v. Regents of the University of California et al.* (S.F. No. 23042, Supreme Court of California, July 1, 1976).

9 There is an excellent discussion of the questions about and meanings of privacy in medicine in A. Allen, "Privacy and Medicine," in E. N. Zalta (Ed.), *The Stanford Encyclopedia of Philosophy* (winter 2016 edition), https://plato.stanford.edu/archives/win2016/entries/privacy-medicine/.

10 His reference is to Viktor Frankl's classic book *Man's Search for Meaning* (Boston: Beacon Press, 1962; first English edition translated by Ilse Lasch).

DAVID

1 From "Doctors" by Anne Sexton, in *The Complete Poems of Anne Sexton* (Boston: Houghton Mifflin Harcourt). Copyright © 1981 by Linda Gray Sexton and Loring Conant, Jr.

2 Mindfulnessfordoctors.co.uk.

3 From "This Be the Verse" by Philip Larkin, in P. Larkin, *High Windows* (New York: Farrar, Straus and Giroux; London: Faber & Faber, 1974).

4 G. E. Vaillant, N. C. Sobowale, and C. McArthur, "Some Psychologic Vulnerabilities of Physicians," *New England Journal of Medicine* 287, no. 8 (1972): 372–75.

5 Derek Perkins, whose work I've referenced above with regard to Ian, offers valuable insight on this. One recent review—"Child Exploitation Materials Offenders," *European Psychologist*, May 2018—can be found here: https://econtent.hogrefe.com/doi/abs/10.1027/1016-9040/a000326.

6 K. M. Beier, D. Grundmann, L. F. Kuhle, G. Scherner, A. Konrad, and T. Amelung, "The German Dunkelfeld Project: A Pilot Study to Prevent Child Sexual Abuse and the Use of Child Abusive Images," *Journal of Sexual Medicine* 12, no. 2 (2015): 529–42.

7 Excerpt from "Herman Melville" by W. H. Auden. Copyright © 1940 by W. H. Auden, renewed. Reprinted by permission of Curtis Brown, Ltd.

JAMAL

1 There's a similar level of controversy in the UK about segregation units and the attendant human rights issues: https://www.theguard ian.com/society/2021/jul/26/52-held-close-supervision-prison-units -may-amount-torture.

2 For more information about Section 47, see https://www.mind.org.uk/ information-support/legal-rights/courts-and-mental-health/section -47/#WhatIsASection47.

3 From *De Profundis* by Oscar Wilde (London: Methuen and Co., 1905).

4 Out of a total of 396 full-time forensic psychiatrists in the UK, 120 are women. https://www.rcpsych.ac.uk/improving-care/workforce /our-workforce-census.

5 Solitary Watch: https://solitarywatch.org/2013/02/16/voices-from -solitary-what-solitary-confinement-does-to-the-mind/. Professor Craig Haney interviewed by the American Psychological Association on the subject: https://www.apa.org/education-career/guide/paths/craig-haney.

6 This is according to a comprehensive report by the Muslim Coun-cil of Britain, "British Muslims in Numbers," January 2015, https:// www.mcb.org.uk.

7 Georgina Sturge, "UK Prison Population Statistics," briefing paper number CBP-04334, July 3, 2020, provides a useful overview of the 2019 Ministry of Justice findings, including religious affiliations.

8 Excerpt from "September 1, 1939" by W. H. Auden. *In Another Time* (New York: Random House). Copyright © 1940 by W. H. Auden.

FURTHER READING

There are so many authors whose work in this field has had a great impact on me over the course of the last three or four decades, only a handful of whom I've been able to reference or give credit to within this book. For those readers who might be prompted by these stories to go a little deeper into the vast literature on the study of the mind, and of human cruelty and its treatment, here is a selection of my personal favorites. I have included some works of crime fiction because this genre can be a useful resource for a student of forensic psychiatry, and it always has been for me. Crime fiction requires an exercise in imagination and empathy, and the best authors are very strong on the relationships involved in crimes of violence.

Bateman, A., and P. Fonagy. *Handbook on Mentalizing in Mental Health Practice*, 2nd edition. Washington, DC: American Psychiatric Association, 2019.

Browning, C. *Ordinary Men*. New York: Harper Perennial, 1998.

Burleigh, M. *Death and Deliverance: "Euthanasia" in Germany, c.1900 to 1945*. Cambridge: Cambridge University Press, 1995.

Chesterton, G. K. *Father Brown: The Essential Tales*. New York: Modern Library Classics, 2005.

Christie, A. *The Murder of Roger Ackroyd: A Hercule Poirot Mystery*. Reprinted edition. New York: William Morrow and Co., 2020. Also the complete Miss Marple series.

Clare, A. *Psychiatry in Dissent: Controversial Issues in Thought and Practice*. London: International Behavioural and Social Sciences Library/Tavistock Institute, 2001.

Cox, M. *Shakespeare Comes to Broadmoor: "The Actors Are Come Hither"—The Performance of Tragedy in a Secure Psychiatric Hospital*. London: Jessica Kingsley, 1992.

Doidge, N. *The Brain That Changes Itself: Stories of Personal Triumph from the Frontiers of Brain Science.* New York: Penguin Books, 2007.

Dunbar, R. *Grooming, Gossip, and the Evolution of Language.* London: Faber & Faber, 1996/2004.

Fine, C. *Delusions of Gender: How Our Minds, Society, and Neurosexism Create Difference.* New York: W. W. Norton and Co., 2011.

Fox Keller, E. *Reflections on Gender and Science.* New Haven: Yale University Press, 1996.

Gill, A. *The Journey Back from Hell.* New York: William Morrow, 1989.

Gilligan, C. *In a Different Voice: Psychological Theory and Women's Development.* Boston: Harvard University Press, 1982.

Holmes, J. *John Bowlby and Attachment Theory.* Abingdon: Routledge, 2009.

James, P. D. *Innocent Blood.* London: Faber & Faber; New York: Scribner, 1980.

Kandel, E. *In Search of Memory: The Emergence of a New Science of the Mind.* New York: W. W. Norton and Co., 2006.

Leon, D. *Death at La Fenice.* New York: Grove Atlantic, 2004. And the other Commissario Brunetti series.

Levi, P. *If This Is a Man.* New York: Orion, 1959.

Livesley, W. J. *Practical Management of Personality Disorder.* New York: Guilford Press, 2003.

McAdams, D. *The Art and Science of Personality Development.* New York: Guilford Press, 2015.

McDermid, V. *The Wire in the Blood.* London: Harper Collins, 1997. And her collected works

Miller, E. J., T. Miller, and G. V. Gwynne. *Life Apart.* New York: Van Nostrand Reinhold, 1972.

Parker, T. *Life After Life: Interviews with Twelve Murderers.* London: Secker and Warburg, 1990. And *The Twisting Lane: Some Sex Offenders.* London: Hutchinson, 1969.

Rankin, I. *Knots and Crosses.* London: Orion, 1987. Also all the Rebus novels and his other works.

Rohr, R. *Falling Upward: A Spirituality for the Two Halves of Life.* San Francisco: Jossey-Bass, 2011.

Sapolsky, R. *Junk Food Monkeys: And Other Essays on the Biology of the Human Predicament.* London: Headline, 1997.

Shem, S. *The House of God.* New York: Richard Marek, 1978.

Stone, I. *The Passions of the Mind: A Biographical Novel of Sigmund Freud.* New York: Doubleday, 1971.

Szasz, T. *The Myth of Mental Illness: Foundations of a Theory of Personal Conduct.* London: Secker and Warburg, 1962.

Tuckett, D. *Minding the Markets.* London: Palgrave Macmillan, 2011.